STREET
VEGAN

STREET VEGAN

Recipes and Dispatches from the Cinnamon Snail Food Truck

Adam Sobel

Photographs by Kate Lewis

CLARKSON POTTER/PUBLISHERS

NEW YORK

Published in the United States by Clarkson Potter/
Publishers, an imprint of the Crown Publishing
Group, a division of Random House LLC, a Penguin
Random House Company, New York.
www.crownpublishing.com
www.clarksonpotter.com

CLARKSON POTTER is a trademark and POTTER
with colophon is a registered trademark of Random
House LLC.

All photographs are by Kate Lewis with the exception
of: pp. 4–5 by Ina Yang; p. 9 by Maryloyise Atwater-
Kellman; pp. 11, 219 (left) by Christopher Patrick
Ernst; pp. 218, 219 (right), 221 by Clay Williams;
p. 227 by Alex Jagendorf. The photograph on
page 181 is courtesy of the Street Vendor Project.

Photographs courtesy of the author: pp. 67, 116,
152, 196.

Photograph on page i (Grunge Tire Tracks) © Four
Leaf Lover/Dreamstime.com. All illustrated artwork
by Shutterstock: © adsheyn; © VoodooDot;
© jadimages.

THIS BOOK IS DEDICATED TO NANA. YOU TAUGHT ME ALL OF THE GOOD THINGS I KNOW, AND THE TREE PLANTED ABOVE YOUR ASHES STILL BRINGS BEAUTY TO THIS WORLD. YOU ARE ALWAYS WITH ME.

Library of Congress Cataloging-in-Publication Data
Sobel, Adam.
  Street vegan : recipes and dispatches from the
Cinnamon Snail food truck / Adam Sobel ;
photographs by Kate Lewis. -- First edition.
     pages cm
  Includes index.
  1. Vegan cooking. 2. Street food—New York
(State)—New York. I. Title.

TX837.S6767 2015
641.5'63609747—dc23
                                    2014047446

ISBN 978-0-385-34619-1
eBook ISBN 978-0-385-34620-7

Printed in China

Book design by Danielle Deschenes
Cover design by Gabriel Levine
Cover photography by Kate Lewis

10 9 8 7 6 5 4 3 2 1

First Edition

CONTENTS

Introduction »» 8
My Vegan Pantry »»»»»»»»»»»»»»»»»»»»»»»»»»»»»»»»»»»» 14

21 **Breakfast**

53 Beverages

71 **Appetizers**

97 Soups

121 **Sandwiches**

149 **Cinnamains**

173 Veggies and Sides

189 **Desserts**

223 Donuts

251 **The Saucy Stuff**

263 «««««««««««««««««««««««««««««««««««« Acknowledgments
266 «« Index

INTRODUCTION

How I Got Started Cooking All These Vegetables

I grew up eating all kinds of animals and never thought I would grow up to help people eat their veggies from the side of a truck. But when I was sixteen, I started hanging out with this really cute girl from Jersey named Joey (now Ms. Snail). Joey was a French fries and canned soup vegan, aka a vegetarian who didn't really eat much in the way of vegetables. (For the record, I really like French fries. Canned soup, not so much.) Joey and I fell in love, and because I really cared for Joey, I wanted her to eat better food. I would spend hours in bookstores copying vegan and soon-to-be-veganized recipes from cookbooks into a notebook, which I would experiment on at home. I also decided that to advance my skills, I would look for work in restaurants.

Serving humans and piggies at the Woodstock Farm Animal Sanctuary.

The first restaurant I worked in was Tom Valenti's Ouest, on Manhattan's Upper West Side. Ouest was far from a vegan restaurant—I mean, come on, they had a dish with a poached duck egg deep-fried in duck fat, not exactly animal-loving. But I learned a lot of skills and cooking methods from working with the extremely talented crew and chef: my care for the integrity of our ingredients, respect for the customer's experience, and the creative treatment of food that preserves its natural appeal (for instance, not making savory watermelon sauces and sweets involving mushrooms just because it *can* be done).

As I experimented with creating meals for Joey, and developing my culinary skill set, I came to understand the ethics behind veganism. I learned about factory farming, the suffering caused to

animals, the harmful effects on agriculture, workers' rights, and the disrupted balance of life on the planet caused by the Standard American Diet. I woke up to the fact that our dietary choices are responsible for a lot of things that we'd like to change in this world. Folks would occasionally come into Ouest and ask for modifications of dishes to make them vegan or vegetarian. The cooks would grumble, but I found myself standing up for the desire these customers had to avoid animal products. Finally one day, the cook asked, "Well, then why aren't YOU vegetarian?" "Maybe I should be," I said, and it was done.

The thing that had stopped me from becoming vegetarian sooner was that I thought it would be a limitation on my freedom, another dogma to have to follow . . . but the truth is, vegetarians and vegans have no rules. When you commit to a vegan lifestyle, all of a sudden there is a wide-open culinary frontier to explore. You are sort of forced into checking out new cuisines, cooking methods, and ingredients from all over the world, on your mission to seek out nourishing, interesting, and satisfying flavors. Before I was vegan, there were probably twenty to thirty different things I would eat. Now I have the freedom and inspiration to check out everything this earth has to offer. Rather than being limited in my choices, I am finally really free!

And while you *can't* consume dead animals, you also no longer want to. You are aware of the suffering you cause by harming animals, and it's just not

---

Once you are aware that you can live a happy, fully satisfied life without causing harm to animals, being a carnivore is a tough thing to justify.

---

something you feel okay with anymore. Once you are aware that you can live a happy, fully satisfied life without causing harm to animals, being a carnivore is a tough thing to justify.

I became fully vegan on the day my first daughter was born. I was nineteen years old, and we had a fantastic, natural home birth, during which my wife labored for twenty-two hours. The whole time she labored, I thought about how important breast-feeding was going to be for our child, both physically and spiritually. Knowing how sacred that connection is between a mother and child, I decided I could never get in the way of that process for any living creature again. How could I drink milk when that milk had always been intended for a baby calf or goat? So I left my love of fancy cheeses behind and never looked back. When your intention is to cause

as little suffering as possible, you begin to discover many ways in which you have been harming others, and become determined to root those behaviors out.

Sure, eating roadkill or leftover hamburgers out of the garbage causes no direct suffering to animals; but I'd prefer to eat a nourishing salad of wild edibles, or greens from my front-yard garden, any day. Without wanting to be a real downer or to get too technical, I want to just suggest that perhaps taking eggs, milk, honey, skin, and other "by-products" from animals causes them suffering. If you have some kind of free-range fantasy about the lives modern farm animals live, you need to do some diligent research. No question about it, our modern factory farms, as well as those smaller farms that claim to produce "happy," humanely raised meat, are terrifying, sad places. Here's a good way to judge if an animal is being raised humanely: Ask yourself if you would put yourself, your mother, or your child in the place of the animal. Would you be happy seeing your child held captive against its will to produce milk or eggs all of its life? What happens then after your child is "spent"? Where does it go from there?

✳

I had been working for years at a vegan restaurant that abruptly went out of business. That closing was an opportunity for me to finally go out on my own and do my own thing. For a couple of years, I did vegan catering, taught cooking classes, and Joey and I had a stand at the farmer's market in Red Bank, New Jersey. We would stay up for almost forty-eight hours every weekend, baking nonstop, and by the time we opened the stand on Sunday, we were so tired. But our stand got popular really fast, and we sold out of food almost every week. Our kids grew up going to the farmer's market with us; Red Bank is also where we live, and it's such a treat to be able to serve our community every week. I have been making food for some of these folks for a decade, since long before I had my own business. There are customers whose kids we have watched grow up, and Joey has made every birthday cake for them since their mom's baby shower.

Red Bank Sundays are really differently paced from the other days of the week for us—nothing like the lunch rush in New York City. Most everyone on the Snail's line takes the time to hang out with complete strangers, and the community sparks. We serve a diverse crowd in Red Bank, including families, farmers, people of all economic and social backgrounds, and more than a few doggies; even the cops know where the best donuts can be found. This is really one of my favorite things to see while I am hustling hard on the grill: people from all walks of life uniting on behalf of yummy nonviolent food. I like to think that beautiful connections and special friendships get formed at the Red Bank farmer's market. I hope we can always be part of it and continue to form the backdrop with the aroma of pancakes.

❋

For about eight years I had been dreaming of running a vegan food truck, and Joey and I had started looking for used food trucks to realize that dream. We had such pure intentions: We simply wanted to have a vegan food truck to change the world, to end factory farms and bring on absolute animal and human liberation worldwide. We saw a gorgeous food truck for sale near scenic Keansburg, New Jersey. They were asking seventy thousand dollars, way more than we could possibly get together; but Joey had a great plan! Since we were doing this project as a means to end suffering for countless beings, we would get a lottery ticket. And because of our mission, we would definitely win, and that meant we would be able to buy the truck.

That afternoon, I went to our corner store to purchase the ticket. I had never played the lottery before, but because we were going to win no matter what, it didn't even matter what numbers I picked. A couple of days later, Joey told me to claim our winnings so we could buy the truck. I walked into the bodega, waving my ticket in the air, announcing, "I'm here to claim my money!" The lovely Gujarati woman at the counter scanned my ticket, then said, in a very matter-of-fact tone, "Sorry." I burst into hysterical laughter. I hadn't even considered for a second that we didn't have a winning ticket. It was so funny. We still ended up getting a food truck started, of course—just not *that* way.

As it turned out, we didn't know anything about the mechanics or economics of mobile food vendors when we finally got our first truck. Joey and I hunted around car lots, eBay, and Craigslist for something within our very small budget. The truck we found was a twenty-year-old box truck that had been a halal food truck (and before that a Southern food truck, and before that a bread delivery truck). It had well over one hundred thousand miles, and when it arrived it came with more problems than we realized. When we took it on its first test drive, we hit a bump and heard a nasty crashing thud. Everything from the catalytic converter and back was just lying there on the ground; the whole exhaust system had fallen off. But I was in love. The guys selling us the truck took off another five hundred dollars, and I purchased the truck that day for eleven thousand dollars in cash.

Okay, I was a total sucker—but a sucker with a dream. I had the truck parked in my driveway under a tarp while I worked on it for months. People would come over and I'd show them this wreck, and to most of them the thing just looked like the wheels might fall off. Maybe only I could see the potential locked deep inside the bad brakes and the walls in desperate need of a power-washing.

> ## *I don't make food that pretends to be something it isn't—just food that's overwhelmingly made with love and with intentions to make the world a more blissful, peaceful place.*

I didn't really think I would do much to the truck before opening it—maybe just make the outside look pretty and give it a serious deep cleaning. Our friend Billy Dolan, who is a general contractor, came to check it out one day, and before we knew it, we had gutted the whole truck. Close friends pitched in, helping with everything from plumbing to stainless fabrication, to the beautiful artwork that adorns the outside of the truck. So many people helped transform this gross thing that had been a morgue, a purveyor of dead animal–based food, into a beautiful sanctuary, destined to bring plant-based food to thousands of people, and maybe, I hoped, have a hand in helping people switch to a plant-based diet. People regularly ask me how to turn devout meat eaters on to yummy vegan food, and that mission

is at the core of everything I do with cooking. I'm less interested in feeding people who already "get" veganism than I am in impressing people who think vegan food sucks. I think the strategy that works the best is to make food that is textured, flavorful, and *just happens to be* vegan. I don't make food that pretends to be something it isn't—just food that's overwhelmingly made with love and with intentions to make the world a more blissful, peaceful place.

❋

Most days on the truck are really fun, and we get to make a lot of people happy. Maybe our karma for having such a great time most of the time is that sometimes the world gets turned upside down, and we end up in food truck hell. Here's how a day like that went back in 2013.

I got to the truck at five A.M. to stock it and drive it into Manhattan. Upon getting to the Financial District, I found that pretty much the entire neighborhood was blocked off for a film shoot, and any streets that weren't blocked off were loaded with parked cars. I REALLY hate to skip the FiDi, but when there is filming it's just not possible to park. To turn a bad situation around, I decided we would head up to West Fifty-Fifth Street.

We got to Midtown and started up the generator. It sounded really bad, like a jackhammer, and now in addition to that, our refrigerator wasn't maintaining the proper temperature. If we couldn't get it cold fast, we'd have to throw out all our food. I tried to call everyone I could think of to come fix the truck on the road, but no one was available. I weighed my options: One of our employees hadn't shown up, leaving us short-staffed, and since we really needed to deal with the generator and fridge, the best thing would be to give away all our donuts before spending the rest of the day trying to repair ol' Snaily. (Keep in mind that our donuts cost us a lot to make: Every ingredient is organic, even the oil we fry them in, and our bakers get paid more than anyone, because they work overnight.) Still, giving away those donuts was the glimmer of light and happiness in my day; seeing an endless stream of people coming up to the truck and getting really happy is one of the biggest joys for me.

After I waited at the shop to check out the generator for almost four hours, the mechanic told me that they would need to remove the generator and work on it for at least twenty-four hours. That would make it impossible to do the next day's event that we had booked weeks earlier. Then our refrigeration people told me that we would need to replace the fridge with a custom-made update. Before leaving, I checked our Twitter account and found angry comments about our not having been in the FiDi. Some of them were very mean and trollish, and it made me feel really bad to have disappointed so many people.

Finally, to top off an already frustrating day, I was rear-ended about a mile away from our kitchen. Our truck sustained some damage, but, thankfully, nothing too major, mostly just body work. While we were waiting for the police to arrive, someone in a big SUV started trying to go down the road we were all on. The driver was a really pissed-off muscle man, and he came up to me, screaming and cursing, saying that if I didn't immediately move the truck, he was going to drive it out of the way himself. I thought for sure he was going to kick my ass, but by some miracle, I convinced him to go another way. I collapsed in the truck, tears welling up in my eyes. Why does it have to be so hard to make people yummy vegetarian food?

Even if every day went like this, I know I don't really have anything to complain about. I have traveled with my family to third-world countries where people make their children into beggars, or watch them starve to death. I have seen so much real suffering in this world, and my petty little Cinnamon Snail problems are, in the scheme of things, not a big deal at all. And I really have so much to be grateful for: I love my kids and wife. My staff and crew are amazing, and they are like family to me. Our customers are so supportive, and their compassion is inspiring to me. I get to make yummy food for a living, and because I'm my own boss, no one can force me to cut corners or compromise the integrity of my food to make it more profitable.

No matter how stressful running a food truck can be, we are married to the game, and we will always fight through the nightmares into the light.

MY VEGAN PANTRY

SOME KOOKY (AND NOT-SO-KOOKY) THINGS IN THE SNAIL'S PANTRY

Just going vegan today? Yay! I am out buying you balloons right now and getting ready to shower you with a bucket of confetti! So how are you going to make all this new food? Oh wait, that's probably why you got this book!

There are likely a ton of vegan ingredients you already have in your kitchen, but here are some other fun items you can use that you may not already know and love. (And anywhere you see the (GF) icon, that means the recipe is also gluten-free!) These ingredients will make your mouth travel far and wide with brand new flavors, and will make you so good at mastering the vegan universe, you'll never go back to boring food again.

NON-MEAN PROTEINS

Don't be mean to cows and chickens! These are some ingredients to use as "the meat" of a recipe.

✳ (GF) **Tofu** is coagulated soy milk that has been strained of most of its liquid. Tofu comes in lots of varieties, which are suitable for different uses. For most of my grilling, frying, and roasting recipes, I use extra-firm tofu, which has very little water in it and doesn't fall apart easily. If you want to try a super-firm tofu, try getting a firm or extra-firm *sprouted* tofu, which is more nutritious and easier to digest than tofu made from unsprouted beans.

I occasionally use **silken tofu**, which is very watery, falls apart easily, and is suitable for being pureed into creams or puddings. Most people are familiar with this form of tofu from its appearances in tiny cubes in miso soup.

✳ (GF) **Tempeh** is an Indonesian food made by fermenting whole soybeans and rice into long, half-inch-thick cakes. Tempeh tends to be very firm, and has a subtle cultured flavor. Most tempeh available in supermarkets is pretty uninspiring, so I often roast tempeh in a marinade, or simmer it in a flavorful broth to soften and give it a base flavor before grilling, frying, or sautéing it.

✳ **Seitan** is a traditional Buddhist substitute for meat, made by simmering wheat gluten dough in a flavorful broth. The result is a sliceable vegan protein that has a texture similar to muscle fibers in various meats. Try to find store-bought seitan that is not preseasoned, so it can be as versatile as possible.

ALTERNAMILKS, BUTTERS, AND CHEESES

✱ (GF) **Soy Milk** is made from blending cooked soybeans with water, straining and boiling the liquid, and often flavoring it to cover up the slightly beany, proteiny flavor. When shopping for soy milk, try to find unsweetened varieties and look for brands with the shortest list of ingredients (organic, non-GMO brands will be best for this, and kindest to our planet).

✱ (GF) **Almond Milk** (and many other nut milks, see pages 55 to 60) is made from blending soaked almonds with water. It tends to be a bit thinner than soy milk, but has a really fantastic subtle flavor. Look for unsweetened varieties with short ingredient lists.

✱ (GF) **Coconut Milk** is made by emulsifying coconut meat and coconut water, and filtering out the fiber. Canned organic coconut milk is rich and creamy, so don't get "lite" or "low fat," or you will miss out on the main awesome thing coconut milk can lend to your cooking.

✱ (GF) **Margarine** has gotten a bad reputation from the mediocre old-school version, but now you can find excellent margarines made naturally that have no hydrogenated oils and

lots of great flavor to replace butter in vegan baking and cooking. I prefer to use Earth Balance brand, which is widely available in health food stores and comes in premeasured sticks.

✱ (GF) **Vegan Cream Cheese** You can totally make your own **tofu cream cheese**, but there are a few vegan tofu cream cheeses on the market that function almost exactly like dairy-based cream cheese.

✱ (GF) **Vegan Mayonnaise** is pretty simple to make, because mayonnaise is basically oil emulsified with acid. There are also some excellent store-bought vegan mayonnaises, my favorite of which is Vegenaise, which can be found at any health food store.

OILS, VINEGARS, AND BOTTLED SAUCES

✱ (GF) **Umeboshi Plum Vinegar** is probably my desert-island ingredient—it's in an embarrassing number of my recipes, because IT IS THE BEST. I know what you are thinking . . . "Plum vinegar? Sounds sweet and fruity." But this vinegar, made from bright pink, pickled Japanese plums, is super tart, salty, and rich in umami flavor. It really brightens up almost any

dish and brings flavors alive, if used in moderation.

✱ (GF) **Rice Vinegar** is made from fermented white or brown rice and has a sharp and slightly funky flavor. It's great for emulating the acidity of dairy (see Dilly Tofu Sour Cream, page 38) and is right at home in Asian soups and sauces.

✱ Extracted from very mature coconuts, **Coconut Oil** (GF) is a rich fat that becomes solid at temperatures below the upper 70s. This stuff is unbelievable for baking, sautéing, and frying. I use both natural unrefined and refined coconut oil. (Whatever you do, don't confuse coconut oil with the packaged coconut butter—that fibrous stuff is costly and not useful for much beyond making macaroons. If you use it instead of coconut oil, it will do nothing for your recipe, and make panda bears all over the planet so, so sad. (Boohoo. Sad pandas.)

✱ (GF) **Toasted Sesame Oil** comes from toasted pressed sesame seeds and is best for dressings and light sautéing, as it will give a nutty flavor to the dish. (It's not suitable for heavy cooking or frying, as it will burn and smoke at a fairly low temperature.)

THE SWEET STUFF

✳ Folks get thrown off by the term **"Evaporated Cane Juice"** (GF) because this is not a liquid sweetener. Instead, sugar cane is juiced, and the liquid is then boiled or evaporated off, until only the crystallized sugar remains. It is the most versatile and suitable natural substitution for bleached white sugar in any recipe.

✳ (GF) **Sucanat** (an abbreviation for SUgar CAne NATural) is probably the most minimally processed granulated sugar on the market. It is flavorful and medium brown, with plenty of molasses and minerals still intact. It's great for sweetening teas and other beverages, but because of the large crystals, avoid using it for cakes, donuts, frostings, and glazes.

✳ (GF) **Agave Nectar** is a thick, very sweet syrup made from the agave cactus (the same plant that gives us tequila). Like many liquid sweeteners, agave becomes thicker if it is cold, so store agave at room temperature for easy and accurate measurements.

✳ (GF) **Yacón Syrup** comes from the yacón tuber that grows in the Andes mountains. The flavor is like a deep, naturally occurring caramel. Yacón syrup can be found at good health food stores or online from shops that specialize in raw foods.

BAKERY ODDS AND ENDS

✳ (GF) **Shredded Coconut** generally comes in two types. Supermarkets sell a variety of what I call "embalmed" shredded coconut, which is filled with tons of preservatives, as if it is being preserved for its coconutty funeral. Health food stores carry organic desiccated (dried), unsweetened shredded coconut, which packs a more authentic coconut flavor and texture than the supermarket garbage.

✳ (GF) **Coconut Flakes** are large, semiround, thin slices of dried mature coconut meat. Toasted and salted, they make a yummy snack, or are a great texture and flavor for a cake or donut topping.

✳ (GF) **Egg Replacer Powder** is a commercially available mixture of different starches. Several brands (such as Bob's Red Mill and Ener-G) make egg replacer powders containing tapioca starch, potato starch, and sometimes arrowroot. When whisked rapidly together with liquid, the starches become an aerated foam, which can behave like egg whites in baking recipes.

IF YOU WANT TO SHOW ME LOVE, BUY ME FLOURS

✳ **Spelt** is an heirloom variety of wheat whose use dates back to around 5,000 B.C.E. As a type of wheat, it does contain gluten, just not as much as all-purpose flour. There are several types, but I only use white spelt flour here.

✳ (GF) **Amaranth** used to be an essential part of the Aztec diet and spiritual practices. When the Spanish colonized South America, they saw how important the grain was to the indigenous people, and in an attempt to control the Aztecs, they made its cultivation a crime punishable by death. But now amaranth is being cultivated in several varieties. Amaranth flour contains a ton of minerals and amino acids, including a whole heck of a lot of lysine.

✳ **Vital Wheat Gluten** is the pure protein of wheat. When you knead a dough together, gluten is created from stretchy chains of proteins. That elasticity allows the dough to expand around bubbles of gas excreted by leavening agents during baking. Vital wheat gluten is the pure protein extracted from wheat flour with all of its bran and other starches removed. This ingredient is key for making seitan, but you can also add it to dough to increase the amount of air the dough can hold.

❋ (GF) **Buckwheat Flour** is nutty and a bit bitter, and its glutinous batter performs nicely when combined with milder flours. Most grains need to be paired with a bean or legume to give your body the right selection of amino acids to become a protein source, but buckwheat is a complete protein by itself.

❋ (GF) **Rice Flour** is made by grinding rice down to a fine powder. It has a nice neutral taste that works well as part of flour mixes. Try to buy finely milled rice flour, as coarser ground rice flour can have a gritty, unpleasant mouthfeel, even after baking.

❋ (GF) **Sorghum Flour** comes from a grain that is often cultivated for use as a sweetener. As a grain, it has a pleasant malty flavor and is best when used in small doses.

❋ (GF) **Garbanzo / Fava Bean Flours** are finely milled and help absorb moisture to make soft and fluffy gluten-free baked goods. Unfortunately, these flours have a noticeable beany flavor, so don't use them for more than about a quarter of the volume of flours used in a gluten-free flour mix.

❋ (GF) **Chestnut Flour** inspires warm wintertime feelings for me. Dried roasted chestnuts are milled into a fine flour that is fantastic in pancakes, waffles, and donuts. Chestnut flour is fairly subtle on its own, so I usually like to augment it with some chopped, sliced, or ground whole chestnuts when I want a stronger flavor.

❋ (GF) **Arrowroot Starch** is a super-fine starchy powder extracted from the tubers of the arrowroot plant. This fine starch is great for thickening liquids into puddings, and helps to replace the binding and stretching actions of gluten in dough. Arrowroot is frequently adulterated with potato starch or tapioca starch, but neither added starch will affect the functionality or flavor of the arrowroot, and they are all naturally derived starches.

❋ (GF) **Gluten-Free Flour Mixes** can now be found from several flour companies. These mixes tend to be heavy on fava, garbanzo, and rice flour, so they can have a beany flavor and dense quality.

❋ (GF) **Xanthan Gum** is a by-product of the metabolic activity of natural bacteria cultures. In minute doses, xanthan gum helps bind flour mixes and aids in the emulsion of fats and liquids to create creamy dressings and beverages.

❋ (GF) **Agar Agar** is a clear sea vegetable which, in a small dose, can really thicken things up, similar to the way gelatin works. Agar agar comes in sheets, flakes, and powder. The powder is easiest to measure accurately and will help you avoid small gelatinous flecks mixed into your food.

SUPERFOODS (ALL ANIMAL-FRIENDLY FOODS ARE SUPER!)

❋ (GF) **Cacao** comes as either whole beans (yummy in trail mix), nibs (coarsely crushed pieces of bean, lovely for garnishing desserts or pulsing into drinks), or powder (to be used in place of cocoa for more bitter chocolate flavor). See page 57 for more on cacao.

❋ (GF) **Maca** is a turniplike root from the Andes that has some powerful nutrition behind it. It is sold at health food stores and online in a powdered form, which is great in drinks and raw desserts.

❋ (GF) **Lucuma** is an orange-fleshed Peruvian fruit, rich in calcium, magnesium, and potassium. Fresh lucuma has a flavor similar to, but sweeter than, mamay, and dried powdered lucuma has a slightly bitter, burnt-caramel flavor.

❋ (GF) **Flax Meal** is a coarse flour produced by milling flax seeds. Flax meal is an easy way to make the omega fatty acids, for which flax is prized, easily digestible (because otherwise the whole seeds can pass through the body intact and undigested). The meal can be used for making raw crusts and breading, and can be whisked into liquid to form a slurry to replace eggs in baking recipes.

❋ (GF) **Hemp Seeds** are the nonpsychoactive (sorry) seeds of the cannabis hemp plant. The seeds are a great source of protein and omega fatty acids. It is possible to find shell-on hemp seeds (and they make a great snack!), but in my recipes, I use shelled hemp seeds, which are sometimes also referred to as hemp nuts. Shelled hemp seeds are great for making smooth milk that doesn't need to be strained, because the hemp seeds aren't very fibrous and don't have a hull.

❋ (GF) **Cacao Butter** is unheated fat from cacao beans. I like it most for naturally emulating the flavor of white chocolate (which is often made from artificial ingredients).

THAI AND INDIAN FLAVORS

❋ (GF) **Fresh Lemongrass** has a gorgeous, citrusy flavor that is essential to a lot of Thai dishes. It comes in long stalks (sometimes as long as 18 inches!), and is very fibrous. By simmering it or steaming it, lemongrass becomes easier to blend or puree.

❋ (GF) **Kaffir Lime Leaves** impart a strong citrusy bay leaf flavor to sauces and broths. Fresh lime leaves can be tough to find. At home, I often substitute leaves from my potted Meyer lemon tree.

❋ (GF) **Red Curry Paste** is usually made from ground chiles, lemongrass, lime leaves, galangal (Thai ginger), and garlic. You can easily make it at home, or purchase vegan brands like Thai Kitchen.

❋ (GF) **Tamarind Concentrate** is made from the tart cherrylike fruits of the tamarind pod, and it's an essential flavor in pad Thai and other Thai dishes. We use it in dressings, lemonade, and even donut glaze for its bright, exotic, fruity flavor.

❋ **Asafetida** is made from the dried resin of a root that is cultivated in India. Its pungent flavor is somewhere between that of garlic and feet . . . but in a good way! It's excellent in Indian dishes and those that require a slightly cheesy, eggy tang.

❋ Bright reddish-orange **Sambar Masala** contains fried dals, chiles, fenugreek, cumin, and other spices. It's wonderful on curried nuts and in marinades, and we sprinkle it on the curried lentil puff pastries on our truck.

JAPANESE AND CHINESE INGREDIENTS

❋ I use two variants of **Soy Sauce**, tamari (GF) and nama shoyu. The use of soy sauce dates way back to ancient China, where its salinity was used for preserving and fermenting. Soy sauces also provide umami flavor, which can really broaden the spectrum of flavor in a dish. Tamari is a dark thin Japanese-style soy sauce that is produced with little (or no) wheat. Nama Shoyu (raw soy) is a raw fermented soy sauce, which has a broader flavor palette.

❋ (GF) **Wasabi Powder** is made from Japanese horseradish (compared to the neon green wasabi found in most sushi restaurants, which contains little to no actual horseradish.) Real unadulterated wasabi powder can be found in some health food stores and in Asian markets.

❋ (GF) *Mirin* is a very mellow sweet rice vinegar, with a barely acidic yet pleasant flavor, best for dressings, glazes, marinades, and light broths.

❋ (GF) *Miso*, in its paste form, is traditionally made from ground fermented rice and soybeans. It has a brothy base flavor that can add saltiness to marinades, dressings, gravy, and vegan burger patties. Miso comes in hundreds of varieties, but I recommend white miso, which has a fairly neutral flavor.

❋ (GF) *Kombu* is a dark green sea vegetable that usually comes in long, wide strips. Cooking dried beans with some kombu in the cooking water makes them more flavorful and digestible, not to mention more nutritious.

❋ (GF) *Hijiki* is my favorite sea veggie, because it really has an unmistakable sea-vegetable flavor. It is easy to find dried, and rehydrates quickly for use in salads and dishes like our New England–Style Chickpea "Crab" Cakes (page 74).

❋ (GF) *Five-Spice Powder* is a spice mix made from ground star anise, Chinese cinnamon, cloves, hot chile peppers, and fennel seeds. You can make it yourself or find it at Asian food stores.

KOREAN INGREDIENTS

❋ (GF) *Korean Ground Chiles* have more flavor than heat, and are usually found dried and coarsely ground. The flakes are a little smaller than Italian crushed red pepper flakes, and the seeds have been sifted out before processing.

❋ (GF) Most *Kimchi* is made from napa cabbage and radishes, fermented in a paste made from chiles, scallions, salt, and sometimes ginger. There are some great kimchi recipes in this book (see page 175). Most commercially available kimchi is made with anchovies or fish sauce, but vegan kimchi can be found in good health food stores, though it will never be as good as the homemade stuff.

❋ *Gochujang* is a fermented Korean chile paste, and can happily go wherever you might think to put ketchup (burgers, veggie dogs, scrambled tofu, etc.). It is made with sweet glutinous rice flour, which gives it a thick, sticky texture.

BOURBON HAZELNUT
PANCAKES WITH
CARDAMOM BROWN
BUTTER

BReaKfast

23 Blue Corn Pancakes

24 Fried Dandelion Greens

27 Maple Mustard Breakfast Seitan Strips

28 Bourbon Hazelnut Pancakes

30 Fresh Fig Pancakes

32 Yacón and Cherry Pancakes

34 Poached Pear–Stuffed French Toast

37 Cranberry Brazil Nut Granola

38 Kasha and Fried Onion Blintzes

41 Almond Milk French Toast

45 White Chocolate Macadamia Granola

46 Beer-Battered French Toast

48 Cashew Oat Waffles

51 Shredded Root Vegetable Hash Browns

WHEN I STARTED THE CINNAMON SNAIL, there were very few exceptional breakfast options for vegans in New Jersey and New York City, and certainly there was nothing really yummy that you could grab on the run. I wanted to make sure we had a couple of unbelievable breakfast burritos, huge selections of freshly baked pastries, and other delights such as our Fresh Fig Pancakes with Chamomile–Blood Orange Syrup (page 30) and Beer-Battered French Toast with Juniper Salted Caramel and Rummy Cranberries (page 46).

Okay, don't get me wrong, it's a real victory for vegans all over New York City that you can now get bagels with tofu cream cheese in some delis—but isn't that kind of boring? Don't vegans also deserve an absolute bomb of a decadent breakfast? Shouldn't your breakfast be more ridiculously wonderful than anything you could get at a non-vegan restaurant, just as a reward for caring about animals?

Breakfast is the first meal a lot of people learn to make for themselves, and if you are lucky, you're taught by someone you love. My grandmother taught me how to make blintzes: I remember when she was making the crepes for them, she insisted on lifting up the edges with her fingertips and quickly peeling each crepe off the pan and flipping it with her bare hands. I got smacked on the wrists if I tried to do it with a spatula; Nana just had her way, and since she had a good seventy years on me, she was right.

Nana and I were really great friends, and I owe my unrelentingly positive attitude to her. I often slept at her apartment, not far from what is now our Midtown East stop with the truck. We would go for walks together and stay up late playing word games and just talking. In her mid-nineties, it was getting hard for Nana to still cook for herself, and she eventually moved in with my parents when she needed full-time care. There were fewer things she could do on her own, and she couldn't be the spontaneous person she had been for so many years. Around that time, we brought Nana in her wheelchair to watch a ballet class for my daughter Idil, who was about four years old. I watched her smiling in her wheelchair at her great-granddaughter. Nana passed away in her sleep later that week, just as Idil and I were on our way to visit her. To this day, I can't share my recipe for blintzes without telling you about the person who taught me how to cook them. She sits deep within me, and I still flip the crepes by hand for her.

Breakfast is a meal you can put a lot of love into, and often a place where I find that old notions about the limitations of vegan foods are proven wrong. Included in this chapter are a variety of the most popular breakfast items that we serve on the truck, as well as some special breakfast fantasies that just aren't possible on our little truck, but that you can enjoy at home.

BLUE CORN PANCAKES

This is one of the few menu items on our truck that has been on the menu since day one, proudly boasting its hardy Southwestern influence on our breakfast offerings. It's a flavorful, hearty, wholesome breakfast. We make these with spelt and blue cornmeal, so it's low in gluten (though read LOW, not gluten-free).

Why *Vermont* maple syrup? Vermont has a proud history of maple sugaring, and is close to New York, so the syrup doesn't need to travel far from tree to plate. We get organic maple syrup from a farm that has great integrity about their growing, harvesting, and processing. We honor and respect that.

MAKES 8 TO 10 PANCAKES

⅔ cup blue cornmeal

⅔ cup white spelt flour

1 teaspoon baking powder

½ teaspoon sea salt

1¼ cups unsweetened soy milk

3 tablespoons agave nectar

3 tablespoons plus ¼ cup canola or safflower oil

1½ teaspoons pure vanilla extract

Pine Nut Butter (page 255), for serving

⅓ cup Vermont maple syrup, for serving

1 Whisk together the cornmeal, spelt flour, baking powder, and sea salt in a mixing bowl. In a separate bowl, mix together the soy milk, agave nectar, 3 tablespoons oil, and vanilla extract. Make a well in the center of the dry ingredients, and add the wet ingredients. Whisk together to form a smooth, light blue batter. Set aside.

2 Heat a griddle, frying pan, or cast-iron skillet over medium heat. Once the pan is hot, heat about 1 tablespoon of oil, and spread it around the surface of the pan. Ladle out about ¼ cup of batter to form each pancake. Cook the pancakes for 2 to 3 minutes until bubbles form on the surface and the edges start lifting off the pan. Flip and fry on the other side for about 2 minutes, or just until cooked through. Add oil to the pan before frying the next batch.

3 Plate 3 pancakes per person with 1 to 2 tablespoons of pine nut butter spread between the layers of pancakes and dolloped on top. Serve syrup in a small pitcher on the side, warmed if preferred.

Fried Dandelion Greens

WITH LEMON GARLIC POTATOES

My twelve-year-old daughter, Idil, knows dandelion greens well: She did a research paper on this wild edible and medicinal plant. As fantastic as they are for you, dandelion greens are pretty bitter. But frying them mellows them out, and they go really well with loads of garlic and lemon. This recipe will help you fall in love with dandelion greens. You can serve these as a savory side to Blue Corn Pancakes (page 23) or alongside the Maple Mustard Breakfast Seitan Strips (page 27).

In addition to roasting on the potatoes, a fresh garlic paste is added right on the finished dish so that you get two different garlicky influences. I'm a big fan of cooking this way, because it brings you a more complete sense of an ingredient's spectrum of flavor.

SERVES 3 (GF)

7 garlic cloves

Grated zest and juice of 2 lemons

2 tablespoons white miso paste

1 tablespoon dried oregano

1 tablespoon dried thyme

2 teaspoons crushed red pepper flakes

6 tablespoons extra-virgin olive oil

4 medium Yukon Gold potatoes, with skins on, cut into ¼-inch cubes

2 tablespoons brown mustard seeds

1 bunch of dandelion greens, coarsely chopped (about 2 cups)

1 medium jalapeño pepper, stemmed, seeded, and sliced

3 tablespoons umeboshi plum vinegar

½ teaspoon sea salt

1 Preheat the oven to 350°F. Line a rimmed baking sheet with parchment paper and lightly oil the paper.

2 Mince 5 of the garlic cloves and add them to a mixing bowl with the lemon zest and juice, miso, oregano, thyme, red pepper flakes, and 3 tablespoons of the olive oil. Add the potatoes to the mixture. Spread the potatoes and all of the marinade on the prepared baking sheet, and bake for 18 to 22 minutes, stirring once, until the potatoes are golden brown and soft.

3 Heat the remaining 3 tablespoons of olive oil in a large cast-iron skillet or wok. Once hot, add the mustard seeds. Once the mustard seeds start to pop, add the dandelion greens and let cook, stirring occasionally, for about 3 minutes. Stir in the jalapeño, umeboshi vinegar, and roasted potatoes. Cover the pan, turn the heat off, and allow the greens to steam for a few minutes until the stems are tender and the leaves are wilted.

4 Mince the remaining 2 garlic cloves as small as you can. Sprinkle the salt onto the minced garlic and, using the side of your knife, press and smear the garlic into a coarse paste. Stir the garlic paste into the cooked potatoes and greens. Serve warm.

maple mustard Breakfast seitan strips

This is not your typical seitan recipe: This is extra-naughty fried gluten. Seitan makes for a great ribs/sausage texture; just make sure to toss the strips in the glaze (or alternatively, in massive amounts of your favorite hot sauce) before eating them, because on their own they are kinda plain. The dough is made from vital wheat gluten (the protein of wheat, removed from wheat's starches and bran) and pureed tofu and veggies. The trick to getting them just right is to form pieces that are not too thick; you want to make sure the inner dough gets cooked without the outside having to fry excessively.

SERVES 6

For the seitan strips
½ block extra-firm tofu
3 tablespoons soy sauce
½ medium yellow onion, chopped
1 celery stalk, chopped
1 medium carrot, chopped
3 garlic cloves, chopped
1¼ cups vital wheat gluten
2 tablespoons paprika
1 tablespoon ground coriander
1 tablespoon ground cumin
1 tablespoon Mexican chili powder
2 cups canola oil, for frying
Minced scallions, crushed red pepper flakes, and smoked paprika (optional; for garnish)

For the maple mustard glaze
3 tablespoons pure maple syrup
2 tablespoons unsulphured molasses
¼ cup whole-grain mustard
2 tablespoons brown rice vinegar
1 tablespoon tamari
1 tablespoon chopped fresh thyme leaves (or 2 teaspoons dried thyme)

1 **Make the seitan:** In a food processor, puree the tofu and soy sauce until completely smooth. Add the chopped onion, celery, carrot, and garlic. Process for about 60 seconds, so that the veggies are broken down into a fine meal. (If the veggies are still in larger pieces, they will be more likely to fall out during frying, and you will have fewer veggies in the seitan and more burnt-up crud in your oil.)

2 In a mixing bowl, combine the wheat gluten, paprika, coriander, cumin, and chili powder. Mix in the blended tofu and vegetables, kneading for a minute or so to form a thoroughly combined dough.

3 On a cutting board, press the dough into a 3½ by 10-inch rectangle, ½ inch thick. Slice the length of the dough into twenty ½-inch-wide strips.

4 **Make the glaze:** In a mixing bowl, whisk together the ingredients for the maple mustard glaze.

5 Heat the canola oil to about 355°F in a skillet or pan with high sides. In two batches, fry the strips of dough in the hot oil, turning as needed to thoroughly brown and crisp the outsides, about 5 minutes total. Remove the fried strips to a paper-towel-lined plate just long enough to soak up any residual oil.

6 Toss the hot seitan strips in the glaze until they are completely coated. To serve, garnish the seitan strips with sliced scallions and sprinkle with red pepper flakes and smoked paprika, if desired.

Bourbon Hazelnut Pancakes
WITH CARDAMOM BROWN BUTTER

This is exactly what breakfast at the Cinnamon Snail is about. Why would you serve yourself boring plain pancakes? Don't you love life? Why aren't you making your kitchen smell like hazelnuts, freshly roasted with bourbon and spices? WHY? Slow your roll—I am sure you are a nice person. So you deserve yummy breakfasts, and the people around you deserve them as well. What about your dad—he thinks your vegan diet is weird, right? Why don't you feed him the best damn pancakes he ever ate in his life? Make everyone you know who doesn't get your veganism some SERIOUSLY BOMB, absurdly good pancakes. They will connect the dots later, somewhere at the bottom of their first stack, as to why you went vegan in the first place. . . . But whatever ingredients you're adding, this is a lovely all-around versatile pancake recipe that you can trust for yielding stacks of tasty fluffies. If you feel creative, use this as a base recipe to add all kinds of absolutely fun things, too.

Quick warning: You'll want to make the cardamom butter in advance, so it can set up nicely in the refrigerator. Plan to make it the day *before* (or at least a few hours before) you make the pancakes, so you'll have a nice, pretty butter pat to top your steaming hot pancakes, along with a generous drizzling of Ginger Stout Syrup (page 253).

MAKES 8 TO 12 PANCAKES

For the cardamom brown butter
¼ cup unsweetened soy milk
½ teaspoon rice vinegar
4 teaspoons pure maple syrup
¼ teaspoon sea salt
¼ teaspoon ground cardamom
¼ teaspoon ground cloves
½ cup refined coconut oil
   (melted to 75° to 100°F, if not
   already in liquid form)
2 tablespoons extra-virgin olive oil
¼ teaspoon xanthan gum

For the bourbon candied hazelnuts
2 cups hazelnuts
½ cup evaporated cane juice
¼ cup bourbon
½ teaspoon sea salt
1 teaspoon ground cinnamon
2 tablespoons canola oil

For the pancakes
1½ cups all-purpose flour
2 teaspoons baking powder
2 teaspoons baking soda
½ teaspoon sea salt
¼ cup pure maple syrup
1⅔ cups unsweetened soy milk
3 tablespoons canola oil, plus more for
   frying the pancakes
1 teaspoon pure vanilla extract
Ground cinnamon and/or vegan
   powdered sugar (optional; for
   garnish)

1 **Make the cardamom butter:** Place the soy milk, rice vinegar, maple syrup, salt, cardamom, and cloves in a high-speed blender and mix on high speed for 10 seconds. Let sit for a minute or so—the mixture will have a curdled, thick consistency like buttermilk. Add the melted coconut oil, olive oil, and xanthan gum. Blend on high speed for 60 seconds to thoroughly emulsify. Pour into an airtight container, and chill in the freezer for an hour. Transfer the tub to the refrigerator, and use as needed. (You will have about 1 cup butter.)

2 **Make the candied hazelnuts:** Preheat the oven to 350°F. Line a rimmed baking sheet with parchment paper. Pulse the hazelnuts a few times in a food processor to break them into smaller pieces. Mix the ground nuts and all the remaining ingredients together in a medium bowl and distribute evenly on the prepared baking sheet. Bake for 12 minutes, flipping the nuts

halfway through to ensure even baking. Allow the nuts to cool, and break up any large clusters; store in an airtight container at room temperature. (The nuts will keep for up to a month.)

3 **Make the pancakes:** In a mixing bowl, whisk together the flour, baking powder, baking soda, and salt. Make a well in the center, and add the maple syrup, soy milk, oil, and vanilla extract. Whisk together to form a smooth batter.

4 Heat a skillet or griddle over medium heat. Lightly oil the pan and ladle the pancake batter evenly onto the hot surface, forming pancakes in any size you like. Sprinkle 1 to 2 tablespoons of the bourbon hazelnuts onto each circle of batter and let cook for about 2 minutes. Carefully flip the pancakes when bubbles appear in the center and the edges start to brown lightly and lift away from the pan. Flip and allow to cook on the second side for an additional 2 minutes.

5 Place 3 or 4 pancakes on each plate. Top with a pat of the cardamom butter, a sprinkle of bourbon hazelnuts, and a dash of cinnamon and/or powdered sugar for garnish, if desired.

Fresh Fig Pancakes
WITH CHAMOMILE-BLOOD ORANGE SYRUP

This is really one of my favorite items on the truck, but it only gets to live on our menu for a couple of months every fall, while fresh local figs are available. I like to use Brown Turkey figs for these, but Black Mission figs will work great, too. The idea is simple: It's a fairly plain batter on which fresh fig slices are placed after the batter has been poured on the griddle. That way, when they are flipped, the figs caramelize and become tender within, but really crisp on the surface. The syrup has flavors of a great orange preserve, but with the wonderful floral aroma of chamomile. Naturally, I think chamomile just begs to have a culinary play date with pine nuts, both of which party well with the figs; so you'll want to get out your container of Pine Nut Butter (page 255) for this recipe.

MAKES 8 PANCAKES

For the syrup
½ cup loose chamomile flowers
2 blood oranges
1¼ cups brown rice syrup
¼ teaspoon orange extract
1 teaspoon mirin

For the pancakes
¾ cup all-purpose flour
⅔ cup chestnut flour
2 teaspoons baking powder
2 teaspoons baking soda
½ teaspoon sea salt
3 tablespoons evaporated cane juice
1⅔ cups unsweetened soy milk
1 teaspoon pure vanilla extract
6 tablespoons canola oil
10 ripe figs, sliced, plus more for garnish
2 tablespoons vegan powdered sugar (optional; for garnish)
¼ cup toasted pine nuts (optional; for garnish)

1 **Make the syrup:** Place the chamomile flowers and 1 cup water in a small saucepan and bring to a boil over high heat. Turn the heat off and cover the pot; let steep for 5 minutes.

2 Zest and juice the oranges into a separate pot, discarding only the seeds. Add the rice syrup, orange extract, and mirin, and strain the steeped tea into the pot. Whisk the syrup together and bring to a boil over medium heat. Serve the syrup warm, or store in the refrigerator for up to a week.

3 **Make the pancake batter:** Whisk together both flours, the baking powder, baking soda, and salt in a mixing bowl. Make a well in the center of the dry ingredients, and add the evaporated cane juice, soy milk, vanilla extract, and 3 tablespoons of the oil. Whisk together to form a smooth batter.

4 **Cook the pancakes:** Heat a skillet or griddle over medium heat. Lightly oil the pan with some of the remaining oil. Ladle ¼ cup of batter for each pancake onto the griddle. Sprinkle 3 or 4 fig slices onto each circle of batter. Let cook for about 2½ minutes, then carefully flip the pancakes when bubbles start to appear closer to the center and the edges start to brown lightly and lift away from the pan. Allow to cook on the second side for an additional 2 minutes or so until perfectly cooked through. Repeat with the batter, adding oil to the pan as needed.

5 Plate 2 or 3 pancakes per person; top with a generous drizzle of the chamomile syrup, a few fresh fig slices, and, if you like, a dash of powdered sugar and a few toasted pine nuts.

yacón AND CHERRY pancakes

WITH LEMON CASHEW CREAM AND RED WINE CHERRIES

A really hooked-up breakfast is not easy for folks avoiding gluten, but these pancakes don't miss the gluten one bit. They laugh at gluten! They pick up gluten and crush it in their pancake hands, hurling it into the sun. Basically, this is a recipe that makes a sweet brunch treat for someone you love, right before you ask them to marry you. You can use any fresh cherry that is available to you, but I really do love Bing cherries the most. They have a great balance of tart and sweet, with a deep, classic unmistakable cherry flavor. What's that? You think cherries suck? Well, replace them with something you like more. (Even though you are wrong about cherries sucking.)

As for the syrup, yacón syrup has a great natural caramel flavor, but it requires no time or skill to put together like sugar-based caramel does. It's also really great for your digestive flora. (If you can't find yacón syrup, try brown rice syrup instead or even the Red Wine Syrup on page 253.)

MAKES 12 PANCAKES (GF)

For the lemon cashew cream
1 cup cashew pieces, soaked in water at least 20 minutes, then drained and rinsed
2 tablespoons unrefined coconut oil
3 tablespoons agave nectar
¼ teaspoon sea salt
½ teaspoon pure vanilla extract
Grated zest and juice of 2 lemons

For the red wine cherries
1 tablespoon extra-virgin olive oil
2 cups halved, pitted sweet cherries
1 cup dry red wine
¼ cup evaporated cane juice
1 tablespoon grated lemon zest, plus more for serving
2 teaspoons arrowroot

For the pancakes
½ cup rice flour
½ cup sifted coconut flour
⅓ cup sorghum flour
⅓ cup garbanzo or fava bean flour
½ teaspoon xanthan gum
2 teaspoons baking powder
½ teaspoon sea salt
¼ cup yacón syrup (or brown rice syrup), plus more for serving
1⅔ cups unsweetened soy milk
3 tablespoons canola oil, plus more for frying the pancakes
1 teaspoon pure vanilla extract
1 cup pitted chopped cherries, plus more for serving
2 tablespoons chopped candied lemon rind (optional; for garnish)
Ground cinnamon (optional; for garnish)

1 **Make the cashew cream:** Place the drained cashews, coconut oil, agave nectar, salt, and vanilla in a blender with 2 tablespoons water, and blend on high speed for 40 seconds. Add the lemon zest and juice and pulse a few times to evenly distribute. Pour the contents of the blender into an airtight container and chill until ready to use (it will last up to 3 days).

2 **Cook the cherries:** Heat the olive oil in a small saucepan over medium heat. Sauté the cherries in the hot oil, stirring, for 2 minutes to sear the cherries. When the skins are blistered, add the red wine, evaporated cane juice, and lemon zest. Bring the mixture to a boil.

3 In a small bowl, mix the arrowroot with ¼ cup water. Pour the arrowroot slurry into the boiling cherry mixture and stir to distribute. Turn off the heat and cool the mixture for 15 minutes. Transfer the simmered cherries to an airtight container to cool until use, or keep on the stove to keep warm.

(You will have about 1 pint cherries; any leftovers can be stored in the refrigerator for up to 4 days.)

4 **Make the pancakes:** Whisk together all four flours, the xanthan gum, baking powder, and salt in a mixing bowl. In a separate bowl, mix together the yacón syrup, soy milk, canola oil, and vanilla extract. Make a well in the center of the dry ingredients, and pour the wet ingredients into the center. Whisk together to form a smooth batter.

5 Heat a skillet or griddle over medium heat, and lightly oil the pan with canola oil. Cook 3 pancakes in the pan at a time, measuring each one out with about ¼ cup of batter. Sprinkle 2 tablespoons of chopped cherries onto each pancake. Let the pancakes cook until bubbles start to appear close to the center and the edges start to lift away from the pan, about 2 minutes. Flip and allow the pancakes to cook on the second side for as much time as it took on the

first side. Transfer the finished pancakes to a plate and cover to keep warm; repeat with the rest of the batter.

6 Plate 3 or 4 pancakes per serving and top with a dollop of lemon cashew cream and a generous spoonful of the simmered cherries. Drizzle the stack of pancakes with yacón syrup; garnish with additional chopped cherries, additional lemon zest, and candied lemon rind, if using; and dust with a sprinkling of cinnamon, if desired.

Poached Pear-Stuffed French Toast
WITH SPICED PECANS

There's nothing fancier than putting on a golden jumpsuit and making this fancy stuffed French toast. To stuff the toast, you will need a crusty, soft Pullman (rectangular loaf-style) bread. I usually use a fresh-baked seven-grain bread from my local bakery, and I buy the bread unsliced, so I can make nice thick slices that are big enough to stuff without falling apart. Leftover bread is perfect for French toast, since it's firmer and can put up with more abuse without stretching or tearing. This stuff is best drenched in Red Wine Syrup (page 253), which brings out the more savory notes in the French toast.

MAKES 6 THICK SLICES

For the spiced pecans
1 cup pecan pieces
½ teaspoon ground nutmeg
½ teaspoon ground cinnamon
¼ teaspoon ground cayenne
3 tablespoons pure maple syrup
¼ teaspoon sea salt

For the French Toast
2⅔ cups all-purpose flour
1 teaspoon baking powder
1 teaspoon baking soda
½ teaspoon sea salt
2 cups unsweetened soy milk
⅓ cup pure maple syrup
¼ cup canola oil
1 medium-size soft Pullman bread of your choice
Vegan margarine, for frying
3 tablespoons vegan powdered sugar (optional; for garnish)
½ teaspoon ground cinnamon (optional; for garnish)
Fresh shaved pear slices (optional; for garnish)

For the pear filling
1½ cups dry red wine
½ cup evaporated cane juice
1 tablespoon grated lemon zest
1 cinnamon stick
½ teaspoon sea salt
3 Bartlett pears, peeled, cored, and halved
4 teaspoons cornstarch
3 tablespoons pure maple syrup

1 **Make the spiced pecans:** Heat a medium-size frying pan or cast-iron skillet over medium heat. Add the pecans, nutmeg, cinnamon, and cayenne to the pan and toast, tossing frequently, for about 4 minutes until the pecans become golden and fragrant. Add the maple syrup and sea salt. Continue to stir for about 2 minutes, while the maple syrup caramelizes around the nuts. Pour the nuts out onto a plate to cool.

2 **Make the batter:** Whisk together the flour, baking powder, baking soda, and salt in a mixing bowl. Add the soy milk, maple syrup, and oil, and whisk well. Set aside until ready to fry.

3 **Make the pear filling:** Mix the wine, evaporated cane juice, lemon zest, cinnamon stick, and salt in a saucepan and bring to a boil over high heat. Reduce the heat to medium low, add the pear halves, cover the pot, and allow the pears to cook for 8 minutes, until soft.

4 Whisk together the cornstarch and maple syrup in a small bowl, and pour it into the pot. Continue to cook for about 1 minute, stirring very gently to prevent lumps from forming. Remove the pot from the heat and allow to cool to room temperature. Remove the pears and chop them into ¼-inch pieces, then mix them back into the remaining liquid.

5 **Batter the toast:** Cut the bread into 6 slices, each about 1 inch thick. Place each slice flat on a cutting board. Carefully cut a 3-inch slit into one side of each slice of bread, extending the knife three quarters of the way through the width of the bread. If possible,

carefully remove a small amount of the bread from the inside of the "pocket." Pack ¼ cup of pear filling into each bread pocket.

6 **Fry the toast:** Heat a cast-iron skillet or griddle over medium heat. Coat the surface of the pan with vegan margarine. Dip one stuffed bread slice into the batter, coating all sides. Immediately remove the slice of bread from the batter and place it in the hot pan. When the

bottom edges appear golden and bubbly, flip the French toast and fry the other side for 2 minutes. Repeat with the remaining slices.

7 **To serve:** Place 1 slice in the center of each plate, and sprinkle with the spiced pecans. Garnish with powdered sugar and cinnamon, if using, and top with a couple of fresh pear shavings, if desired.

Cranberry Brazil Nut Granola ✿

1 cup Brazil nuts

½ cup unsalted, hulled sunflower seeds

⅓ cup shredded coconut

2¼ cups quick-cooking oats

3 tablespoons amaranth flour

⅓ cup pure maple syrup

Grated zest and juice of 1 orange

¼ teaspoon sea salt

1½ teaspoons ground cinnamon

1 teaspoon pure vanilla extract

3 tablespoons extra-virgin olive oil,
   plus more for greasing the pan

⅔ cup dried cranberries

Once upon a time we offered granola on our breakfast menu, with fun flavors like this one. In my first Food Network appearance, I was filmed for a show all about food trucks. Filming went on all day—we showed them some really crazy interesting entrées, acted really silly, and had a lot of fun. But when I finally caught the edited segment, eight hours of filming had been reduced to about four minutes, and one of the only pieces of dialogue they had was of me saying in a nerdy, cracking voice, "Yes, and we make our own granola." So typical of mainstream TV, to have all these manly barbecue trucks on their show, and then the wimpy vegan guy who sputters, "Yes, and we make our own granola." I decided that if I wanted to show the world some of the most impressive, badass vegan food possible, I was never going to mention granola's delicious dirty name again. Until now. (Serve this up with fresh blueberries and plenty of almond or soy milk.)

MAKES 1 QUART

1 Preheat the oven to 350°F. Line a rimmed baking sheet with parchment paper and lightly grease with olive oil.

2 Pulse the Brazil nuts in a food processor a few times to yield coarsely chopped pieces. Transfer the chopped Brazil nuts to a medium bowl. Add the sunflower seeds and coconut to the food processor, and process for 1 minute, to yield a coarse meal. Add the contents of the food processor to the bowl with the nuts. Mix in the oats, amaranth flour, maple syrup, orange zest and juice, salt, cinnamon, vanilla, the 3 tablespoons of olive oil, and 2 tablespoons water.

3 Evenly spread the granola onto the prepared pan. Bake for 8 minutes, then mix the contents of the pan around with a spatula, especially bringing pieces that were close to the edge into the center. Bake for an additional 6 to 8 minutes, until golden and fragrant.

4 Remove the pan from the oven, and while the granola is still hot, pour it into a medium bowl and mix in the dried cranberries. When the granola is cooled to room temperature, store in an airtight container. Serve in bowls with almond or soy milk and fresh berries.

Kasha AND Fried Onion Blintzes
WITH DILLY TOFU SOUR CREAM

This is probably my family's favorite breakfast that I make at home, and possibly the yummiest thing I can make. This is exactly how my nana would want me to cook this up, and I think of her every time I make them. Of course, you don't have to flip your crepes by hand as my grandmother taught me to do, and if you don't have Teflon fingertips, you probably shouldn't. To flip the crepes, using a very thin metal spatula, make sure the crepe is fully detached from the bottom of the pan before flipping.

No matter how you flip them, these blintzes are delicious with a big dollop of the vegan sour cream on top, as well as a spoonful or two of my Perfect Homemade Applesauce (page 254).

MAKES 4 BLINTZES WITH ALL THE FIXIN'S

For the dilly tofu sour cream
½ block extra-firm tofu, crumbled (about 1¼ cups crumbled)
2 teaspoons rice vinegar
2 teaspoons umeboshi plum vinegar
4 teaspoons evaporated cane juice
3 tablespoons melted coconut oil
1 teaspoon caraway seeds (optional)
3 tablespoons minced fresh dill

For the crepes
1¼ cups unsweetened soy milk
½ teaspoon apple cider vinegar
5 tablespoons extra-virgin olive oil
1½ teaspoons evaporated cane juice
1 cup all-purpose flour
3 tablespoons cornstarch
¼ teaspoon sea salt
2 tablespoons coconut oil
2 cups baby greens of your choice (optional; for serving)
¼ cup chopped fresh flat-leaf parsley (optional; for garnish)

For the kasha and fried onion filling
2 garlic cloves, minced
⅔ cup kasha (toasted buckwheat groats)
½ teaspoon sea salt
½ teaspoon freshly ground black pepper
½ teaspoon dried thyme
3 tablespoons extra-virgin olive oil
1 large yellow onion, chopped

1 Make the sour cream: Add the tofu, both vinegars, evaporated cane juice, coconut oil, and caraway seeds (if using) to a high-speed blender. Blend on high for 60 seconds to produce a very smooth cream. Pulse in the fresh dill to evenly incorporate. Chill the sour cream for at least 30 minutes, to achieve a slightly richer consistency. (This can be kept refrigerated for up to 4 days.)

2 Make the crepe batter: In a small bowl, whisk together the soy milk, vinegar, 3 tablespoons of the olive oil, and the evaporated cane juice. Whisk in the flour, cornstarch, and salt. Allow the batter to sit for 10 minutes, so that the flour becomes fully hydrated.

3 Cook the crepes: Heat a crepe pan or very shallow frying pan over medium-low heat. Melt about 1½ teaspoons of the coconut oil in the pan. Pour about ¼ cup of batter into the pan, and tilt the pan around to spread the batter out as thin as possible, covering as large a surface as possible. Allow the crepe to cook for about 3 minutes, until the top shows bubbles throughout and is partially dry. Work a very thin metal spatula around the perimeter of the crepe, to fully loosen it from the pan. When the crepe is completely detached, flip it and cook the other side for only about 1 minute, just to seal the batter. Transfer the crepe to a covered plate or pie pan, and repeat with the rest of the batter, adding more coconut oil as you make each crepe.

4 Make the filling: Toast the garlic and kasha in a frying pan or cast-iron skillet over medium heat for 3 minutes, stirring constantly. Stir in the salt, pepper, and thyme. Pour 1 cup water into the pan, and cover the pan. After a minute or so, lower the heat and let the mixture simmer for about 7 minutes to allow to the kasha to cook until tender.

5 Meanwhile, heat the olive oil in a separate pan over high heat. Once the oil is hot, cook the onions for about 6 minutes, stirring frequently, until the onions are golden brown. Scrape the onions and any remaining oil into the pan with the kasha, and fluff together with a fork.

6 To fill the crepes: Lay each crepe flat out on a cutting board. Place about ¼ cup of the kasha filling in the center of each crepe. Roll each crepe up like a burrito, tucking in all sides so that no filling can escape. When all the blintzes are formed, heat the remaining 2 tablespoons of olive oil in a cast-iron skillet or frying pan over medium heat. Carefully place all the blintzes into the pan, with the seams placed down onto the pan. Allow the blintzes to fry and brown longer on this first side to help seal them, 2 to 3 minutes. Carefully roll each blintz one quarter of the way around to fry one side, and continue frying and turning every 2 minutes until all surfaces are well browned.

7 Plate the blintzes over a bed of the baby greens, if using, and top with a dollop of the cool sour cream. Garnish the blintzes with the chopped parsley, if desired.

ALMOND MILK FRENCH toast WITH....

RASPBERRY-GRAPEFRUIT COULIS AND SMOKY ROASTED ALMONDS

Around the time we finished construction on our second truck, we'd been struggling with our waffle iron for a solid year. For whatever reason, our totally top-of-the-line commercial Belgian waffle maker kept having one problem after another. Though we kept a spare, it was getting annoying and expensive, and too often we had to tell people that they couldn't get waffles that day. We had to put up a sign (more than once) that read: "Today is National Waffle Iron Vacation Day! Even waffle irons need a break sometimes." It became evident that continuing to serve waffles on two trucks was going to be twice the headache as offering them on one truck.

So, much to the dismay of waffle fans everywhere, we stopped offering them and put a couple of hooked-up types of French toast on the menu in their place. This is one of those first substitute recipes, and I can personally say, I love it more than any waffle we ever offered. It's just yummy as heck, and I always love being able to offer a great gluten-free breakfast item.

SERVES 4 (GF)

For the roasted almonds
2 tablespoons pure maple syrup
2 tablespoons evaporated cane juice
2 tablespoons extra-virgin olive oil, plus more for greasing the pan
¼ teaspoon sea salt
1 teaspoon pure vanilla extract
1 teaspoon liquid smoke
½ teaspoon ground nutmeg
1 cup slivered almonds

For the raspberry-grapefruit coulis
1¼ cups frozen raspberries, thawed
Grated zest and juice of 1 ruby red grapefruit
⅓ cup pure maple syrup
2 teaspoons balsamic vinegar

For the French toast
1¼ cups almond milk
1 tablespoon ground cinnamon
3 tablespoons pure maple syrup
1 teaspoon pure vanilla extract
3 tablespoons oat flour
½ teaspoon sea salt
2 tablespoons extra-virgin olive oil
3 tablespoons coconut oil, for frying
8 slices gluten-free bread of your choice
1 cup fresh raspberries (optional; for garnish)
8 fresh mint leaves (optional; for garnish)
2 tablespoons vegan powdered sugar (optional; for garnish)
4 teaspoons grated grapefruit zest (optional; for garnish)

1 **Make the roasted almonds:** Preheat the oven to 350°F. Lightly oil a small pie pan or loaf pan.

2 In a small bowl, whisk together the maple syrup, evaporated cane juice, the 2 tablespoons of oil, the salt, vanilla, liquid smoke, and nutmeg. Add the slivered almonds and toss thoroughly to coat all surfaces of the almonds.

3 Spread the contents of the bowl out in the oiled pan. Bake for 7 minutes, then thoroughly flip the contents around. Bake for another 6 minutes, until the nuts are golden brown. Allow to cool completely before breaking apart the clusters.

4 **Make the raspberry-grapefruit coulis:** Place the raspberries, grapefruit zest and juice, maple syrup, and balsamic vinegar into a small saucepan, then cover and cook over medium heat for 6 minutes. Turn off the heat and allow the contents to cool to room temperature. Place the berry mixture into a blender and blend on low speed for 20 seconds, to macerate the berries without grinding the seeds too much. Run the resulting puree through a very fine mesh strainer to remove any seeds or pulp. Warm in a small saucepan for immediate use, store in an airtight container in the refrigerator for up to 3 days, or freeze for up to a month.

5 **Make the French toast dredging liquid:** Whisk together the almond milk, cinnamon, maple syrup, vanilla, oat flour, salt, and olive oil in a medium bowl.

6 **Cook the French toast:** Heat a frying pan or cast-iron skillet over medium heat. Melt about 1½ teaspoons of the coconut oil in the pan.

7 Cut the slices of bread on a diagonal, creating a total of 16 triangles. Soak 4 triangular pieces of bread in the batter, letting the excess liquid drain back into the bowl. Immediately transfer the pieces to the pan and fry on each side for about 4 minutes, until golden brown. Continue with the remaining slices of bread, adding coconut oil to the pan as needed.

8 Stack up 4 triangular pieces of bread per serving. Drizzle liberally with the raspberry-grapefruit coulis, and garnish with ¼ cup roasted almonds per plate. Garnish with the fresh raspberries, mint leaves, powdered sugar, and grapefruit zest, if desired.

White Chocolate macadamia Granola
WITH CHERRIES AND HUNZA RAISINS

Who says granola has to be bird food? Who doesn't want this heavenly white chocolate bar of a breakfast cereal? Only people who listen to Nickelback don't want it. The truth is, though, vegan white chocolate isn't so easy to come by, so this granola gets its white chocolate flavor from cacao butter and chocolate extract.

Hunza raisins are a variety of golden raisins grown way up in the Himalayas. They have a bright sweet-tart flavor and a great chewy texture. The Hunza people, for whom the raisins are named, supposedly have one of the longest, healthiest lifespans on earth. Rumor has it, their diet includes these raisins, plus fresh and dried fruit year-round, and NO animal fat. (If you can't get out to the Himalayas any time soon, look for these at your local Middle Eastern market, or use ordinary golden raisins instead.)

MAKES 1 QUART

1 cup unsalted, unroasted macadamia nuts
½ cup unsalted, hulled sunflower seeds
⅓ cup shredded coconut
2½ cups quick-cooking oats
½ cup pure maple syrup
½ teaspoon sea salt
¼ teaspoon ground cardamom
1 teaspoon chocolate extract
1 teaspoon pure vanilla extract
¼ cup melted cacao butter
2 tablespoons extra-virgin olive oil, plus more for greasing the pan
⅔ cup chopped dried cherries
½ cup yellow Hunza raisins

1 Preheat the oven to 350°F. Line a rimmed baking sheet with parchment paper and lightly grease it with olive oil.

2 Pulse the macadamia nuts in a food processor a few times to yield coarsely chopped pieces. Transfer the chopped macadamias to a medium bowl. Add the sunflower seeds and coconut to the food processor and process for 1 minute to yield a coarse meal. Add the contents of the food processor to the bowl with the nuts. Add the oats, maple syrup, salt, cardamom, chocolate extract, vanilla extract, melted cacao butter, the 2 tablespoons olive oil, and 3 tablespoons water, and thoroughly mix to combine.

3 Evenly spread the granola onto the prepared baking sheet. Bake the granola for 8 minutes, then remove the pan from the oven and mix the contents of the pan around with a spatula, especially moving pieces that were on the edges into the center. Bake for an additional 6 to 8 minutes, until everything is golden brown and fragrant. Remove the pan from the oven, scrape the hot granola into a medium bowl, and mix in the dried cherries and raisins. When fully cooled to room temperature, store in an airtight container for up to a month.

Beer-Battered FRENCH Toast

WITH JUNIPER SALTED CARAMEL and RUMMY CRANBERRIES

This French toast came up when I started thinking about what Thanksgiving would be like if it were a breakfast instead of a dinner. (It's really taken over the top when you add a dollop of Pumpkin Brown Butter, page 258.) It makes for an exciting seasonal brunch, and it's wonderful in tiny portions as a fun dessert for a really special winter dinner. Use a thick, crusty artisan bread for this (unless you are avoiding gluten—in which case, substitute your favorite gluten-free bread, flour, and beer, just like the Pilgrims did for their decadent, celiac-sensitive breakfasts back in the day). Serve it with the caramel syrup warmed up, because there's nothing in the world like warm caramel sauce. Breakfast of champions.

SERVES 4

For the rummy cranberries
½ cup spiced rum
3 tablespoons pure maple syrup
1 teaspoon molasses
Grated zest and juice of 1 orange
½ teaspoon tamari
1½ cups fresh cranberries, coarsely chopped

For the juniper salted caramel syrup
6 juniper berries
¼ cup coconut milk
¼ cup brown rice syrup
½ teaspoon pure vanilla extract
1 cup evaporated cane juice
6 tablespoons vegan margarine (such as Earth Balance)
2 teaspoons fleur de sel (large-crystal sea salt)

For the French toast
1⅔ cups all-purpose flour
1 teaspoon ground cinnamon
¼ teaspoon allspice
¼ teaspoon sea salt
2 tablespoons melted coconut oil
One 12-ounce bottle of beer
3 tablespoons pure maple syrup
⅔ cup unsweetened soy milk
¼ cup vegan margarine or coconut oil, for frying
8 slices bread of your choice
Ground cinnamon and vegan powdered sugar (optional; for garnish)

1 **Make the cranberries:** Whisk together the rum, maple syrup, molasses, orange zest and juice, and tamari in a small saucepan over medium-high heat. Once the liquid comes to a boil, add the cranberries, cover the pot, and lower the heat to a simmer for 20 minutes. Keep warm.

2 **Make the syrup:** Place the juniper berries, coconut milk, rice syrup, and vanilla in a saucepan, and cook over medium heat until bubbling. Remove from the heat and allow to steep, uncovered, for 10 minutes.

3 In a 2- to 3-quart saucepan over medium-high heat, melt the evaporated cane juice and margarine, whisking very frequently as the sugar melts and becomes slightly golden. Once the sugar has reached a reddish brown color (about 350°F) remove the pot from the heat, and strain the pot of juniper coconut milk into the sugar. Whisk thoroughly to dissolve all sugar and emulsify. Mix in the fleur de sel, and keep warm until ready to serve. (Any remaining syrup can be stored in the refrigerator for up to a month. If crystallization occurs, bring the syrup to a boil again before serving.)

4 **Make the French toast batter:** In a medium bowl, whisk together the flour, cinnamon, allspice, and salt. Add the coconut oil, beer, maple syrup, and soy milk, and whisk together to form a smooth, thin batter.

5 **Cook the French toast:** Melt 2 tablespoons of the margarine (or coconut oil) in a large skillet or frying pan on the stove over medium heat. Cut the slices of bread in half, if desired, and submerge them on both sides in the batter. Fry all slices for about 3 minutes on each side, until golden brown. Add more margarine or coconut oil to the pan for subsequent batches of toast.

6 Place 2 pieces (or 4 halves) of toast on each plate. Top each serving with a heaping ¼ cup of warm simmered cranberries and 2 tablespoons of warm caramel, and garnish with cinnamon and powdered sugar, if desired.

Cashew Oat Waffles
WITH CARAMELIZED APPLES

Unlike regular flour-based waffles, these are hearty and packed with protein. They happen to be gluten free, but never mind that—they taste and smell like heaven. The apples also rock all on their own, served hot right on top of vegan ice cream or oatmeal. Serve these bad boys with lots of maple syrup and a big pat of our Pine Nut Butter (page 255).

MAKES 8 SMALL WAFFLES (GF)

For the caramelized apples
4 teaspoons extra-virgin olive oil
2 crisp apples of your choice, cored
    and cut into thin ½-inch-long pieces
Grated zest and juice of 1 lemon
1 tablespoon pure maple syrup
2 tablespoons evaporated cane juice
¼ teaspoon sea salt
1 tablespoon coconut oil

For the waffles
2 cups rolled oats
⅔ cup cashew pieces
½ cup gluten-free all-purpose flour
4 teaspoons agave nectar
4 teaspoons extra-virgin olive oil
½ teaspoon ground nutmeg
1 teaspoon ground cinnamon,
    plus more for serving
½ teaspoon sea salt
1 teaspoon pure vanilla extract
2 tablespoons coconut oil

1 **Pre-caramelize the apples:** Heat the olive oil in a sauté pan over medium heat. Once the oil is hot, sauté the apples for 4 minutes, flipping frequently, until they are very lightly browned. Stir in the lemon zest and juice, maple syrup, evaporated cane juice, and sea salt, and cook, stirring, for 3 minutes, until the apples are lightly browned. Set aside.

2 **Make the waffle batter:** Place the oats in a food processor and process them for about 2 minutes into a coarse flour. Transfer the oat flour to a medium bowl. Process the cashews in the food processor for about 2 minutes, until the cashews are finely ground. Transfer the ground cashews to the bowl with the oat flour and add the all-purpose flour, agave nectar, oil, nutmeg, cinnamon, salt, vanilla, and 1⅔ cups water. Mix thoroughly to combine—the batter should be thick, almost a very loose dough. Let the batter sit for at least 20 minutes.

3 **Make the waffles:** Heat the waffle iron fully. Thoroughly oil both sides of the waffle iron with about 1 heaping teaspoon of coconut oil on each side.

4 Place about ½ cup of the batter onto the waffle iron, then close and let cook for about 5 minutes. Remove the waffles when they are golden brown on both sides. Repeat with the remaining batter, adding 1 teaspoon of coconut oil to each side of the waffle iron for each batch.

5 While the waffles cook, heat the tablespoon coconut oil in a sauté pan over medium-high heat. Once the oil is hot, add the partially caramelized apples. Allow them to brown nicely on one side before flipping them to caramelize them completely, about 5 minutes total. The sugars should become deeply brown and gooey.

6 Place each waffle on a plate. Top with the hot apples and garnish with a dash of cinnamon.

SHredDED root Vegetable Hash Browns
WITH FIG OLIVE TAPENADE

Damn straight—you can have things like parsnips, turnips, and celery root for breakfast. They are starchy, so they have a lot in common with the humble potato (and when I say humble, I mean, it's also the best thing in the world). But unlike potatoes, these root veggies are super-flavorful, and probably also a lot better for you. The tapenade, which is just slightly sweet from the figs and balsamic, really kicks them into high gear. You wouldn't think so, but figs and olives are a match made in heaven, and they come together with a sophisticated savory sweetness.

SERVES 4 (GF)

For the fig olive tapenade
3 tablespoons balsamic vinegar
¼ cup dry red wine
¼ cup chopped dried figs
¾ cup pitted kalamata olives
2 tablespoons extra-virgin olive oil

For the hash browns
1 large parsnip, peeled
1 medium turnip, peeled
½ medium celery root, peeled
1 large russet potato, peeled
2 garlic cloves, minced
2 tablespoons chopped fresh rosemary
   leaves, plus whole sprigs for garnish
1 teaspoon paprika
½ teaspoon sea salt
3 tablespoons extra-virgin olive oil

1 **Make the tapenade:** Bring the vinegar, wine, and figs to a boil in a small saucepan over high heat. Cover the pot, turn off the heat, and allow the figs to steam and soften for 10 minutes. Pour the contents of the pot into a food processor along with the olives and oil, and process for 3 minutes until a fairly smooth tapenade is formed. The tapenade will keep in an airtight container in the refrigerator for up to a week.

2 **Make the hash browns:** Shred the parsnip, turnip, celery root, and potato with either a grater or a food processor equipped with a shredding blade. Place the shredded vegetables into a bowl with 4 cups cold water, and massage them by hand, squeezing out the extra starch. Allow the vegetables to sit in the water for 5 minutes. Drain the vegetables in a colander, and rinse them off under cold running water. Allow the vegetables to dry as much as possible, squeezing out extra liquid through the colander.

Transfer the drained vegetables to a small bowl, and mix in the garlic, chopped rosemary, paprika, and salt.

3 Heat the olive oil in a large skillet or frying pan over medium-high heat. Once the oil is hot, scatter the shredded vegetables evenly over the surface of the pan. Allow them to fry and brown on the first side for about 3 minutes. Start flipping around the shredded vegetables every 2 minutes or so, so that after about 15 minutes, all sides are nicely browned and there are no remaining pockets of uncooked vegetables.

4 Serve with the tapenade on the side in a small ramekin, and garnish if desired with fresh sprigs of rosemary.

BRAZIL
NUT MILK

CHOCOLATE
CASHEW MILK

PISTACHIO MILK
WITH CLOVE AND
ROSEWATER

VANILLA
SESAME MILK

COCONUT
STAR ANISE
MILK

CHAMOMILE
PINE NUT
MILK

BEVERAGES

NUT MILKS AND MILKSHAKES

55 Vanilla Sesame Milk

56 Coconut Star Anise Milk

57 Chocolate Cashew Milk

58 Brazil Nut Milk

60 Pistachio Milk

60 Chamomile Pine Nut Milk

61 Supreme Raw Fudge Brownie Milkshake

62 Creamy Strawberry Pink Drink

LEMONADES AND AGUA FRESCAS

63 Cucumber Ginger Agua Fresca

63 Watermelon Habanero Refresco

63 Honeydew Mint Agua Fresca

65 Plain Old Agave-Sweetened Fresh Lemonade

65 Maple–Mashed Blackberry Lemonade

65 Icy Strawberry Thai Basil Lemonade

65 Hibiscus Limeade

66 Fresh Fig Arnold Palmers

HOT BEVERAGES

69 Toasted Hazelnut Hot Chocolate

69 Hot Ragi

69 Peppermint Hot Chocolate

ON A BLAZING SUMMER DAY SOME YEARS BACK, I was driving through Manhattan with Anatole, my yoga and meditation teacher. We stopped outside his apartment on the Lower East Side so that he could run inside, and he soon returned with an ice-cold jar filled with some mysterious white liquid. On the lid was an Om symbol etched into the metal, and what was under the lid was pure magic: fresh, icy Brazil nut milk.

That was the first freshly made nut milk I had ever experienced, and it convinced me that Anatole is the great master of tasty drinks. If there were an interplanetary beverage-making throw-down, I wouldn't think twice about who we should send as Earth's ambassador. Anatole taught me most of what I know about really yummy drinks, and a lot of yummy food, and he's inspired me to extract flavors in sippable form from all kinds of ingredients.

People ask me often what my family prefers to drink in place of milk. Years ago, we used to make our own soy milk, but the process took a long time. We had to boil the beans for hours, filling our home with a chicken–gym locker room–beany fragrance. (Thirsty yet?) After blending and straining the soy beans, the milk needed to be simmered for a long time and then flavored to hide the beany taste. We'd then have to drink the milk fast, as it would go sour in a few days. All of this left me with a great big *meh* . . .

Now, we prefer tree nut–, seed-, or coconut-based milks. They require about as much time and labor as a smoothie, are much more affordable, and are much more nourishing than soy or rice milk. Because they are such a snap to put together, I don't flinch about making them often, so we can enjoy them as fresh as possible. And I definitely don't miss washing all those big pots of beans, or the B.O. smell of soy wafting throughout my home.

Anatole taught me about making cocktails from fresh juices, making ice-cold guanabana (soursop) smoothies, nut milks, and all forms of absolutely orgasmic potions. I can only hope that our beverages make people feel the same way, as if they are being nourished with blissful heavenly nectars.

Vanilla Sesame Milk

Sesame seeds are an unbelievable source of plant-based calcium. A cup of sesame seeds provides more than 1,400 milligrams of calcium. In addition, these little seeds cause no harm to adorable cows in the process of delivering their calcium. So there!

I'll be honest, though: The calcium isn't what gets me excited about sesame; I'm in it for the taste. The real sesame flavor is the same as that in my guilty pleasure halva, the ultra-sweet Mediterranean dessert made from sesame paste and TONS of sugar. Vegan versions *can* be found, and my family and I ate so much of it in Greece that I nearly lost all my teeth. So now, instead of gorging on candy, I can enjoy the goodness of sesame as a more naturally sweetened, heavenly alternative to dairy milk. (You can try this sesame milk as a really yummy base for ice creams and milk shakes.)

MAKES 1 QUART GF

⅔ cup unroasted white sesame seeds
1½ teaspoons pure vanilla extract
1 tablespoon unrefined coconut oil
¼ cup pure maple syrup
½ teaspoon sea salt

1 Place the sesame seeds in the pitcher of a high-speed blender and cover them with 1 cup water. Let the seeds soak for at least 20 minutes, or up to an hour.

2 Blend the seeds and their soaking water on high speed for 40 seconds. Add the vanilla, coconut oil, maple syrup, salt, and 3 cups water and blend for another 40 seconds, until as smooth as possible. Pour the sesame milk through a very fine mesh strainer or strainer bag to remove any grit. Store the milk in an airtight container in the refrigerator for up to 3 days.

WHAT TO DO WITH THE NUT/SEED PULP?

When I make nut or seed milk, I add the strained pulp to the food I feed my dogs: With the minerals and fat the pulp contains, it's a nice treat for them and keeps their coats looking awesome. Just don't give them pulp from making any form of chocolate milk, because chocolate and cute doggies don't mix. Neither do macadamias and doggies. You can also use the pulp as a base for raw dehydrated cookies and bars.

Coconut Star Anise Milk

This rich, creamy elixir is one of our favorite light breakfasts. You can warm it slightly and sprinkle it with fresh ground nutmeg on top during the winter, or use ice in place of the water for this beverage's summertime incarnation as a super-food milk shake!

If you've never had maca before, you're missing out: It's an Andean root with a smoky caramel flavor. It's known to be a super-food and has been proven to have beneficial effects on libido, sperm health, and a bunch of other dirty stuff like that.

MAKES ABOUT 1 QUART, depending on the yield of the coconut (GF)

1 medium young Thai coconut
½ cup cashews
1 tablespoon coconut oil
1 teaspoon pure vanilla extract
3 tablespoons agave nectar
½ teaspoon pink Himalayan salt
  or sea salt
2 tablespoons maca powder
1 tablespoon tocotrienols (see
  page 58; optional)
7 star anise seeds (about
  1½ whole stars)

1 Using my coconut guide (below), crack open and remove the meat and water from the coconut. Transfer the coconut water and meat to a blender.

2 Add the cashews, coconut oil, vanilla, agave nectar, salt, maca powder, tocotrienols (if using), and star anise seeds to the blender. Let the mixture sit for 15 minutes for the cashews to soften. (Soaking the nuts will result in a smoother, creamier milk.)

3 Blend the mixture at a high speed for 45 seconds. Add 2½ cups water, and continue blending for 30 seconds. If the tiny flecks of star anise bother you, strain the milk through a fine-mesh strainer. Store the milk in an airtight container in the refrigerator for up to 3 days.

GETTING INTO THE COCONUT!

People get really intimidated about opening young Thai coconuts (young Thai coconuts are preshaved into a white houselike shape), and then you know what they do? They get really creative, finding the most complicated, weirdest way to get into the damn things. People pull out drills, and saws, and dynamite . . . but listen, it's really not that difficult, and you don't need to risk blowing up your kitchen sink or accidentally drilling into your dinner table, okay? Here's what I like to do to get into young Thai coconuts:

1 Place the coconut, flat side down, on a stable counter or work surface.

2 Using a heavy knife or cleaver (not a delicate or valuable knife), use a lot of force to whack one partial cut into the top of the coconut.

3 Take two more whacks to form a triangle shape that cuts through the woody part of the coconut, just into the water within. With the tip of the knife, pry the triangle out.

4 Pour the water from within the coconut through a strainer and into a measuring cup (so you can get rid of any hull fragments that may have fallen into the water).

5 With two strong blows, crack the coconut in half. Rinse out the two halves, and use a spoon to scoop the thin, soft meat into a bowl.

Chocolate Cashew Milk

This chocolate milk is a hit with everybody, especially those with chronic chocolate dependency. Chocolate addiction runs deep in my family, and we self-medicate often. For serious chocolate fixes, pure unroasted cacao powder provides the most intense flavor and is the best way to access all of chocolate's antioxidants and alkaloids. For a more subtle, traditional chocolate milk, replace half the cacao powder with roasted or Dutch-process cocoa.

MAKES 1 QUART (GF)

1 cup cashew pieces
¼ cup cacao powder
¼ cup agave nectar
¼ teaspoon sea salt
2 tablespoons coconut oil

1 Place the cashews, cacao powder, agave nectar, salt, coconut oil, and 1 cup water in a blender. Let the mixture sit for 15 minutes, to start softening the cashews.

2 Blend for 40 seconds at high speed. Add another 2¾ cups water and blend for 20 more seconds, until the milk is creamy, smooth, rich, and just a wee bit thicker than regular chocolate milk. Store the milk in an airtight container in the refrigerator for up to 3 days.

CACAO

Cacao beans are *unroasted* "cocoa" beans, scooped from the fruits of the cacao tree, fermented, then dried. Cacao has an ancient history in South America: It was first cultivated as food by the Olmec people of Central America more than two thousand years ago. Cacao is a powerhouse of antioxidants and is proven to be a mood elevator. Ms. Snail (my loving wife) has told me that, if our industrial society and transportation fail, she is prepared to walk from the New York metro area down into South America to be once again reunited with cacao!

The flavor of cacao "nibs" is intensely chocolaty and bitter—akin to that of espresso beans but, dare I say, MORE wonderful. I personally have a thing for sprinkling them on roasted root vegetables or butternut squash. On the truck, we use cacao in our Raw Chocolate Pudding (page 199), in our Mint Matlock Took All His Clothes Off cookies (page 202), and in our raw chocolate milk.

Brazil Nut Milk

Brazil nuts really make my favorite milk. Brazil nuts come from one of the largest and longest-living types of tree that grow throughout the Amazon rain forest. (The trees that bear Brazil nuts can live up to one thousand years.) The name is misleading, as, like pine nuts, Brazil nuts are actually a seed. Brazil nuts are an exceptional source of Omega-6 fatty acids and also contain selenium, which has anticarcinogenic effects on prostate and breast cancer. (A quick note: Because they are such fibrous nuts, you really need an extremely fine mesh strainer to pass the milk through, as the pulp of this milk really isn't so fun to have to drink.)

MAKES 1 QUART (GF)

¾ cup Brazil nuts, soaked in water for at least 1 hour

1 tablespoon coconut oil

3 tablespoons agave nectar

½ teaspoon pure vanilla extract

1 tablespoon tocotrienols (optional)

¾ teaspoon soy lecithin (optional; for a more smoothly emulsified milk)

½ teaspoon sea salt

1 Drain and rinse the soaked Brazil nuts. Add the nuts to a high-speed blender along with the coconut oil, agave nectar, vanilla, tocotrienols and lecithin (if using), salt, and 2 cups cold water. Blend on high speed for 45 seconds.

2 Add 2 more cups cold water, and blend for an additional 60 seconds on high, until only the tiniest flecks of brown skin can be seen floating about the milk. Strain the milk through cheesecloth or a fine-mesh strainer, and chill for 30 minutes. Store the milk in an airtight container in the refrigerator for up to 3 days. Stir or shake before serving.

WTF, Tocotrienols?

Is it foot medicine? Is it spaceman food? Actually, tocotrienols are essentially the soluble form of rice bran, containing the highest concentration of vitamin E. But I love this stuff because its flavor and texture does kinda remind me of astronaut ice cream. When is someone going to be a food pioneer out there, and invent vegan astronaut ice cream out of this stuff!?! WHEN!?

You can find tocotrienols on raw foods websites and in health food stores, sometimes in the area where you find supplements and other astronaut ice cream ingredients.

Pistachio Milk WITH CLOVE AND ROSEWATER

This light green milk captures the flavor of baklava, without the low-quality honey and high-fructose corn syrup that's usually in that delicious treat. Aside from being straight-up awesome to drink, this recipe makes an excellent milk to use in iced chai or in grain-filled breakfast porridges.

MAKES 1 QUART (GF)

⅔ cup shelled unroasted pistachios, soaked in water for 20 minutes

3 tablespoons pure maple syrup

¼ teaspoon ground cloves

1½ teaspoons rosewater

½ teaspoon sea salt

⅛ teaspoon ground cardamom, or 4 cardamom seeds (not full pods)

Drain and rinse the soaked pistachios. Add the nuts to a high-speed blender along with the maple syrup, cloves, rosewater, salt, cardamom, and 4 cups cold water, and blend on high for 90 seconds, until the milk is smooth and frothy. Strain the milk through a fine-mesh strainer, and chill for 30 minutes. Stir or shake well before serving. Store in an airtight container in the refrigerator for up to 3 days.

Chamomile Pine Nut Milk

I think chamomile and pine nuts were destined to come together. They are a winning combination in a lot of dishes, such as salads that are garnished with roasted pine nuts and have chamomile tea in their dressing, or in Fresh Fig Pancakes with Chamomile–Blood Orange Syrup (page 30) slathered with Pine Nut Butter (page 255). The delicate complexities of each harmonize to create a gentle, gorgeous bouquet of flavor. You can't beat a cold glass of this elixir after a hard yoga class or workout.

MAKES 1 QUART (GF)

⅓ cup loose chamomile tea, or 4 chamomile tea bags

2 cups boiling water

⅔ cup pine nuts

3 tablespoons pure maple syrup

½ teaspoon pure vanilla extract

½ teaspoon grated lemon zest

¼ teaspoon sea salt

2 cups ice-cold water

1 Place the chamomile flowers in a small heat-proof bowl, and pour the boiling water over them. Cover the bowl with a plate, and allow the chamomile to steep in the hot water for 6 minutes.

2 Strain the resulting tea into a high-speed blender, discarding the flowers. Allow the tea to cool to room temperature (about 20 minutes). Add the pine nuts, maple syrup, vanilla, lemon zest, and salt to the blender. Blend on high speed for 60 seconds to create a loose cream. Add the ice water and blend for 30 seconds to yield a smooth, fragrant milk. Chill before serving. Refrigerate the milk in an airtight container for up to 2 days.

SUPREME Raw Fudge BROWNIE Milk Shake

Here's a totally badass beverage that is as decadent as they come, without using sugar, soy, or any other such stuff that's not 100 percent beneficial to your body. Instead, this is creamy and yummy, relying on the richness of nuts and coconut oil. Raw cacao lends its super-food goodness here, too, and laughs with maniacal mega-force at the nutritional emptiness of a chocolate milk shake made with crappy store-bought soy ice cream.

MAKES 1 QUART (GF)

2 tablespoons melted coconut oil, plus extra for greasing the pan

¾ cup almond butter

2 tablespoons agave nectar

4 tablespoons cacao powder

1 tablespoon cacao nibs, plus more for garnish

⅔ cup unroasted cashew pieces, soaked in water for 15 minutes

3 tablespoons pure maple syrup

1 tablespoon carob powder

1 teaspoon pure vanilla extract

½ teaspoon sea salt

2 cups ice cubes

Ground cinnamon (optional; for garnish)

1 Lightly grease a 9 by 9-inch baking pan or pie pan with coconut oil.

2 In a small bowl, or food processor, thoroughly combine the 2 tablespoons coconut oil, the almond butter, agave nectar, 2 tablespoons of the cacao powder, and the cacao nibs. With wet hands, press the mixture flat into the prepared baking pan. Freeze the pan for 1 hour, until it has set into a stiff fudge.

3 Drain and rinse the cashews. Blend the cashews, maple syrup, the 2 remaining tablespoons of cacao, the carob, vanilla, and salt with 2 cups water in a high-speed blender on high speed for 60 seconds, until the mixture is smooth, thick, and creamy. Add the ice to the blender, and blend on medium speed for 40 seconds to yield a thick milk shake.

4 Remove the frozen fudge from the freezer and score it into ½-inch squares. Add the pieces of fudge to the blender, and pulse several times to distribute small bits of fudge throughout the milk shake. Pour the milk shake into 2 or 3 tall glasses, and garnish with a light dusting of cacao nibs and of cinnamon, if desired.

Creamy strawberry pink drink
WITH CACAO NIBS

This is one of my favorite milk shake–like things to drink. It's like a good-for-you version of a strawberry milk shake with chocolate chips. It takes just about as long to make as your average smoothie, but is way more like a radical 1980s summer block party in your mouth—as if someone opened up the fire hydrant and ice-cold strawberry Nesquik is gushing out all over a street that is paved with chocolate.

MAKES 1 QUART (GF)

Water and meat of 1 young coconut (see page 56 on cracking open a coconut)

2 tablespoons coconut oil

⅓ cup unroasted cashew pieces

1½ cups frozen strawberries

½ teaspoon pure vanilla extract

2 tablespoons pure maple syrup

¼ teaspoon sea salt

2½ cups ice cubes

2 tablespoons cacao nibs, plus more for garnish

2 thinly sliced fresh strawberries (optional; for garnish)

Place the coconut water, coconut meat, coconut oil, cashews, frozen strawberries, vanilla, maple syrup, and sea salt into a high-speed blender. Blend on high speed for 60 seconds to make a smooth pink puree. Add the ice and continue blending for 45 seconds to form a smooth, creamy milk shake. Pulse in the cacao nibs a few times to evenly distribute. Serve in tall glasses, and garnish with cacao nibs and fresh strawberry slices, if you wish.

agua Frescas

It's fitting for a food truck to serve cold agua frescas—after all, it was West Coast taco trucks that first popularized these cold, refreshing drinks in North America. Before that, agua frescas were mostly enjoyed in Mexico. Here are a couple of really wonderful ones to try out as the star of your next barbecue or taco party. (Each of these recipes makes 1 quart, except for the Watermelon Habanero Refresco, which yields about 3 quarts, depending on the size of your watermelon.)

Cucumber Ginger Agua Fresca (GF)

This is a refreshing example of a *gaseosa* (a carbonated agua fresca). Because it relies on adding seltzer water for carbonation, it needs to be consumed immediately. Otherwise, you can make the base up to a day in advance, and then add the ice and seltzer when you serve it.

1½ cups chopped peeled cucumber
4 teaspoons minced peeled fresh ginger
Zest and juice of 1 lime
3 tablespoons evaporated cane juice
⅔ cup crushed ice, plus more for serving
2⅓ cups seltzer water

Place the cucumber, ginger, lime zest and juice, evaporated cane juice, and ice into a blender. Blend on high for 60 seconds, until the ice is completely melted. Strain the mixture through a fine-mesh strainer into a 1-quart pitcher. Stir in the seltzer water and pour into glasses over ice.

Watermelon Habanero Refresco (GF)

This is really one of my favorites. Make this drink in summertime, when local watermelons are at their peak ripeness. You can adjust the heat to your liking by cutting back on or adding extra habanero. Because the juicer will get rid of the pulp and seeds anyway, you can use a seeded or seedless melon and get pretty much the same result. The exact yield will depend on the watermelon, but figure a small watermelon will give you 2 to 3 quarts of juice!

1 small ripe watermelon (10 to 12 pounds)
½ habanero pepper, stem and seeds removed
3 medium celery stalks
3 tablespoons agave nectar
2 cups crushed ice

Separate the flesh of the watermelon from the rind, and discard the rind. In a juicer, juice the watermelon, habanero, and celery.

Strain the juice well, and place it in a large pitcher or gallon jar. Stir in the agave nectar, ice, and 2½ cups cold water. Serve immediately, or store in a sealed jar in the refrigerator for up to 2 days.

Honeydew Mint Agua Fresca (GF)

2 cups freshly juiced honeydew melon, pulp discarded
¼ cup minced fresh mint leaves, plus extra for garnish
Grated zest and juice of 1 lime, plus lime slices for garnish
3 tablespoons evaporated cane juice
1 cup crushed ice

Mix together the juiced melon, the mint, lime zest and juice, evaporated cane juice, and crushed ice with 2 cups cold water in a 1- to 2-quart pitcher. Serve immediately.

Several Rad Lemonades

Lemonade is the undisputed heavyweight champion of hot-weather beverages, but did you know lemonade doesn't *just* have to be a great guy? He can also be a supernatural flavor drag queen, or a rapping hockey-playing bank robber. He can be a superhero who rides off into the sunset on a two-story-tall rescue dog.

What on earth is it that I am trying to tell you? As great as plain old lemonade is, it doesn't have to be plain. Here are some killer lemonade recipes that will make you also ride a two-story dog into the sunset, cold glass in hand. (Each of these recipes makes 1 quart of lemonade.)

MAPLE-MASHED BLACKBERRY LEMONADE

HIBISCUS LIMEADE

ICY STRAWBERRY THAI BASIL LEMONADE

Party

Street Vegan

Plain Old Agave-Sweetened Fresh Lemonade (GF)

½ cup strained freshly squeezed
   lemon juice
¼ cup plus 1 tablespoon organic
   agave nectar

In a 1- to 2-quart pitcher, whisk together the lemon juice and agave nectar. Mix in 3¼ cups cold water. Add ice to the pitcher to fill, or chill and pour over ice-filled glasses.

Maple–Mashed Blackberry Lemonade (GF)

½ cup fresh blackberries
½ cup strained freshly squeezed
   lemon juice
⅓ cup pure maple syrup

Crush the blackberries either by hand or using a potato masher in a small bowl, until all the berries are mashed into tiny bits. Pour the mashed berries and their juice into a 1- to 2-quart pitcher. Mix in the lemon juice, maple syrup, and 3 cups cold water. Add ice to the pitcher to fill, or chill and pour over ice-filled glasses.

Icy Strawberry Thai Basil Lemonade (GF)

⅓ cup chopped fresh strawberries,
   stems removed, plus more for
   garnish
2 tablespoons chopped fresh Thai basil
   leaves, plus more for garnish
⅓ cup strained freshly squeezed lemon
   juice
¼ cup agave nectar
1⅓ cups ice cubes, plus extra crushed
   ice for serving

Place the strawberries, basil, lemon juice, agave nectar, and 2½ cups of cold water into a blender, and blend on high for 60 seconds until completely smooth. Add the ice cubes and pulse a few times to crush the ice and incorporate. Serve in glasses with crushed ice, and garnish each glass with Thai basil leaves and strawberry slices.

Hibiscus Limeade (GF)

1 cup boiling water
2 hibiscus tea bags (containing ONLY
   hibiscus)
⅓ cup strained freshly squeezed lime
   juice
¼ cup plus 1 tablespoon organic agave
   nectar
3 cups crushed ice

Place the boiling water and tea bags into a 1- to 2-quart heat-proof pitcher. Allow the tea to steep for 5 minutes.

Remove the tea bags and stir in the lime juice, agave nectar, and ice while the tea is still warm, so that it mostly melts the ice and makes the pitcher nice and cold. Serve immediately.

FRESH FiG arNold PalMeRs

We on the Cinnamon Snail are really into golf. Our truck staff sometimes has to cook in hot, sweaty foam golf-ball costumes. We watch our TVs with bated breath as world-renowned golfers like Lee Travino putt their way to victory in miniature golf courses all over the planet. We are so into golf, that we commemorate Arnold Palmer, one of the most famous golf personalities of all time, with this lovely drink. A traditional "Arnold Palmer" is simply lemonade mixed with iced tea. The addition of fresh figs makes for a lovely, late-summer refreshing golf potion. Whether you know who Lee Travino is or not, you are still allowed to partake.

MAKES 1 QUART (GF)

1 black tea bag (assam or orange pekoe are both nice choices)

½ cup evaporated cane juice

½ cup stemmed and chopped fresh figs, plus more for serving

2 cups boiling water

½ cup strained freshly squeezed lemon juice

2 cups ice cubes, plus extra crushed ice for serving

1 Place the tea bag, evaporated cane juice, and chopped figs in a small heat-proof bowl and pour the boiling water over them. Let the mixture sit for 30 minutes, to cool to room temperature.

2 Discard the tea bag, and pour the contents of the bowl into a blender, along with the lemon juice and ice cubes. Blend on high speed for 45 seconds, until smooth. Strain through a fine-mesh strainer into a large pitcher (or leave the bits of fig in if you prefer). Add the crushed ice and additional fig pieces to the serving glasses and pour in the lemonade.

Street Vegan

Hot Beverages

Sometimes New York City rears its beastly head and does something really gentle and kind. One early morning, I'm driving the truck into Manhattan. During the two-hour drive to Midtown, I'm drinking my hot tea and chanting along to a recording of the mantra *om mani padme hom*, so by the time I'm parked, I'm in a fantastic mood.

Just after parking, I hear a knock on the truck door. It's a cop—I figure he's here to tell me to move, or to ticket the truck. But this cop tells me he's parking his car behind us, and asks me if that's okay. "Um, yeah, sure. Of course," I say. "This is the first time a police person has ever asked me if it was okay with me where *he* parked." The officer smiles and says, "Well, I wanted to make sure that wasn't your spot. Everyone's got to make a living."

It doesn't happen often, but when New York wants to be nice and sweet, it's really the best thing ever. I need to start EVERY day with a hot tea and mantra, so that all the bad guys will turn into donut-loving butterflies.

TOASTED HAZELNUT
HOT CHOCOLATE

Toasted Hazelnut Hot Chocolate (GF)

MAKES 2 CUPS

⅓ cup hazelnuts
1¾ cups unsweetened soy milk
3 tablespoons pure maple syrup
2 tablespoons cacao butter
¼ cup vegan dark chocolate chips
2 tablespoons finely ground toasted hazelnuts (optional; for rimming the cup)

1 Toast the hazelnuts in a dry pan over medium heat, stirring, for about 6 minutes, until fragrant.

2 Place the hazelnuts, soy milk, and maple syrup in a blender, and blend on high speed for 45 seconds, until thoroughly pureed.

3 Melt the cacao butter in a 1-quart saucepan over medium heat. Strain the contents of the blender into the pot, discarding the pulp. Once the milk has come to a boil, turn off the heat and whisk in the chocolate chips. Continue whisking until all the chocolate chips have broken down and the hot chocolate is smooth.

4 If you intend to coat the rim of the cup, spread the ground toasted hazelnuts on a wide plate. Place the rim of the cup down in a plate of warm water, about ⅛ inch deep. Roll the slightly wet rim of the cup in the ground hazelnuts. Carefully pour the hot chocolate into each cup, so as not to disturb the ground nuts on the edges.

Hot Ragi with Cloves and Cardamom (GF)

MAKES 2 CUPS

2 whole cloves, crushed
1 full cardamom pod, crushed
2 cups unsweetened soy milk
4 teaspoons evaporated cane juice
Pinch of sea salt
3 tablespoons ragi flour

Place the cloves, cardamom, soy milk, evaporated cane juice, and salt into a large saucepan. Heat the mixture over medium-high heat, stirring occasionally, until almost boiling. Whisk in the ragi flour until smooth. Lower the heat for a couple of minutes, and allow the ragi to thicken a little, like thick grainy hot chocolate. Strain the drink into a mug, discarding the cloves and cardamom.

Peppermint Hot Chocolate (GF)

MAKES 2 CUPS

2 cups unsweetened soy milk
4 teaspoons evaporated cane juice
⅔ cup vegan dark chocolate chips
½ teaspoon peppermint extract
Small pinch of ground cloves
Vegan marshmallows, for garnish

Bring the soy milk to a boil in a small saucepan over high heat. Turn off the heat immediately, and whisk in the evaporated cane juice, chocolate chips, peppermint extract, and cloves. Continue whisking until all of the chocolate chips have fully broken down and a smooth, rich hot chocolate is ready to make your day wonderful. Pour into mugs and top with your favorite vegan marshmallows.

RAD RED RAGI

I fell in love with *ragi* while staying in Mysore, India, to study yoga in my early twenties. Ragi is a kind of Indian red millet, and is often made into drinks, balls, and dosas, with rich red whole-grain color. It's one of my favorite drinks on cold winter days. If you can't find ragi flour, make an imitation by grinding red millet or quinoa in a spice grinder or blender until a fine flour is produced.

BEER-BATTERED
HABANERO
BUFFALO WINGS

appetizers

73 Pan-Fried Kimchi Dumplings

74 New England–Style Chickpea "Crab" Cakes

77 Polenta Sage Cashew Cheese Wedges

79 Beer-Battered Habanero Buffalo Wings

81 Rosemary White Bean Croquettes

84 Grilled Tomato–Olive Bruschetta

86 Smoky Portobello- and Potato-Stuffed Poblanos

88 Truffled Potato and Fried Onion Pierogies

90 Tequila Lime Tostones

92 Flaky Spinach Pie

94 Chimichurri Tempeh Empanadas

WITHIN THE FIRST FEW MONTHS OF OPENING THE CINNAMON SNAIL, I was contacted about doing a "super-adoption" event, where many animal-rescue centers collaborate to have hundreds of pets adopted over one weekend. The organizers anticipated eighty thousand attendees, and they wanted us to be the only food vendor. It sounded perfect. But I needed to get my "A team" together.

But what did my A team look like? I was baking pastries at night and running the truck all day by myself, so I needed a few friends to help me work the event. In my naiveté, I thought I would be able to feed at least ten thousand people, and I planned for a big tent next to the truck with a giant vegan buffet. Since it was summer, I assumed I would need an absurd amount of water, and so I ordered four hundred cases of biodegradable water bottles (a total of ninety-six hundred bottles). I also rented a van to carry all the water and extra catering gear for the weekend.

I arranged to have the water dropped off in the driveway of my home. The day of delivery, I got home late to start my all-night baking, and that's when the ridiculousness of my water estimate really hit me. There were dozens of pallets of water, stacked all the way out to the street. What the hell was I thinking? After a night of baking a zillion pastries, my helpers and I did our best to get as much water into the extra van, but we barely made a dent.

Yet day one of the event was slow as hell, and day two ended early due to a giant thunderstorm. Out of ninety-six hundred water bottles, we had sold about forty. So much food went to waste that weekend, and I lost thousands of dollars.

After that weekend I took the day off to clean the truck and recover. When I opened up the leftover cases of water, I found that nearly every bottle was leaking! The biodegradable bottles had just gone on the market, and so each bottle was leaking from a scuff on the bottom corner. After I complained, the company took back all 9,560 leftover bottles, apologizing profusely and giving me twenty cases for free.

That's when I really learned about the challenges of special events. Every promoter presents you with exciting numbers and factoids to make you want to vend (and pay them fees for participating), but you soon learn what questions to ask, and how to verify the answers. And now we kill it so hard on the streets that our normal days are more predictable than special events ever are. We can accurately estimate and prep the right amount of food for the day. But ninety-six hundred water bottles? Never again.

We still love catering private events like weddings, and these kinds of appetizers allow us to serve a variety of exciting vegan food to a big crowd without getting them too stuffed to party. The recipes in this chapter will provide you with some fun things to try out, whether you want to make an appetizer for dinner at home, or you want something great for a potluck.

PaN-FrieD KiMCHi DUMPLiNGS
WITH FIERY MISO DIPPING SAUCE

These are really easy and addictive dumplings. They're great as an appetizer, or as a meal over dark leafy greens like fried dandelion greens (see page 24) or Lemon-Garlic Swiss Chard (page 187). In 2013 I taught a series of Southeast Asian Street Food cooking classes at the Institute of Culinary Education in New York City, and these were a class favorite.

MAKES ABOUT 20 DUMPLINGS

For the miso dipping sauce
3 tablespoons white miso paste
3 tablespoons toasted sesame oil
1 teaspoon minced peeled fresh ginger
4 teaspoons rice vinegar
2 tablespoons mirin
2 tablespoons agave nectar
½ jalapeño pepper (keep the seeds to increase the heat)
1 teaspoon chipotle powder

For the dumplings
4 cups all-purpose flour, plus more for rolling the dough
¼ cup sesame seeds, plus more for garnish (optional)
1 tablespoon crushed red pepper flakes
1 tablespoon sea salt
1¼ cups chopped kimchi, homemade (see page 175) or store-bought
Canola oil, for frying the dumplings
Minced scallions, light green and white parts (optional; for garnish)

1 Prepare the dipping sauce: Place the miso paste, sesame oil, ginger, vinegar, mirin, agave nectar, jalapeño, and chipotle powder in a blender with ¾ cup water, and blend on high for 20 seconds. Set aside. If not using immediately, store the sauce in an airtight pint container in the refrigerator for up to 6 days.

2 Make the dumpling wrappers: Combine the flour, sesame seeds, red pepper flakes, and salt in a mixing bowl. Add 1½ cups warm water, a little bit at a time, while kneading the mixture with your hands, until a smooth dough is formed. Allow the dough to rest for at least 20 minutes, covered, before rolling for dumplings.

3 Fill the dumplings: On a lightly floured surface, roll the dough out into a ⅛-inch-thick rectangle. Cut the dough into 2½-inch squares. Place a tablespoon of chopped kimchi in the center of each square. Working with one dumpling at a time, bring the corners together in the center above the filling and pinch them closed, fold any open sides in, and firmly roll together the little stem of dough that sticks out from the top. Place the formed dumplings on a lightly floured baking sheet.

4 Fry the dumplings: Once all the dumplings are assembled, heat a few tablespoons of canola oil in a large pan. Fry the dumplings in the hot oil for about 90 seconds on each side, until the dumplings are fully cooked, crispy, and golden on all sides. Serve with the dipping sauce, and garnish with sesame seeds and minced scallions if desired.

New England-Style Chickpea "Crab" Cakes
WITH LEMON DIJON TARTAR SAUCE

These cakes don't taste like ground-up adorable sea creatures, and that's one of the many reasons why I love them a lot. Japanese bread crumbs (panko) give them a crispy golden exterior, and they get their summer-vacation happiness (and a gentle seaside flavor without the fish) from nourishing sea vegetables, fresh parsley, and plenty of lemon zest.

SERVES 5

For the tartar sauce
2 tablespoons coconut oil
5 garlic cloves, chopped
1 small sour pickle, chopped
1 teaspoon dried thyme
1 teaspoon dried oregano
Juice of 1 lemon
1 tablespoon mirin
1 tablespoon umeboshi plum vinegar
2 tablespoons Dijon mustard
1 tablespoon agave nectar
4 ounces soft tofu
1 minced scallion, green and white parts, plus more for garnish
1 tablespoon grated lemon zest

For the cakes
¼ teaspoon dried hijiki
2 tablespoons dried wakame
2 tablespoons extra-virgin olive oil
2 shallots, finely chopped
2 garlic cloves, minced
1 celery stalk, finely chopped
1½ cups cooked chickpeas, rinsed and drained
3 tablespoons white miso paste
¼ cup chopped fresh flat-leaf parsley, plus more for garnish
2 tablespoons chopped fresh dill
1 tablespoon grated lemon zest, plus more for garnish
½ teaspoon freshly ground black pepper
¾ cup all-purpose flour
⅓ cup canola oil
1 cup unsweetened soy milk
2 tablespoons Dijon mustard
2 cups panko bread crumbs
1¼ cups coarsely chopped frisée, mustard greens, or arugula, for serving

1 **Make the tartar sauce:** Melt the coconut oil in a sauté pan set over medium heat. Sauté the garlic, pickle, thyme, and oregano in the hot oil for about 3 minutes, until the garlic turns golden. Turn off the heat and stir in the lemon juice, mirin, plum vinegar, mustard, and agave nectar.

2 Scrape the contents of the pan into a blender. Crumble the tofu into the blender and blend at high speed for 40 seconds, until a mostly smooth puree is formed. Pulse in the scallion and lemon zest until just combined. Chill for at least 1 hour, or up to 3 days in an airtight container.

3 **Make the cakes:** Place the hijiki and wakame in a small bowl and pour 2 cups hot water over them. Allow the sea vegetables to rehydrate for 15 to 20 minutes.

4 Heat the olive oil in a sauté pan set over medium heat. Sauté the shallots, garlic, and celery for 4 to 5 minutes, until the shallots start to soften. Drain and rinse the sea vegetables and add them to the sauté pan. Transfer the contents of the pan, along with the chickpeas, miso, parsley, dill, lemon zest, pepper, and flour, to a food processor. Process for about 30 seconds, to evenly distribute all ingredients, but leaving the mixture chunky. Divide the contents of the food processor into 20 round silver-dollar-size fritters, about ½ inch thick, smoothing the outside with wet hands.

5 **Fry the cakes:** Heat the canola oil in a frying pan set over medium-high heat. In a small bowl, combine the soy milk and mustard, which will cause the milk to curdle and thicken; place the bread crumbs in a separate bowl. Dip each chickpea cake in the curdled soy milk, then in the bread crumbs, and then slip each cake into the hot oil. Working in batches, fry the cakes for about 2 minutes on each side, until each is heated through and has an even golden crust. Drain the fried cakes on a paper-towel-lined plate. Serve immediately, or reheat anytime within 24 hours.

6 On each plate, place ¼ cup mixed greens, 4 hot chickpea cakes, and a ramekin with 3 or 4 tablespoons of the tartar sauce. Garnish with lemon zest, scallions, and parsley.

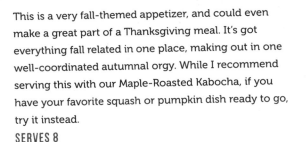

PoleNta SaGe Cashew CHeeSe WeDGeS

WITH CARAMELIZED SHALLOT CHESTNUT RAGOUT

This is a very fall-themed appetizer, and could even make a great part of a Thanksgiving meal. It's got everything fall related in one place, making out in one well-coordinated autumnal orgy. While I recommend serving this with our Maple-Roasted Kabocha, if you have your favorite squash or pumpkin dish ready to go, try it instead.

SERVES 8

For the cashew cheese
2 cups cashews, soaked in water
  for 30 to 60 minutes, drained
¼ cup white miso paste
2 tablespoons rice vinegar
1 tablespoon dried thyme
1 tablespoon dried oregano
1 teaspoon asafetida
½ cup extra-virgin olive oil

For the polenta
9 tablespoons extra-virgin olive oil
1 tablespoon sea salt
1½ cups medium-coarse ground
  polenta
½ cup minced fresh sage, plus more
  sliced leaves for garnish
1 tablespoon crushed red pepper flakes
Maple-Roasted Kabocha (page 180),
  or your squash of choice
1 cup baby arugula
Micro radish greens (optional; for
  garnish)

For the chestnut ragout
3 tablespoons extra-virgin olive oil
2 medium shallots, thinly sliced
3 garlic cloves, minced
1 medium celery stalk, finely chopped
1 cup sliced roasted chestnuts
2 tablespoons tamari
1 tablespoon umeboshi plum vinegar
2 tablespoons pure maple syrup
2 teaspoons dried thyme
2 teaspoons ground coriander
½ teaspoon freshly ground black
  pepper
3 cups vegetable broth
1 tablespoon arrowroot

1 **Make the cashew cheese:** Place the cashews, miso paste, rice vinegar, thyme, oregano, asafetida, and olive oil into a high-speed blender. Blend on high for 50 to 60 seconds to form a smooth puree, stopping occasionally to scrape the sides of the blender down, to ensure everything is fully incorporated. Set aside.

2 **Make the polenta:** Use 2 tablespoons of the olive oil to grease a parchment-lined 9 by 9-inch baking pan.

3 In a saucepan, bring 2¾ cups water to a boil. Add the salt, 3 tablespoons of the olive oil, and the polenta and cook, whisking constantly, for 2 minutes. Whisk in the sage, red pepper flakes, and cashew cheese. Continue to cook for about 3 more minutes, stirring with a wooden spoon, until the mixture is the consistency of stiff dough. Working quickly with a lightly oiled rubber spatula, transfer the polenta into the prepared baking pan. Brush the surface of the polenta with 2 tablespoons olive oil. Allow to cool to room temperature, then chill for at least 1 hour (or up to a full day).

4 **Make the chestnut ragout:** Heat the olive oil in a sauté pan set over medium-high heat. Add the shallots and cook for 4 minutes, stirring occasionally, until they are golden brown. Add the garlic, celery, chestnuts, tamari, plum vinegar, maple syrup, thyme, coriander, and black pepper. Continue to sauté, stirring frequently, until the celery softens, about 2 minutes.

5 In a blender, combine the broth and arrowroot for 15 seconds, until the arrowroot is fully dissolved. Pour the contents of the blender over the cooking vegetables, bring the mixture to a boil, and allow to boil until the ragout has thickened slightly.

6 **To serve:** Slice the chilled polenta into 16 triangles. In a thick-bottomed skillet or frying pan, heat the remaining 2 tablespoons of olive oil. Fry the polenta triangles on both sides for about 90 seconds to warm the pieces through and get them crispy and golden brown on the outside. Drain the polenta on a plate lined with paper towels. Warm the chestnut ragout and the kabocha squash, if serving.

7 You can plate all this yummy stuff in any way you like, but this is what I think is the most pleasant: Evenly distribute the arugula into small mounds on each plate. Stack two pieces of warm polenta against one another on top of the greens. Place 4 pieces of your squash of choice in the center of the polenta on each plate. Spoon out 2 to 3 tablespoons of the chestnut ragout onto each serving, and garnish with the sliced sage and microgreens, if desired.

Beer-Battered Habanero Buffalo Wings
WITH ROASTED GARLIC RANCH DIP

Many people don't know that blocks of tofu actually have wings, and if you aren't careful removing them from the packages, sometimes they fly away to a heavenly tofu sanctuary high up on an edible cloud made of ranch dip.

One of the really nice things about making something like this out of tofu is that you can make them any shape and size you like. I like to form them into smaller nuggets, which gives you a higher ratio of spicy, textured crust on each piece. You can make it as an appetizer, but it can even work as a component of a meal. Try serving it for din-din with stewed collard greens, vegan mac 'n' cheese, and Coconut Mashed Yams (see page 166). It's pretty much the best meal ever, and I want to eat it every day.

SERVES 4

For the roasted garlic ranch dip
8 garlic cloves
2 tablespoons extra-virgin olive oil
⅔ cup vegan mayonnaise
Grated zest and juice of 1 lemon
2 teaspoons stone-ground mustard
1 tablespoon agave nectar
1 dill pickle, minced
1 minced scallion, light green and white parts
2 tablespoons minced fresh flat-leaf parsley, plus more for garnish
1 tablespoon minced fresh dill

For the beer batter
1 cup vegan beer
¼ cup unsweetened soy milk
1 teaspoon apple cider vinegar
1 teaspoon stone-ground mustard
1 tablespoon evaporated cane juice
1 tablespoon paprika
1 teaspoon dried thyme
1 teaspoon sea salt
1⅓ cups all-purpose flour

For the wings
⅔ cup canola or safflower oil, for frying
One 14-ounce block extra-firm tofu
⅓ cup all-purpose flour
⅓ cup habanero hot sauce, or other thick hot sauce of your choice
2 tablespoons finely minced red onion (optional; for garnish)
3 tablespoons micro radish greens (optional; for garnish)

1 **Make the dip:** Preheat the oven to 400°F. Line a small rimmed baking sheet with parchment paper.

2 Toss the garlic cloves in the olive oil in a small bowl, and spread them on the prepared baking sheet. Roast the garlic for 12 to 14 minutes, until golden brown. Place the pan on a wire rack and allow the garlic to cool for 10 minutes. Transfer the garlic and oil to a blender along with the mayonnaise. Blend on high speed for 45 seconds,

recipe continues

until smooth. Add the lemon zest and juice, mustard, agave nectar, pickle, scallion, parsley, and dill and pulse a few times to incorporate, just until you have a dip speckled with bits of fresh herbs and pickle throughout. If not using immediately, store in an airtight container in the refrigerator for up to 4 days.

3 **Make the beer batter:** Whisk the beer, soy milk, vinegar, mustard, evaporated cane juice, paprika, thyme, salt, and flour in a medium bowl until well combined.

4 **Make the wings:** Heat the oil in a large frying pan over medium-high heat. Cut the tofu into about 20 pieces (of whatever shape you like). Gently toss the tofu in a medium bowl with the flour, until all sides are well coated.

5 Working with 3 or 4 pieces at a time, submerge the tofu in the beer batter, letting the excess drip back into the bowl, and quickly place them into the hot oil. Fry in batches, making sure that the tofu pieces aren't touching one another while they cook. Once the pieces have turned golden brown on the bottom side, flip them and fry for another 2 to 3 minutes. Remove the tofu pieces and drain on a plate lined with paper towels.

6 Toss the tofu pieces in a small bowl with the hot sauce (using more or less, depending on your heat tolerance). Serve family style or on small plates, with the ranch dip in a ramekin on the side, and garnish with chopped parsley. Sprinkle with the minced red onion and microgreens, if desired.

RoSEMaRy wHiTe BeaN CROQUETTES
WITH ROASTED FENNEL AND WHITE WINE JUS

These miniature white bean croquettes are lovely served as an hors d'oeuvre, or on top of a simple salad with arugula and mustard greens. Save the delicate fennel tops, as the fronds make a lovely fresh garnish.

SERVES 4

For the white wine jus
2 medium shallots, chopped
2 garlic cloves, sliced
1 medium celery stalk, chopped
2 bay leaves
2 tablespoons Dijon mustard
¼ teaspoon sea salt
2 tablespoons evaporated cane juice
3 cups dry white wine
1 tablespoon cornstarch, mixed into
   3 tablespoons water

For the roasted fennel
2 tablespoons rice vinegar
1 tablespoon stone-ground mustard
1 teaspoon fennel seeds
½ teaspoon crushed red pepper flakes
2 tablespoons agave nectar
3 tablespoons extra-virgin olive oil
1 cup diced fennel (¼-inch cubes), plus
   a few fronds for garnish
¼ cup drained brined capers
¼ cup finely minced shallots
¼ cup chopped fresh basil leaves

For the croquettes
1 cup cooked Great Northern beans,
   rinsed and drained
¼ cup chopped celery
¼ cup chopped onion
2 tablespoons minced fresh rosemary
   leaves
3 garlic cloves
½ teaspoon sea salt
2 teaspoons stone-ground mustard
⅓ cup all-purpose flour
3 tablespoons plus ¼ cup extra-virgin
   olive oil
⅔ cup wheat germ
⅔ cup unsweetened soy milk
1 teaspoon apple cider vinegar
1 cup bread crumbs
8 medium pieces Boston lettuce or
   red radicchio, for serving

1 **Make the white wine jus:** Place the shallots, garlic, celery, bay leaves, mustard, salt, evaporated cane juice, and wine in a medium saucepan, cover, and bring to a boil over high heat. Once the mixture has come to a boil, add the cornstarch slurry, lower the heat, and allow

recipe continues

the liquid to simmer for 10 minutes. Turn off the heat and let cool to room temperature. Pour the jus through a sieve into an airtight container; use immediately, or refrigerate for up to 3 days.

2 **Make the roasted fennel:** Preheat the oven to 350°F. Lightly oil a small baking pan.

3 In a small bowl, whisk together the rice vinegar, mustard, fennel seeds, red pepper flakes, agave nectar, and olive oil. Mix in the diced fennel, capers, shallots, and basil. Pour the contents of the bowl into the baking dish and roast for 15 to 17 minutes, until the fennel pieces are lightly browned and softened. Set aside.

4 **Make the croquettes:** Process the beans, celery, onion, rosemary, garlic, salt, mustard, and flour with the 3 tablespoons olive oil in a food processor until you have a mostly smooth dough, about 2 minutes. Add the wheat germ, and continue to process until well incorporated. Divide the dough into 12 portions, then shape each portion into a round, flat croquette about ½ inch thick and 1½ inches in diameter.

5 Combine the soy milk and cider vinegar in a shallow bowl or pie pan; the mixture will curdle. Place the bread crumbs in a separate bowl. Heat the ¼ cup olive oil in a frying pan over medium-high heat. One at a time, coat each croquette in the curdled soy-vinegar mixture,

and then coat it thoroughly in the bread crumbs. Working in batches, transfer the breaded croquettes into the hot oil, and fry them on both sides until golden brown, 2 to 3 minutes per side. Drain the croquettes on a plate lined with a paper towel.

6 To serve, pour ¼ cup of the white wine jus onto the center of each plate. Arrange 3 lettuce or radicchio pieces on each plate, and top with 3 croquettes per serving. Top each croquette with the warm roasted fennel and capers, and garnish with the fennel fronds.

GRILLED TOMATO-OLIVE BRUSCHETTA
WITH BASIL-PINE NUT CREAM

Everyone loves bruschetta made with ripe tomatoes. Luckily, tomato season and grilling season coincide, and you are going to put your outdoor charcoal or wood grill to work in a couple of different ways in this recipe. First, your favorite rustic bread gets brushed with a garlicky marinade and charred on the grill, and then it's topped with a smoky mixture of grilled tomato and olives, and rich, tangy pine nut cream flavored with basil.

SERVES 4

For the bread toasts

1 cup extra-virgin olive oil

8 garlic cloves

2 scallions, light green and white parts

1 teaspoon fennel seeds

½ teaspoon crushed red pepper flakes

½ teaspoon sea salt

8 slices crusty rustic bread (no larger than about 3 by 3 inches)

16 small fresh basil leaves (optional; for garnish)

¼ cup toasted pine nuts (see Note)

For the basil–pine nut cream

⅔ cup toasted pine nuts (see Note)

¼ cup extra-virgin olive oil

3 tablespoons chopped fresh basil leaves

1 tablespoon white miso paste

1 tablespoon freshly squeezed lemon juice

½ teaspoon asafetida

3 tablespoons unsweetened soy milk

For the bruschetta topping

3 tablespoons extra-virgin olive oil

1 tablespoon freshly squeezed lemon juice

2 teaspoons balsamic vinegar

2 teaspoons red wine vinegar

1 medium leek, trimmed, halved, and rinsed of grit

2 large beefsteak tomatoes, cut into thick slices

½ cup chopped kalamata olives

¼ cup chopped fresh basil leaves

½ teaspoon dried oregano

½ teaspoon crushed red pepper flakes

1 tablespoon evaporated cane juice

½ teaspoon sea salt

1 **Make the garlic oil for the toasts:** Place the oil, garlic, scallions, fennel seeds, red pepper flakes, and salt in a blender and blend on high speed for 40 seconds, until mostly smooth. Set aside.

2 **Make the basil–pine nut cream:** Place the pine nuts in a high-speed blender along with the olive oil, basil, miso paste, lemon juice, asafetida, and unsweetened soy milk. Blend on high speed for 60 seconds to form a smooth, creamy puree. Use immediately, or store in

Toasting Pine Nuts

In a dry sauté pan over medium-low heat, toast the pine nuts, tossing frequently, until they are fragrant and very lightly golden. Cool on a wire rack. The toasted pine nuts can be stored in an airtight container for later use, but freshly toasted pine nuts have the best flavor.

an airtight container in the refrigerator for up to 3 days. (If using a cream made in advance, let the cream return to room temperature, or whisk in a small amount of soy milk, as the cream may thicken as the fats solidify in the refrigerator.)

3 **Make the bruschetta topping:** Preheat a charcoal or wood-fired grill. In a mixing bowl, combine the olive oil, lemon juice, and vinegars. Toss the leeks and tomatoes in the marinade gently, so that all surfaces are coated but the leeks do not completely fall apart. Grill the tomatoes and leeks on both sides for about 2½ minutes, so that light grill marks are formed. Return the leeks and tomatoes to the bowl and allow them to cool for at least 20 minutes.

4 Taking care not to lose too much of their fantastic juices, transfer the leeks and tomatoes to a cutting board and chop them into ¼-inch pieces. Return the chopped leeks and tomatoes to a medium bowl and combine them with the olives, basil, oregano, red pepper flakes, cane juice, and sea salt. Use immediately, or store in an airtight container in the refrigerator for up to 3 days.

5 **Make the bruschetta:** Soak both sides of the bread slices with 1 to 2 tablespoons of the garlic oil. Grill the bread on both sides for about 60 seconds, depending on the heat of the grill, to sear the bread with grill marks. While the bread is still hot, spread 2 tablespoons of the tomato-olive tapenade onto each slice and top with 1 to 2 tablespoons of the basil–pine nut cream. Garnish with whole basil leaves, if desired, and toasted pine nuts.

YUMMY FOOD COMA STORY

The First Annual NYC Vegetarian Food Festival in 2011

We knew it would be big, and we came prepared. The event organizers, on the other hand, didn't see it coming. We were parked out in front of the event, which took place in a small ballroom on West Eighteenth Street. Within hours the line to enter the food festival was more than four blocks long, and it was taking hours for people to get into the cramped space, which was stuffed with free samples and prominent vegetarian guest speakers.

So naturally, many people gave up on entering the festival and ate at our truck instead. For a full eight hours, Sean (my beloved window guy) and I alone served a line that was a full block long. Occasionally, friends supplied us with bags of arugula, small bills for change, or extra bread as needed. But then our electrical system failed. It was our luck that the week before the event, I had had our electrician install an inverter to run our refrigeration from our truck's alternator while driving. So when we lost power, I turned the truck on to idle, and the inverter converted the engine power to electricity to keep our food cold. It worked pretty great—that is, until the inverter exploded in the last hour of the event, which was pretty scary. Sparks, zapping sounds, the smell of wires frying—you know, general unsafe electrical fire type stuff. By the grace of God, we made it through the event.

As I lowered the awning, there were still people trying to slip under the closing metal awning to nab a last pastry. It was one of those days where if we hadn't finally shut the window, we would have stayed there serving people all night; but we were exhausted, in a bit of a food trance, and eager to go home and get ready to rock the next day!

Smoky Portobello— and Potato— Stuffed Poblanos

It's tempting at a vegan barbecue to overdo it on soy and fake hot dogs (yes, I love any excuse to deliver condiments to my face). But here's something fun and plant-based to throw on the grill, and to be a playground for yummy condiments. Try it with fried onions, Chipotle Mayonnaise (page 256), or Grilled Mango Salsa (page 260).

MAKES 4 STUFFED POBLANOS (GF)

For the marinade

3 tablespoons loose Lapsang souchong tea leaves
3 tablespoons stone-ground mustard
3 tablespoons tamari
2 garlic cloves
1 teaspoon crushed red pepper flakes
¼ cup minced fresh cilantro
¼ cup freshly squeezed lime juice
1 tablespoon evaporated cane juice
⅔ cup extra-virgin olive oil

For the filling

Caps of 2 medium portobello mushrooms
2 medium russet potatoes
2 tablespoons coconut oil
¼ cup minced onion
½ teaspoon sea salt
1 tablespoon nutritional yeast
1 tablespoon paprika
1 teaspoon chipotle powder
1½ teaspoons ground coriander
3 tablespoons minced fresh cilantro

For the poblanos

4 medium poblano peppers
¼ cup thinly sliced scallions, light green and white parts (optional; for garnish)

1 **Make the marinade:** Heat 1 cup water in a small saucepan. Once the water is boiling, add the tea leaves to the pot. Cover the pot, turn off the heat, and allow the tea to steep for 6 minutes. Strain the hot tea into a blender along with the mustard, tamari, garlic, red pepper flakes, cilantro, lime juice, evaporated cane juice, and oil. Blend on high speed for 30 seconds to emulsify, then set aside. (You will have about 2 cups marinade.)

2 **Prepare the filling:** Preheat a barbecue grill or char broiler. Clean the mushroom caps with a dry paper towel, and place them in a small bowl. Add 1 cup of the marinade, toss well, and set the mushrooms aside to absorb the liquid.

3 Peel and slice the potatoes into ½-inch cubes. Place them in a covered pot with 3 cups water set over medium-high heat. Bring the water to a boil, then immediately turn the heat off and drain the potatoes in a colander.

4 Heat the coconut oil in a sauté pan set over medium heat. Add the onions and sauté for about 5 minutes, until golden brown. Add the par-cooked potatoes, the salt, nutritional yeast, paprika, chipotle, and coriander. Continue to cook, tossing frequently, for about 10 minutes, until the potatoes are soft and gently smashed. Remove from the heat and set aside.

5 Once the grill is hot, grill the mushroom caps, starting with the rounded side facing you. Grill both sides for about 3 minutes, until the mushrooms are tender and well charred. Remove to a plate and allow the mushrooms to cool slightly. Place the mushrooms on a cutting board and chop into ¼-inch pieces. Stir the chopped mushrooms and the cilantro into the potatoes. (Leave the grill or barbecue nice and hot.)

6 **Finish the poblanos:** Bring 3 cups water to a boil in a large pot. Place the poblano peppers into the pot, then turn off the heat and cover the pot, allowing the peppers to blanch and steam for 2 minutes. Carefully remove the peppers and allow them to cool; they should be just slightly softened. Remove the stems and seeds of the peppers while leaving them whole. Toss the hollowed peppers in the remaining marinade in a small bowl, then carefully divide the potato-mushroom filling among them, packing it into each pepper.

7 Grill the stuffed poblanos on all sides for about 2 minutes to cover the peppers in charred grill marks. Brush the hot peppers with additional marinade to glaze them before serving. Garnish with the sliced scallions, if desired.

Cleaning Mushroom Caps

Mushrooms are quite unlike other vegetables when it comes to cleaning them. Because mushrooms are made of porous mycelium, they act like sponges. If you try to clean them under running water, the dirt clinging to the outside mixes with the water and gets soaked deeper into the body of the mushroom. So I always clean mushrooms by gently wiping them with a paper towel or clean dish towel. (Much of what appears to be dirt on mushrooms is just spores that have dropped from the mushroom or others around it during cultivation. So clean gently!)

Truffled Potato and Fried Onion Pierogies

WITH HORSERADISH MUSTARD CREAM

When my parents first fell in love, they quickly found that they had grown up with some of the same foods in their childhoods. My father really didn't have a stable home when he was growing up, but he lived in Brooklyn for some of his teenage years with his grandparents from the Ukraine, who were Orthodox Jews. My mother's family was a mix of Polish, Russian, and Hungarian Jews. Thus, Eastern European food was a staple of my diet while I was growing up. Kasha varnishkes, blintzes (see page 38), matzo brie, and of course pierogies dominate my childhood food memories.

Some folks dry and then steam their pierogies before frying them. Those steps are kind of finicky and make the process even longer, so unless you are a real traditionalist, I suggest you just form and fry them as I do. The horseradish mustard cream provides a nice bite to kick these up a notch if you are eating them on their own. Otherwise, eat them the way we always did in my family, as the perfect accompaniment to a great soup.

MAKES ABOUT 30 PIEROGIES

For the horseradish mustard cream

2 tablespoons extra-virgin olive oil
1 shallot, minced
¼ cup shredded fresh horseradish
6 drained brined capers
4 teaspoons Dijon mustard
2 tablespoons agave nectar
1 tablespoon brown rice vinegar
½ block firm silken tofu (typically sold in 12.3-ounce containers)

For the pierogies

5 large russet potatoes (about 2 pounds), peeled
3 tablespoons canola or safflower oil
1 large yellow onion, chopped
3 tablespoons truffle oil
3 tablespoons almond milk
1 teaspoon sea salt, plus more to taste
3 cups all-purpose flour, plus more for rolling out the dough
¼ cup tofu sour cream, store-bought or homemade (see page 38)
¼ teaspoon freshly ground white pepper
¼ cup extra-virgin olive oil, for frying
1 cup baby spinach leaves (optional; for plating)
¼ cup coarsely chopped fresh flat-leaf parsley (optional; for garnish)
Cracked black pepper (optional; for garnish)

1 **Make the horseradish mustard cream:** Heat the olive oil in a small saucepan over medium heat. Once the oil is hot, stir in the shallots and sauté for about 2 minutes to soften. Stir in the horseradish and capers, and continue to sauté for 4 minutes. Add the mustard, agave nectar, and vinegar. Place a lid on the pot, lower the heat to a simmer, and allow the horseradish to steam for 5 minutes. Turn off the heat and allow the mixture to cool for about 10 minutes. Pour the mixture into a high-speed blender, and add the silken tofu. Blend on high speed for 60 seconds to form a smooth cream. Chill the cream for at least 45 minutes before serving. If not using immediately, store in an airtight container in the refrigerator for up to 4 days.

2 Make the pierogi filling: Quarter the potatoes and place them in a pot along with 4 cups water. Bring the water to a boil, and allow the potatoes to cook for about 7 minutes, until the potatoes are cooked through. Drain the potatoes in a colander.

3 Heat the canola oil in a sauté pan over medium-high heat. Once the oil is hot, fry the onions in the oil, tossing a few times, until they are nicely browned. Turn off the heat, then add the potatoes and the truffle oil, almond milk, and ½ teaspoon of the salt to the pan. Mash until smooth with a potato masher.

4 Make the dough: Combine the flour, sour cream, white pepper, and the remaining ½ teaspoon of salt in a mixer. Gradually add 1 cup water while the mixer is running at a low speed, until you have just formed a firm but not very sticky dough. Continue mixing at low speed for 2 more minutes to develop

the gluten. Allow the dough to sit in a covered bowl for 20 to 30 minutes, so that the flour becomes fully hydrated.

5 Shape the pierogies: On a floured work surface, roll out the dough to about ⅛ inch thickness. Using a 2-inch-wide biscuit cutter or water glass, cut circles out of the dough. (You can reroll the scrap dough to make more pierogies.) Place a heaping tablespoon of the filling in the center of each circle of dough. Gently wet the perimeter of each circle with a finger or a pastry brush dabbed in warm water. Fold the circles of dough in half over the filling to form half-moon shapes, being careful not to push

the filling out into the edges of the pierogies. Use a fork to press the top and bottom edges together. As you work, transfer the sealed pierogies onto a lightly floured cutting board or baking sheet.

6 Heat the olive oil in a large frying pan over medium-high heat. Once the oil is hot, fry the pierogies for 2 to 3 minutes per side until they are golden brown. Remove the cooked pierogies and pat dry of excess oil with a paper towel. Salt the pierogies to taste, and plate them over baby spinach, if desired; garnish with parsley and cracked black pepper, if you like. Serve with the Horseradish Mustard Cream.

Truffle Oil

Truffle oil may not be one of your regular ingredients, but if you want the flavor of the most expensive mushrooms on earth without the expense, this is a good way to get it. In the '80s truffle oil quickly became an overused novelty flavor, thrown onto everything from crappy French fries to wannabe fancy-pants pizzas. Unfortunately, truffle oil is one of the most commonly adulterated ingredients available. Producers will often toss a tiny fleck of dried mushroom into each bottle just to claim that there is real truffle in the otherwise bogus and often petroleum-based product. There are a few expensive but real truffle oils out there, both imported and domestically made. We use the fantastic organic truffle oil from the Brooklyn-based company Da Rosario, which you can buy online.

Tequila Lime Tostones

WITH MASHED BLACK BEANS AND PICANTE HAZELNUTS

These tostones bring together the texture and savoriness I love from classic tostones, with the sweetness I long for from ripe fried plantains, by tossing the tostones in a caramelized mixture of tequila, lime juice, chili, and brown sugar. The glazed tostones get coated in spicy hazelnuts that have been roasted with garlic and habaneros, and I serve them with chunky mashed black beans and cilantro. These make a great side dish for taco night, or a pretty rad snack if you have been coerced into watching the Super Bowl against your will. (Let's face it: Unless you're a die-hard football fan, snacks are the only thing that make the Super Bowl worth dealing with.)

SERVES 4 (GF)

For the picante hazelnuts
½ habanero pepper, stem removed, minced
1 garlic clove, minced
2 tablespoons freshly squeezed lime juice
1 tablespoon tomato paste
1 teaspoon Mexican chili powder
2 tablespoons extra-virgin olive oil
¼ teaspoon sea salt
½ cup hazelnuts

For the mashed black beans
2 tablespoons extra-virgin olive oil
½ teaspoon ground cumin
½ red onion, minced
2 garlic cloves, minced
½ minced jalapeño pepper, stem removed, with seeds or without (depending on how hot you want it)
1 plum tomato, cut into small dice
1 tablespoon tomato paste
1 cup unsalted vegetable broth
½ teaspoon sea salt
3 tablespoons minced fresh cilantro, plus more for garnish
1½ cups cooked black beans, rinsed and drained

For the tostones
3 ripe green plantains
⅓ cup canola or safflower oil, for frying
¼ cup tequila
¼ cup freshly squeezed lime juice
3 tablespoons Sucanat or other brown sugar
1 teaspoon Mexican chili powder, plus more for garnish
½ teaspoon sea salt
1 cup chopped radicchio or baby arugula (optional; for plating)

1 Preheat the oven to 350°F. Line a rimmed baking sheet with parchment paper.

2 **Prepare the picante hazelnuts:** Process the habanero, garlic, lime juice, tomato paste, chili powder, olive oil, and salt in a high-speed blender for 45 seconds to form a smooth marinade. Add the hazelnuts, and pulse a couple of times just to break them up and coat them with the marinade. Spread the mixture onto the prepared baking sheet, and bake for 10 minutes. Remove the pan and stir the hazelnuts. Bake for another 3 to 5 minutes, until the nuts are mostly dry and well toasted. Allow the nuts to cool completely, then break up any clusters. Store in an airtight container for up to 1 week.

3 **Prepare the black beans:** Heat the olive oil in a medium saucepan over high heat. Once the oil is hot, sprinkle on the cumin, and allow it to fry for about 20 seconds before adding the onions, garlic, and jalapeño. Once the onions have softened, stir in the tomato, and continue sautéing for about 1 minute. Stir in the tomato paste, broth, salt, cilantro, and beans, and lower the heat to a simmer. Cover and cook for about 8 minutes, further softening the beans and vegetables. Uncover the pan and turn off the heat. Use either a food processor or a potato masher to roughly mash the beans. Keep warm until ready to serve.

4 **Fry the tostones:** Peel and cut the plantains on the diagonal into 4-inch-thick slices. Heat the oil in a frying pan over high heat. Once the oil is very hot, fry the plantains, working 8 pieces at a time, for 3 minutes on each side. Dry the fried plantains with paper towels and allow them to cool to room temperature. Flatten the plantains between your hands just a little bit, to give them a crushed texture.

5 Heat the tequila, lime juice, Sucanat, chili powder, and salt in a large sauté pan over medium-high heat. Once the liquid in the pan starts to bubble vigorously, add the fried plantains and toss them in the liquid to coat all sides with the caramelizing sauce. (You can also reheat the fried plantains in a warm oven or large dry pan, and then coat them with the sauce in a large mixing bowl.)

6 Serve 3 to 5 tostones per person, over a small scattering of radicchio or arugula, if using. Garnish each plate with 2 tablespoons of the hazelnuts and place a small ramekin of mashed black beans alongside. Garnish the whole plate with cilantro leaves and a dusting of Mexican chili powder.

FLAKY SPINACH PIE

Non-vegans don't think about what's missing in this spinach pie—instead, they think about what's in it: flaky, savory yumminess. That's why we offer this spinach pie every day, and at most of our catered events. To make this as an appetizer for a fancy dinner, you can make the filling up to a few days in advance, leaving the final assembly and baking for the day of serving. Otherwise, you can bake it earlier in the day, and just crisp the entire pie or individual portions briefly in the oven to reheat it and bring it back to life. It's always best served hot and fresh from the oven.

If you can't gather up the combined spices for sprinkling on before baking (or if you feel a little lazy), you can substitute 2 tablespoons of Cajun seasoning for the whole mix.

MAKES 24 PIECES

For the spinach filling

½ cup garlic cloves

¼ cup extra-virgin olive oil

2 bunches of spinach, very well washed, roots removed and leaves separated from stems

2 tablespoons umeboshi plum vinegar

2 tablespoons rice vinegar

1 teaspoon tamari

½ medium yellow onion, chopped

¼ cup drained brined capers

2 teaspoons dried oregano, or 4 teaspoons minced fresh oregano

1 tablespoon dried thyme

1 teaspoon freshly ground black pepper

For the pastry crust

1 tablespoon paprika

1 teaspoon ground coriander

1 teaspoon onion powder

1 teaspoon garlic powder

½ teaspoon dried thyme

½ teaspoon sea salt

⅓ cup extra-virgin olive oil, plus more for the baking sheet

1 package vegan filo dough

1 Preheat the oven to 350°F. Line a small rimmed baking sheet with parchment paper.

2 Prepare the filling: Toss the garlic cloves with 2 tablespoons of the olive oil in a small bowl. Transfer the garlic to the prepared baking sheet and roast for 12 to 15 minutes, until lightly golden brown and fragrant. Remove and set aside.

3 Place the spinach stems in a food processor along with the roasted garlic, plum vinegar, rice vinegar, and tamari. Process for about 90 seconds, until you have a fairly smooth puree.

4 Heat the remaining 2 tablespoons of olive oil in a medium-size heavy-bottomed pot set over medium heat. Once the oil is hot, sauté the onions for about 5 minutes, until translucent. Stir in the spinach leaves, capers, oregano, thyme, and pepper, and continue to sauté for 2 minutes to sweat the spinach leaves. Stir in the garlic and spinach puree, then cover the pot. Lower the heat to a simmer, and allow everything to steam for about 5 minutes. Turn off the heat, then uncover and allow the filling to cool for at least 30 minutes.

5 Make the pastries: Preheat the oven to 350°F. Thoroughly oil a rimmed baking sheet.

6 Combine the paprika, coriander, onion powder, garlic powder, thyme, and sea salt in a small bowl. Pour the ⅓ cup olive oil into a separate small bowl. Unroll the filo dough and spread about one quarter of the sheets (3 to 5 sheets) into the bottom of the oiled baking sheet. Brush the surface of the top sheet liberally with olive oil. Place another 3 to 5 sheets on top of the oiled one. Evenly spread the spinach filling over the prepared filo sheets. Lay out another 3 to 5 sheets of dough over the spinach, brush them with oil, and place the remaining 3 to 5 sheets on top, oiling them thoroughly. With a sharp knife, using smooth downward slices, cut the spinach pie into 24 equal pieces. Sprinkle with the mixed spices.

7 Bake the pie for 14 to 17 minutes, until the crust is golden brown and crisp. Score the pieces again with a knife to break them apart. Serve the spinach pie hot.

CHIMICHURRI TEMPEH EMPANADAS

WITH MINT ONION RELISH

These empanadas are seasoned with the spicy herbal flavor of Argentine chimichurri, baked, rather than fried, in a flaky pastry shell, and then cooled off with a sweet minty onion relish. The dough for this recipe reveals one of the basic truths of easy flaky pie crusts: If you leave the fat unevenly distributed in little flecks throughout the dough, and take care not to overmix, you'll have a nicely textured crust with very little fuss.

MAKES 12 TO 14 MEDIUM EMPANADAS

For the empanada dough and glaze

3 cups all-purpose flour, plus more for shaping the dough

¾ teaspoon sea salt

½ teaspoon ground coriander

½ teaspoon crushed red pepper flakes

¾ cup vegan margarine (such as Earth Balance), chilled and cut into ¼-inch cubes

3 tablespoons pureed silken tofu

2 tablespoons finely minced fresh cilantro

3 tablespoons unsweetened soy milk

2 tablespoons extra-virgin olive oil

4 teaspoons evaporated cane juice

¼ teaspoon ground turmeric

1 teaspoon smoked paprika

2 cups mesclun greens (optional; for plating)

For the mint onion relish

2 tablespoons extra-virgin olive oil

1 medium yellow onion, finely chopped

1 garlic clove, minced

1 medium sour pickle, minced

¼ cup coarsely chopped fresh mint leaves, plus more for garnish

1 teaspoon molasses

1 teaspoon pure maple syrup

½ teaspoon tamari

½ teaspoon apple cider vinegar

For the chimichurri tempeh filling

1 tablespoon dried oregano

1 cup firmly packed chopped fresh flat-leaf parsley

1 garlic clove, minced

1 minced jalapeño pepper (without seeds if you want less heat)

2 tablespoons red wine vinegar

¼ teaspoon freshly ground black pepper

Scant ½ teaspoon sea salt

⅓ cup plus 2 tablespoons extra-virgin olive oil

2 scallions, light green and white parts, chopped, plus more for garnish

One 8-ounce package tempeh, crumbled

⅓ cup shredded carrots

1 Make the empanada dough: Place the flour, ½ teaspoon of the salt, coriander, and red pepper flakes in a food processor, and process for 15 seconds to evenly distribute the ingredients. Add the margarine, pureed tofu, and ¼ cup cold water, and continue processing for 45 to 60 seconds, until a rough dough is formed. Press the dough into a ball, place it in a lightly oiled bowl, and chill, covered, for 30 minutes.

2 Make the empanada glaze: Combine the cilantro, soy milk, olive oil, evaporated cane juice, turmeric, paprika, and remaining ¼ teaspoon salt in a small bowl and whisk together vigorously with a fork. Set aside.

3 **Make the mint relish:** Heat the olive oil in a large sauté pan over medium heat. Once the oil is hot, add the onions and sauté for about 4 minutes, until the onions are lightly brown. Stir in the minced garlic and pickle, and continue sautéing for about 2 minutes until the garlic is softened and fragrant. Stir in the mint, molasses, maple syrup, tamari, and cider vinegar, and lower the heat to low. Allow to cook for a few more minutes until the mint has wilted and the onions have reached a deep brown.

4 **Make the tempeh filling:** Combine the oregano, parsley, garlic, jalapeño, red wine vinegar, black pepper, and sea salt with ⅓ cup of the olive oil in a blender. Pulse the ingredients several times until the parsley is very finely minced; the marinade should look like a very loose, chunky, oily pesto.

5 Heat the remaining 2 table-spoons of oil in a sauté pan over medium-high heat. Once the oil is hot, sauté the scallions for about 2 minutes. Add the crumbled tempeh and shredded carrots and continue sautéing, stirring regularly, for about 4 minutes, until the tempeh is lightly browned and seared all over. Stir in the marinade, lower the heat, and allow the tempeh to soak up most of the sauce as it cooks down for about 3 minutes. Turn off the heat, and allow the mixture to cool to room temperature, to make it less scary and hazardous to handle when filling the empanadas.

6 **Shape and bake the empanadas:** Preheat the oven to 350°F. Line a baking sheet with parchment paper and lightly oil the paper.

7 Remove the dough from the refrigerator, and very briefly knead it on a lightly floured surface to make it smooth and workable. Roll the dough out into a ⅛-inch-thick rectangle. Using a cookie cutter or rim of a glass, cut 3-inch-wide circles out of the dough, rerolling as necessary to cut as many disks out of the dough as possible. (You should be able to get 12 to 14 circles total.)

8 Place 2 tablespoons of the tempeh filling in the center of each disk, and wipe a thin layer of water around the edges of each circle to help seal them. Fold the pastry in half over the filling, and crimp the edges together with the tines of a fork. Brush the top of each pastry with a liberal stroke of the empanada glaze. Transfer the empanadas to the prepared baking sheet, and bake for 10 minutes. Rotate the sheet around in the oven after 10 minutes to ensure even baking. Bake for 4 to 8 more minutes, until golden brown.

9 Place a ramekin of mint onion relish on the side of each serving plate, and garnish it with extra mint. Scatter some mesclun greens on each plate, if desired, then add 2 or 3 empanadas per plate and garnish with chopped scallions.

THAI COCONUT
CURRY SOUP

Soups

99   Jalapeño Corn Chowdah

101   Live Habanero Tomato Soup

102   French Lentil Soup

103   Thai Coconut Curry Soup

104   Maple Butternut Squash Soup

106   Ginger Laphing

107   Creamy Roasted Almond Cauliflower Soup

108   Wild Mushroom, Spinach, and Potato Soup

109   Tomato Sage Bisque with Mizuna

111   Red Wine Minestrone

112   Korean Kimchi Soup

115   Cheesy Broccoli Beer Soup

117   Seitan Asada and Ancho Red Bean Chili

IN OUR EARLY DAYS, I didn't think it would even make sense to have our truck be open during the winter months. Who would want to wait in a line with the icy wind ripping off the Hudson River to freeze their mustache to a crisp? For the first few years, I closed the truck down for the coldest part of the winter and spent much-deserved time with my girls, drinking hot cider and chilling out by our wood stove. Yet after a few years, we had become a sort of institution in New York City, our growing staff wanted to keep working all year, and I thought we would give it a shot staying open all winter.

Much to my surprise, things barely slowed down for us at all. Loyal fans still show up in droves throughout the freezing rain, snow, and temperatures close to zero degrees, and every time, we are humbled by their devotion. When winter hits, it's still lively: A really bundled-up crowd sip on their hot soup while waiting for their sandwiches to come out. We work through the winter, sometimes cooking in thermal underwear, three sweatshirts, and a coat, because the inside of the truck really isn't much warmer than outside at all.

Having really yummy hot soup is just as important to us, freezing our butts off on the truck, as it is for our customers. We need to survive! Somebody please pour a bowl of soup down my shirt, so I can thaw out! In this chapter, you will find some of my favorites that we do on the truck. Please do not pour them down your shirt, unless you are really, really cold.

Jalapeño Corn Chowdah

This creamy soup is *just* spicy enough, and it is best made midsummer when fresh local corn is on its best behavior. The creamy body of the soup is provided by pureed chickpeas, which really make this a nice hearty meal. Serve it with the optional fried pepper garnish for an extra kick. My wife says *chowdah* is a gross word, but I must argue, the word *chowder* is even grosser. What a cringe-worthy word . . . call it *soup* if you want, and it will make Joey (Ms. Snail) happy.

MAKES 1 QUART (GF)

For the fried pepper garnish (optional)
3 tablespoons coconut oil

1 minced jalapeño pepper with seeds, stem removed

1 scallion, light green and white parts, minced

3 tablespoons minced fresh flat-leaf parsley

1 tablespoon freshly squeezed lemon juice

¼ teaspoon sea salt

For the soup
2 tablespoons coconut oil

½ medium yellow onion, finely chopped

1 medium jalapeño pepper, stem and seeds removed, finely chopped

1½ cups fresh corn kernels (from about 2 ears)

⅔ cup cooked and drained chickpeas

2 tablespoons tahini

1 celery stalk, chopped

2 garlic cloves

3 cups vegetable broth

2 tablespoons tamari

2 tablespoons agave nectar

2 teaspoons apple cider vinegar

1 tablespoon ground cumin

2 teaspoons ground coriander

1 teaspoon dried thyme

¼ teaspoon freshly ground black pepper

1 **Make the pepper garnish:** In a small saucepan over high heat, melt the coconut oil. Once the oil is hot, stir in the jalapeño and scallion, and continue to cook, stirring, for about 2 minutes. Turn off the heat, and immediately stir in the parsley, lemon juice, and salt. Use immediately, or store in an airtight container in the refrigerator for up to 3 days.

2 **Make the chowdah:** Heat the coconut oil in a 2-quart pot over medium heat. When the oil is hot, sauté the onions and jalapeño for 3 minutes, stirring occasionally. Stir in the corn and continue to sauté for about 3 minutes, until the onions are lightly golden and the jalapeño has softened.

3 Place the chickpeas, tahini, celery, garlic, vegetable broth, tamari, agave nectar, vinegar, cumin, coriander, thyme, and black pepper into a blender and blend on high speed for 60 seconds to form a smooth puree. Pour the contents of the blender into the pot, and bring the mixture to a boil. Turn off the heat, and serve the soup immediately with a spoonful of the spicy garnish, if using, in the center of each bowl. If not serving right away, let the soup and garnish cool and store separately in the refrigerator for up to 4 days.

Live Habanero Tomato Soup

It's so easy, when you eat primarily raw food, to end up having a lot more sweet things in your diet. Many raw savory dishes take a lot of time and planning to execute. This spicy raw soup, on the other hand, takes mere minutes to whip together, and it packs plenty of essential fatty acids from the hemp seeds and flax oil.

MAKES 1 QUART (GF)

3 ripe medium tomatoes

1 small habanero pepper (or less if you like it less spicy), stem and seeds removed

3 tablespoons hemp seeds

2 tablespoons flax oil

1 garlic clove

2 tablespoons white miso paste

1 celery stalk

½ lime, including the rind

½ teaspoon ground coriander

¼ cup thinly sliced scallions, light green and white parts (optional; for garnish)

Smoked paprika (optional; for garnish)

Place the tomatoes, habanero, hemp seeds, flax oil, garlic, miso paste, celery, lime, and coriander in a blender. Add 1⅓ cups warm water and blend for 45 seconds on high speed. Pour into cups to serve. Garnish with the scallions and a pinch of smoked paprika, if desired.

FRENCH LENTiL SOUP

WITH CAPERS AND FRIED PINE NUTS

I made this rustic soup for the Cinnamon Snail's final week on the streets in 2010. It was twenty degrees outside, but people lined up eagerly for their last Cinnamon Snail fix before the truck's hibernation. Inside the truck, we survived the frigid temperature by downing cup after cup of the steamy lentil soup. Thinking about it makes me look forward to our next winter, when I'll have a perfect excuse for extensive lentil soup field testing.

MAKES ABOUT 2 QUARTS (GF)

7 garlic cloves

½ medium yellow or Vidalia onion, quartered

4 tablespoons extra-virgin olive oil

1 large carrot

One 28-ounce can whole peeled tomatoes

1½ cups French lentils, washed and picked over

5½ cups vegetable broth

1½ teaspoons minced fresh rosemary

2 teaspoons dried oregano

1 teaspoon dried thyme

½ teaspoon freshly ground black pepper

1 crushed dried pepperoncino (or 1 teaspoon crushed red pepper flakes)

2 tablespoons tamari

2 tablespoons balsamic vinegar

½ cup pine nuts

¼ cup drained brined capers, chopped

Fresh herbs, for garnish

1 In a food processor, chop the garlic and onion until all pieces are smaller than peas.

2 In a very large pot, heat 2 tablespoons of the olive oil over medium heat. Add the chopped onion and garlic.

3 While the onion and garlic are cooking, chop the carrot and pulse it in the food processor briefly to create smaller irregular pieces. Once the onion and garlic mixture has become golden, drain the juice from the can of tomatoes into the pot. Add the drained tomatoes to the chopped carrot in the food processor and pulse them briefly to cut each tomato into 3 or 4 large pieces.

4 Add the contents of the food processor, the lentils,

broth, rosemary, oregano, thyme, black pepper, pepperoncino, tamari, and vinegar to the pot, and raise the heat to high. Allow the soup to come to a boil. Place a lid on the pot, lower the heat to medium low, and simmer for 40 minutes.

5 In a small pan, heat the remaining 2 tablespoons of olive oil over medium heat, and add the pine nuts. Stir the pine nuts with a wooden spoon every 20 seconds. After 2 minutes, or when the pine nuts are golden on all sides, remove them from the oil and add them along with the capers to the soup. (At this point, the soup can be stored or frozen if desired.)

6 When ready to serve, garnish each bowl with fresh herbs.

THAI COCONUT CURRY SOUP

WITH CHICKPEAS, THAI BASIL, AND KAFFIR LIME LEAVES

This is one of my favorite Cinnamon Snail soups, and when we make it at home, we dump any of the remaining fall veggies from our garden into it. I've done it with butternut squash, turnips, collard greens, sweet potatoes. Basically, any veggies you have lying around will be much happier surrounded by this spicy coconut broth. You don't have access to lime leaves? LEAVE them out. Get it? Leaf 'em out? #dadjokes

MAKES 2 QUARTS (GF)

3 tablespoons toasted sesame oil

1 tablespoon brown mustard seeds

1 medium yellow onion, diced

2 medium carrots, peeled and diced

3 celery stalks, diced

2 tablespoons minced peeled fresh ginger

2 tablespoons ground coriander

2 tablespoons ground cumin

3 tablespoons Thai red curry paste

¼ cup chopped fresh Thai basil leaves

8 kaffir lime leaves, sliced into strips

2 medium Yukon Gold potatoes, diced

7 cups vegetable broth

One 13.5-ounce can coconut milk

3 tablespoons rice vinegar

3 tablespoons agave nectar

2 tablespoons tamari

2 cups cooked and drained chickpeas

1 Heat the sesame oil over medium heat in a medium soup pot. Add the mustard seeds, and wait for them to pop. Add the onions, carrots, celery, and ginger. Sauté in the hot oil for 3 to 4 minutes, to soften the vegetables.

2 Add the coriander, cumin, red curry paste, basil, and lime leaves, and continue cooking for 2 more minutes, stirring frequently. Add the potatoes, vegetable broth, coconut milk, vinegar, agave nectar, tamari, and chickpeas; raise the heat to high; and bring the soup to a boil. Continue to cook on high for 15 minutes, or until the potatoes are cooked through. Serve hot, or cool and store in an airtight container in the refrigerator for up to 4 days, or in the freezer for up to a month.

maple Butternut squash soup

We often offer this soup on our Thanksgiving catering menu. It's sweet and creamy and smells great. Ginger, cloves, and star anise contribute to its aroma, and coconut milk lends the soup a creamy rich body. When you remove the seeds from the squash, don't toss them in the garbage—they are the best part! Try frying them in a little coconut oil and then tossing them with sea salt and a little nutritional yeast or garam masala as a garnish for the soup.

MAKES 4 QUARTS (GF)

2 tablespoons extra-virgin olive oil

1 medium yellow onion, chopped

2 garlic cloves

2 tablespoons minced peeled fresh ginger

3 celery stalks, coarsely chopped

2 medium carrots, coarsely chopped

1 small butternut squash, peeled, seeds removed, cut into 1-inch cubes

1 full star anise

1 tablespoon ground coriander

1 tablespoon ground cumin

2 teaspoons ground cinnamon, plus more for garnish

½ teaspoon ground nutmeg

½ teaspoon ground cloves

1 teaspoon freshly ground black pepper

3¼ cups vegetable broth

¼ cup tamari

⅓ cup pure maple syrup

Two 13.5-ounce cans coconut milk, plus more for garnish

1 In a 4-quart pot, heat the olive oil over medium heat. Sauté the onions, garlic, and minced ginger in the oil for 3 to 4 minutes, stirring, until the onions begin to soften. Add the celery and carrots and continue to sauté, stirring, for 3 minutes.

2 Add the squash, star anise, coriander, cumin, cinnamon, nutmeg, cloves, pepper, broth, tamari, maple syrup, and coconut milk and raise the heat to high. Bring the soup to a boil. Cook for 6 to 8 minutes, until the squash can easily be cut into with the side of a fork. Turn off the heat and allow the soup to cool for 15 to 20 minutes. Blend the soup in batches at medium speed for 60 seconds, to form a smooth pureed soup. Or if you own an immersion blender, drop that bad boy into the pot, and get the job done right in the darn pot.

3 To serve the soup, garnish the top of each serving with a drizzle of coconut milk and a dash of cinnamon. If not serving immediately, store in airtight quart-size containers in the refrigerator for up to 4 days, or in the freezer for up to a month.

Ginger Laphing

WITH BOK CHOY AND ROASTED PEANUTS

Laphing is a brothy Tibetan soup that you can find on the streets of Dharamsala, the town in northern India that is home to the Tibetan leadership and community in exile. It's really a street-food-heavy town: The narrow streets on the hillside are filled with the sounds and smells of people making *momos* (Tibetan dumplings), and you also find hot bowls of laphing prepared to order from street carts. The soup is nourishing and spicy, and you can eat it at the foot of a temple on a cliff while the sun sets. This is a perfect vegan alternative for chicken soup, if you are feeling a little run down.

MAKES 1 QUART (GF)

2 Yukon Gold potatoes, cut into ½-inch cubes

4 teaspoons toasted sesame oil

2 sliced scallions, light green and white parts; plus 2 tablespoons minced scallions, light green and white parts, for garnish (optional)

4 teaspoons minced peeled fresh ginger

1 teaspoon minced jalapeño (use less if you can't stand the heat), stem and seeds removed

2 garlic cloves, minced

5 cups vegetable broth

3 tablespoons tamari

2 tablespoons brown rice vinegar

1 bundle of buckwheat soba noodles (2 to 3 ounces)

1 head of bok choy, separated into individual leaves

¼ cup chopped roasted peanuts; plus 2 tablespoons ground roasted peanuts for garnish (optional)

1 Place the potatoes in a medium pot with 4 cups water and bring to a boil over high heat. Allow the potatoes to cook for 7 minutes, or until just soft. When the potatoes are cooked, drain them in a colander and set aside.

2 Heat the sesame oil in a separate pot over medium heat. Sauté the sliced scallions, the ginger, chile, and garlic in the hot oil, stirring. After about 4 minutes, once the garlic has softened and turned lightly golden, add the broth, tamari, and vinegar and bring to a boil.

3 Break the bundle of soba noodles in half and stir them into the boiling broth. Continue stirring for 2 minutes or so until the noodles are al dente. Stir in the cooked potatoes, the bok choy leaves, and the chopped roasted peanuts. Turn off the pot and serve immediately, garnishing with the minced scallions and ground roasted peanuts, if desired.

Creamy Roasted almond Cauliflower Soup

This soup gets its creaminess from the garlic and the blanched almonds that are roasted with the cauliflower. A little fresh lemon rind gets roasted with the vegetables to contribute freshness and maximum levels of pizzazz. I mean, you look really happy eating your Top Ramen on New Jersey Transit, but maybe you wouldn't mind a pizzazz-laden soup once in a while? You know—to make you look more confident on the golf course or at the board meeting, accompanied by your Bluetooth earpiece that flashes a blue light every two seconds? CAULIFLOWER. It's true. Cauliflower will give you that pizzazz.

MAKES 3 PINTS (GF)

1 head of cauliflower, coarsely chopped
1 cup blanched almonds
Rind from ½ lemon, plus the rind and juice of 1 whole lemon
7 tablespoons extra-virgin olive oil
2 teaspoons tamari
1 tablespoon dried thyme
1 teaspoon freshly ground black pepper
3 tablespoons evaporated cane juice
¼ teaspoon ground turmeric
½ teaspoon sea salt, plus more to taste
¼ cup shaved or chopped radish of your choice
4 cups vegetable broth
2 tablespoons white miso paste
½ medium yellow onion, diced
4 garlic cloves, minced
3 tablespoons minced fresh flat-leaf parsley
1 small parsnip, cleaned and diced
1 celery stalk, diced

1 Preheat the oven to 400°F.

2 In a large bowl, combine the cauliflower, almonds, ½ lemon rind, 1 tablespoon of the olive oil, the tamari, thyme, and pepper. Spread the mixture in an even layer in a roasting pan and bake for 12 to 14 minutes, until the cauliflower has wilted and the almonds have become slightly golden.

3 Meanwhile, in a small baking dish, combine the full lemon rind and juice, evaporated cane juice, ¼ cup of the olive oil, the turmeric, and the salt. Roast the lemon rind for 9 to 12 minutes, until the lemon pieces brown slightly on the edges. Place the lemon rind and any oil and juice from the pan into a blender and blend on high for 45 seconds, until only very small fragments of lemon rind remain. Combine the lemon rind with the shaved radish and set aside.

4 Combine the vegetable broth with the miso paste and the roasted cauliflower and almonds in a blender. Blend on high speed for 60 seconds to form a smooth puree.

5 In a soup pot, heat the remaining 2 tablespoons of olive oil over medium heat. Sauté the onions, garlic, and parsley in the hot oil for about 5 minutes, or until the onions become translucent. Add the parsnips and celery and continue to sauté for another 3 minutes. Pour the pureed cauliflower mixture into the soup pot, bring up to a boil, and cook for 6 minutes, or until the parsnips are soft. Remove from the heat. Salt to taste. Serve by garnishing each bowl with the shaved radish and lemon mixture.

WILD MUSHROOM SPINACH, AND POTATO SOUP

I'm extra lucky to have a couple of friends who know I'm a total fiend for wild mushrooms. Our area of New Jersey gets enormous chicken of the woods, hen of the woods, oyster, and, on the medicinal end, lion's mane and reishi mushrooms. I wrote this recipe specifically to work with hen of the woods (aka maitake). If those absurdly good mushrooms aren't available, you can still have a wonderful bowl of soup by substituting an equal amount of chopped portobello, shiitake, oyster, or cremini in place of the maitake.

MAKES 2 QUARTS (GF)

4 Yukon Gold potatoes, cut into ½-inch cubes

2 tablespoons extra-virgin olive oil

1 medium yellow onion, finely chopped

2 cups chopped maitake mushrooms

3 garlic cloves, minced

2 tablespoons chopped fresh rosemary leaves

4 cups packed baby spinach

6 cups vegetable broth

2 tablespoons rice vinegar

1 teaspoon dried thyme

½ teaspoon freshly ground black pepper

¼ cup tamari

1 Place the potatoes in a saucepan with 6 cups water and bring to a boil over high heat.

2 Meanwhile, in a separate pot, heat the olive oil over medium heat. Sauté the onions and mushrooms, stirring, for 6 minutes, until the onions become translucent and the mushrooms are tender. Add the garlic, rosemary, spinach, broth, vinegar, thyme, pepper, and tamari. Bring the soup to a slow boil, then turn off the heat.

3 Once the potatoes have become soft enough to cut into with the side of a fork, about 7 minutes of cooking time, drain them into a colander and add them to the soup. Serve immediately, or store in airtight containers in the refrigerator for up to 3 days, or in the freezer for up to a month.

STRANGE SENTIENT FRUITS

Mushrooms are the heroic weirdos of the woods. In nature they break down dense, complicated matter and allow it to degrade to a biologically useful available form. When grown on contaminated material, the mushroom fully transforms the material as it metabolizes it, leaving no traces of hydrocarbons in the medium on which it has been grown.

Similarly, mushrooms perform a medicinal alchemy: they help remove heavy metals, impurities, and environmental contaminants from the body. Of course, they also offer mouth-watering flavors and satisfying textures, so why not fall in love with mushrooms?

One of my heroes is Paul Stamets, a mycologist (mushroom researcher) who has pioneered creative ways in which mushrooms can be used to reverse environmental destruction. I really recommend his book *Mycelium Running*—read it and be inspired, and get excited about how mushrooms can repair our damaged planet.

tomato Sage Bisque WITH MIZUNA

This creamy soup gets its hearty body from brown rice, which is blended with the other ingredients at the end. The soup is a lovely orange red and looks extra pretty with the optional garnishes: a drizzling of coconut milk, a dusting of smoked paprika, and some thinly sliced fresh sage. Mizuna is a mildly spicy green (sometimes green and purple) leafy vegetable available in the spring and fall. If you can't find it, you can substitute mustard greens in this recipe.

MAKES 2 QUARTS (GF)

1 tablespoon extra-virgin olive oil

1 medium red onion, chopped

3 celery stalks, chopped

3 garlic cloves

1 lemon, rind and all, cut into 8 pieces, seeds removed

3 tablespoons chopped fresh basil leaves

1 teaspoon dried thyme

2 teaspoons ground coriander

1 tablespoon brown rice syrup

3 medium tomatoes, stems removed, halved

¼ cup uncooked brown rice

2 bay leaves

1½ cups unsweetened soy milk

8 fresh sage leaves, thinly sliced, plus more for garnish

1 teaspoon crushed red pepper flakes

½ cup thinly sliced mizuna

1 teaspoon sea salt

¼ cup coconut milk (optional; for garnish)

2 teaspoons smoked paprika (optional; for garnish)

1 Heat the olive oil in a soup pot over medium-high heat. Sauté the onions, celery, and garlic for about 4 minutes, to sweat the vegetables. Stir in the lemon, basil, thyme, coriander, and rice syrup. Continue to sauté for 3 minutes.

2 Add the tomatoes, uncooked rice, bay leaves, soy milk, and 3 cups water. Raise the heat to high and bring the mixture to a boil. Cover the pot and reduce the heat to medium. Allow the soup to cook for 20 minutes, or until the rice is tender. Remove the lid and turn off the heat. Discard the bay leaves.

3 Using an immersion blender, or working in batches in a high-speed blender, blend the soup until it becomes smooth. Return the pureed soup to the pot.

4 Add the sage, red pepper flakes, mizuna, and salt. Allow the soup to cool for 10 minutes, while the mizuna becomes tender.

5 To serve, ladle about 1½ cups soup into each bowl. Drizzle each bowl with a pinch of sliced sage leaves, 1 tablespoon coconut milk, if using, and ½ teaspoon smoked paprika, if using.

Red Wine Minestrone

WITH SWISS CHARD AND PEARL ONIONS

Pearl onions are tiny little baby onions. In this soup, they go in first and cook on their own and slightly caramelize, and then soak up lots of the soup's flavors as it simmers. What you ultimately get is these little baby onions in each bowl that are bursting with the flavors of the soup. If you are in a jam and can't find pearl onions, you can get away with using the absolutely tiniest shallots you can find, or boiler onions or cipolline in place of them. Soups with pasta in them, like minestrone, *need* something extra nourishing going on to validate their pasta-laden existence. Swiss chard to the rescue: Added toward the end of the recipe, it is perfectly cooked and kept as nutritionally intact as possible.

MAKES ABOUT 3 QUARTS

2 tablespoons extra-virgin olive oil
16 small pearl onions, peeled
1 small yellow onion, diced
2 celery stalks, finely chopped
2 garlic cloves, minced
1 medium carrot, finely chopped
3 cups vegetable broth
2 cups red wine
One 28-ounce can diced tomatoes, with juice
1 cup pasta (ditalini, or small elbows or shells)
1 cup cooked and drained pinto beans
1 teaspoon crushed red pepper flakes
1 teaspoon dried thyme
1½ teaspoons dried oregano
¼ cup chopped fresh basil leaves
1 bunch Swiss chard, stems removed, chopped
Sea salt

1 Heat the olive oil in a soup pot over medium-high heat. Add the pearl onions and cook, stirring frequently, for about 5 minutes, until the outsides are lightly browned.

2 Add the diced onions, celery, garlic, and carrot and continue to sauté for 4 to 5 minutes to sweat the vegetables. Add the broth, red wine, and diced tomatoes to the pot and raise the heat to high.

3 Once the mixture comes to a boil, add the pasta and cook for about 4 minutes, so that the pasta is still not yet fully cooked. Stir in the beans, red pepper flakes, thyme, oregano, basil, and Swiss chard and continue to cook for about 2 minutes, until the pasta is cooked al dente. Salt to taste.

Korean Kimchi Soup

WITH UDON NOODLES AND FRIED TOFU

Kimchi soup, *or kimchiguk*, is often made with huge cubes of plain blanched tofu, and it can be a little boring. In this recipe we use crispy fried tofu as well as udon noodles, which soak up the spicy broth around them. The soup is best made with homemade Kimchi and homemade gochujang, a chili paste made with glutinous rice flour. Not to fear, though—folks with little time to fool around with such stuff can find vegan store-bought varieties in Asian food stores and health food stores. Just be a diligent label reader: Most store-bought kimchi does contain fish.

This soup packs a pretty great bite, so if you are not as badly addicted to the capsaicin kiss of death as I am, cut back on the gochujang, silly!

MAKES ABOUT 2 QUARTS

One 14-ounce block extra-firm tofu

¼ cup canola oil

2 tablespoons toasted sesame oil

⅔ cup coarsely chopped kimchi, homemade (see page 175) or store-bought

⅓ cup julienned carrots

4 teaspoons evaporated cane juice

4 teaspoons gochujang (see page 145) or store-bought

1 tablespoon rice vinegar

2 teaspoons tamari

5 cups vegetable broth

2 scallions, light green and white parts, sliced thinly, plus more for garnish

One 3-ounce bundle of dry udon noodles

4 teaspoons black sesame seeds (optional; for garnish)

¼ cup micro radish greens (optional; for garnish)

1 Cut the tofu into ½-inch cubes, and pat off as much extra liquid from them as possible with a paper towel.

2 Heat the canola oil in a 9-inch frying pan over high heat. Working in batches if necessary, fry the tofu on both sides in the hot oil for about 7 minutes, or until it is puffed, crispy, and golden. Remove the tofu from the oil, and drain it on a plate lined with paper towels. Turn off the heat under the frying pan, and reserve the oil to use again, if desired.

3 Heat the sesame oil in a soup pot over medium heat. When the oil is hot, sauté the kimchi and carrots for 4 minutes. Stir in the evaporated cane juice, gochujang, vinegar, and tamari. Continue to sauté for 3 minutes.

4 Add the broth, scallions, and fried tofu, then cover the pot and raise the heat to high. Once the soup comes to a boil, stir in the udon noodles. Cook for about 4 minutes, stirring occasionally, until the noodles are just cooked al dente.

5 To serve, ladle about 1½ cups of soup into each bowl, distributing the noodles evenly. Garnish with scallions, sesame seeds, if using, and micro radish greens, if using.

CHEESY Broccoli BEER SOUP
WITH SMOKY SUNFLOWER CHORIZO

Beer soups have been around for centuries, and they usually contain lots of cheese and roux. Instead of too much gloopy floury roux, this soup relies on mashed potatoes. Now that you know that, it's even more exciting, right? Because this is essentially a totally hooked-up stuffed baked potato, masquerading as a soup. This is a perfect soup to serve at a Super Bowl party, by the way.

MAKES ABOUT 2 QUARTS

For the sunflower chorizo

1½ cups sunflower seeds
2 tablespoons tomato paste
2 tablespoons Cajun seasoning
2 teaspoons ground cumin
1 teaspoon asafetida
2 tablespoons tamari
2 tablespoons pure maple syrup
1½ teaspoons liquid smoke
¼ cup extra-virgin olive oil
2 teaspoons fennel seeds

For the soup

3 tablespoons coconut oil
2 large shallots, chopped
3 garlic cloves
1 celery stalk, chopped
2 tablespoons Dijon mustard
¼ teaspoon cayenne pepper
½ teaspoon asafetida (optional; for extra cheesy fun times)
1 tablespoon smoked paprika
4 teaspoons tamari
1½ cups coarsely chopped broccoli
One 12-ounce bottle vegan beer
2 cups vegetable broth
3 small Yukon Gold potatoes, quartered
⅓ cup nutritional yeast

1 **Make the chorizo:** Preheat the oven to 400°F. Line a rimmed baking sheet with parchment paper and lightly oil the paper.

2 Place the sunflower seeds, tomato paste, Cajun seasoning, cumin, asafetida, tamari, maple syrup, liquid smoke, olive oil, and fennel seeds in a food processor and process for about 60 seconds, just until no whole sunflower seeds remain. Crumble the mixture evenly over the surface of the lined baking sheet. Bake for 14 to 18 minutes, until the sunflower mixture is reddish brown and crispy. Set aside.

3 **Make the soup:** Heat the coconut oil in a soup pot over high heat. Sauté the shallots, garlic, and celery in the hot oil for about 4 minutes. Stir in the mustard, cayenne, asafetida (if using), paprika, and tamari and sauté for 3 more minutes. Add the broccoli, beer, broth, potatoes, and yeast, then cover the pot and bring to a boil. Continue cooking until the potatoes are cooked through and can be cut easily with the side of a fork. Remove the lid, turn off the heat, and allow the soup to cool for about 15 minutes.

4 Carefully and thoroughly blend the soup in a high-speed blender or with an immersion blender. Before serving, reheat the pureed soup and stir in the crumbled sunflower chorizo, or top each bowl with a bit of chorizo for garnish.

A WONDERFUL FOOD TRUCK DISASTER

There are times on the truck when everyone gets drenched with a freezing hurricane of water, and we all wish we had a dry change of clothes and a cup of hot soup. Usually, we're cozy inside as the customers bear the brunt, but sometimes we all share in the storm.

One such day was the Bethlehem (Pennsylvania) Vegfest, just a week before the 2012 Vendy Awards. A few days earlier, the truck's generator had died, and we threw in a crappy backup while we waited for our nice new one. Turned out the backup generator wasn't powerful enough, and shut off regularly. Without power, in summer, we had to keep everything in coolers in the absurdly hot truck. Cooking without our exhaust system was like being baked alive in the truck.

After lots of complications and *many* nights of work, we were in the final stages of installing the new generator on the night before Vegfest, just in time for what we expected would be a super busy day. We'd need to leave Jersey by nine A.M. Around seven thirty, the generator was finally tested—nothing! We'd been told by the manufacturer that we would not need an external fuel pump to run the thing, but they were dead wrong. We had just enough time to obtain and install a fuel pump once the auto parts store opened. We fired up the generator again . . . and still nothing. With no time left, we grabbed an extension cord and drove off to Pennsylvania, praying there would be an outlet or generator for us there.

It was a gorgeous day, with a huge turnout, and, thank goodness, an electrical panel we could plug into. For hours we kicked ass, serving amazing food to a never-ending line of folks, many of whom had heard of us and been waiting years to try our food. A few hours in, the sky began to darken, and then we lost power. At the electrical panel, an event personnel was shutting everything off. A rainstorm was coming in, and they were closing down the event.

Back at the truck, I made the announcement, but said that we would still serve the seventy or eighty people waiting in our line. We cooked like crazy as the rain and wind swept across the parking lot, and the entire festival cleared out except for our truck and a huge line of drenched people. Finally, I announced that we'd be giving free food to everyone in line, and people went crazy. It was so much fun, even with the rain.

Seitan Asada and Ancho Red Bean Chili

WITH CILANTRO MINT SOUR CREAM

If there's one thing that turns me off from most chili recipes, it's the whole single-textured-bowl-of-mush thing. I mean, I like a good heap of mush just as much as the next man (Ethiopian food especially), but a full bowl of savory gruel just isn't a real turn-on to me. That's why I came up with this recipe, which features some diverse textures and flavors. The soft, cool, minty sour cream melts into the crisp Southern-style seitan, hearty beans, and tomatoes. Toast up some corn bread in chili oil, and you have a perfect meal for a cold day, one you will never confuse with a ground-up, boiled burlap sack. (And I really, really recommend you add the habanero I've included, unless you have a major aversion to spice. It gives the chili a perfect kick.)

MAKES 2 QUARTS

For the seitan asada
3 tablespoons extra-virgin olive oil
1 small yellow onion, chopped
3 garlic cloves
1 celery stalk, sliced
2 tablespoons Mexican chili powder
2 teaspoons ground cumin
1 tablespoon crushed red pepper flakes
3 tablespoons pure maple syrup
2 tablespoons tamari
1 teaspoon liquid smoke
3 tablespoons apple cider vinegar
2 tablespoons tomato paste
2 tablespoons coconut oil
⅔ cup large shreds of seitan

For the ancho red bean chili
1 cup vegetable broth
2 dried ancho chiles, stems removed
2 tablespoons extra-virgin olive oil
1 small yellow onion, minced
2 garlic cloves, minced
¼ cup finely chopped red bell pepper
¼ teaspoon minced fresh habanero, stem and seeds removed (optional; for extra heat)
1 tablespoon ground cumin
4 teaspoons Mexican chili powder
1 tablespoon smoked paprika
2 cups cooked (or drained canned) red or pink beans
One 28-ounce can diced tomatoes, with juice

1 tablespoon molasses
2 tablespoons tamari
¼ cup chopped fresh cilantro leaves, plus more for garnish
2 scallions, light green and white parts, sliced thin (optional; for garnish)

For the cilantro mint sour cream
½ block soft tofu, crumbled
¼ cup extra-virgin olive oil
2 tablespoons brown rice vinegar
1 tablespoon apple cider vinegar
2 tablespoons agave nectar
½ teaspoon sea salt
½ teaspoon asafetida
1 minced scallion, light green and white parts
2 tablespoons chopped fresh mint leaves
2 tablespoons chopped fresh cilantro leaves

1 **Make the seitan asada:** Heat the olive oil in a sauté pan over medium-high heat. Sauté the onions, garlic, and celery in the oil for about 5 minutes, until the garlic is lightly browned. Stir in the chili powder, cumin, and red pepper flakes, and continue to sauté for about

recipe continues

2 minutes. Stir in the maple syrup, tamari, liquid smoke, cider vinegar, tomato paste, and ⅓ cup water, and cook until the mixture comes to a boil. Place the mixture in a blender, and blend on high for 30 seconds to form a smooth, thick sauce. Set aside.

2 **Fry the seitan:** Heat the coconut oil in a sauté pan over medium-high heat. Add the seitan slivers and cook, flipping the pieces every couple of minutes, for 7 to 9 minutes, until the slivers are well browned and a bit crispy. Pour the pureed sauce over the seitan, and stir the seitan for about 3 more minutes until the sauce caramelizes around the pieces. Set aside.

3 **Make the chili:** Bring the vegetable broth to a boil in a small covered pot. Add the dried chiles, cover the pot, and turn off the heat. Allow the chiles to rehydrate for at least 10 minutes.

4 Heat the olive oil in a medium pot over medium-high heat. Sauté the onions in the oil for about 4 minutes. Stir in the garlic, bell pepper, and, if using, the habanero. Allow the vegetables to cook for 3 minutes. Stir in the cumin, chili powder,

and paprika, and continue cooking for 3 minutes to fry the spices. Stir in the beans, tomatoes, molasses, and tamari, and reduce the heat to low.

5 Place the vegetable broth and rehydrated chiles into a blender, and pulse several times so that the chiles are broken into small fragments. Stir the contents of the blender into the chili. Allow the chili to simmer uncovered for 15 minutes, stirring occasionally. Turn off the heat and stir in the chopped cilantro.

6 **Make the cilantro mint sour cream:** Place the crumbled tofu, olive oil, rice vinegar, cider vinegar, agave nectar, salt, and asafetida in a blender, and blend on high for 60 seconds to form a smooth, thick puree. Add the scallion, mint, and cilantro and pulse several times to just combine. Use immediately, or chill and use within 3 days.

7 Just before serving, stir the crisp seitan into the hot chili. Ladle about 2 cups of chili into each bowl and top with 2 tablespoons of sour cream. Garnish with cilantro and with scallions, if using.

Hold on! Forget about the bowl; you can't eat a stupid bowl.

What are you thinking putting this hooked-up yummy chili in a bowl? Instead, why not go all out and make these into . . .

Stuffed Potato Skins

MAKES 16 POTATO SKINS

8 small russet potatoes
¼ cup extra-virgin olive oil
Sea salt and freshly ground black pepper
1 quart Seitan Asada and Ancho Red Bean Chili with Cilantro Mint Sour Cream (recipe above)
2 tablespoons finely chopped fresh cilantro leaves
2 scallions, light green and white parts, sliced thin

1 Preheat the oven to 350°F.

2 Place the potatoes in a large pot and cover with water. Bring the water to a boil. Allow the potatoes to cook for only 5 minutes after the water comes to a boil. Carefully drain the water from the pot (without removing the potatoes), and replace the hot water with ice and cold water. Allow the potatoes to cool.

3 Cut each potato in half lengthwise. Holding the halved potatoes in one hand, carefully remove the centers of the potatoes with a melon baller or sharp-edged spoon, leaving the skins and a slim ¼-inch rim of potato close to the skin. Transfer the potatoes to a rimmed baking sheet; drizzle olive oil on the skins and lightly season them with salt and pepper. Bake the skins for 15 to 18 minutes, until thoroughly cooked.

4 Mix the hot chili and seitan asada. Ladle a couple of heaping spoonfuls of chili into the potato skins, and top with the sour cream, cilantro, and scallions.

PEKING SEITAN
BAO BUN

SAGE TEMPEH
SAUSAGE SLIDER

THAI BARBECUE
SEITAN RIBS

Sandwiches

123   Miso Teriyaki Seitan

124   Thai Barbecue Seitan Ribs

127   Lemongrass Five-Spice Seitan

130   Korean Barbecue Seitan

132   Brown Sugar–Bourbon Glazed Seitan

134   Bangin' Bao

     135   Sesame Bean Paste Bao Buns

     136   Peking Seitan Bao Buns

     136   Oyster Mushroom Bao Buns

137   Sage Tempeh Sausage Sliders

140   Blue Corn and Hemp Seed–Crusted Tempeh

142   Maple Barbecue Tempeh

145   Gochujang Burger Deluxe

IN THE VERY BEGINNING OF THE TRUCK'S LIFE IN HOBOKEN, a lot of things didn't work. We couldn't afford to park the truck in a garage during the winter, so the pump for our sinks would freeze and burst. The truck's brakes would also lock up and screech really bad, and during our first health inspection, our generator (which controlled our refrigeration, lights, and electrical equipment) wouldn't start up. Luckily, because it was so cold that January, the inside of our refrigerator read twenty-one degrees, and the inspector let us slide, as long as we promised to get it fixed. And we did.

We finally opened on Valentine's Day 2010 to a small line of hungry and in-the-know vegans on the Jersey waterfront. There had been a *huge* snowstorm that week, and while we worked a friend climbed onto our roof to shovel off the snow that was melting down through our exhaust system. We were the new, weird food truck in town, and it took a while for us to catch on. But I knew things would turn around for us if we stuck with it and put a lot of love into our food.

For the truck's first year, I basically did everything on my own on two to four hours of sleep per night. I would get up at two A.M. and make donuts and pastries, then load everything into the truck and drive the ninety minutes to Hoboken. I would cook and work the window alone, rushing around the truck to keep the line moving. After three P.M., I'd drive back to Red Bank, clean up and, if I was lucky, take a brief nap before prepping for the next day.

When business was *really* slow, I started parking closer to downtown Hoboken. That's when I started to run into problems with the police.

One very cold morning, I was confronted by some really surly officers who made me shut down the truck. (I'm pretty sure at least one of them was in a storm trooper costume and the other was a bad guy from *Dick Tracy*. Either way, all these towns have different games the local authorities make you play.) The brakes were locking up so badly that I could barely drive away, and they finally locked up completely as I screeched to a halt, right at the entrance to the closest mechanic's shop. I put out the word to our social media fans that I was stranded with a failing truck and tons of food, and soon vegans flocked in from all over Jersey to the lot. There I was, cooking and giving away yummy food amid a bunch of broken-down cars.

I guess it wasn't a major aspiration in my culinary career, but sandwiches really are the perfect thing to serve people from your broken-down food truck in a parking lot. They truly are a handheld entrée—that's why I have so much fun creating new sandwiches, because the sky's the limit.

miso teriyaki seitan

WITH GRILLED ONIONS AND FIVE-SPICE FRIED SUNFLOWER GOMASIO

This sandwich has developed a cult following. Every day we serve these up to regulars who may have driven over an hour, sometimes from out of state, to treat themselves to this juicy golden glazed seitan. Gomasio, a coarsely ground powder of toasted sesame seeds and salt, is a common condiment in macrobiotic cuisine. We reinvented gomasio for this sandwich, incorporating fried sunflower seeds and spicy, aromatic Chinese five-spice powder. The bite of the five-spice gomasio and the Wasabi Mayonnaise are mellowed by the sweetness of miso glaze and sautéed onions.

MAKES 3 SANDWICHES

For the miso teriyaki sauce
2 tablespoons tamari
¼ cup white miso paste
1 cup extra-virgin olive oil
⅔ cup agave nectar
2 teaspoons rice vinegar
1 tablespoon crushed red pepper flakes

For the gomasio
2 tablespoons toasted sesame oil
⅓ cup sunflower seeds
⅔ cup sesame seeds
1 tablespoon Chinese five-spice powder
¼ teaspoon sea salt

For the seitan
3 tablespoons extra-virgin olive oil
¾ medium onion, sliced into
    ¼-inch-thick rings
2¼ cups chopped seitan (about
    ¾ pound)

For assembly
Three 8-inch sections of wide baguette
    (from one 24-inch-long baguette)
¾ cup Wasabi Mayonnaise (page 256)
3 cups loosely packed fresh arugula

1 **Make the miso teriyaki sauce:** Add the tamari, miso, olive oil, agave nectar, rice vinegar, and red pepper flakes to a blender with ⅓ cup water and blend at a high speed until smooth and emulsified. Set aside.

2 **Make the gomasio:** Heat the sesame oil in a small cast-iron skillet or sauté pan over medium heat. Add the sunflower seeds, sesame seeds, five-spice powder, and salt and stir frequently as the seeds toast for 3 to 4 minutes. When the color is golden brown and you hear frequent popping of seeds, scrape the contents of the pan into a food processor and grind for 2 to 3 minutes, until you have a coarse, fragrant powder. Store in an airtight container for up to 1 month.

3 **Prepare the seitan:** Heat a sauté pan or skillet over medium heat. Add the olive oil, onions, and seitan. Cook, stirring occasionally, until the onions and seitan start to brown, about 6 minutes. Add the miso teriyaki sauce and continue to cook and stir until the seitan and onions are thoroughly coated.

4 **Assemble the sandwiches:** Heat a pan or griddle over medium heat. Cut each baguette portion in half lengthwise. Toast the baguettes in the pan, cut side down. Spread 2 to 3 tablespoons of the wasabi mayonnaise on each baguette half. Place 1 cup of the arugula on each bottom half of baguette, followed by one-third of the seitan filling. Sprinkle with 1 tablespoon of the gomasio and cover with the top half of baguette.

thai Barbecue Seitan Ribs

WITH PICKLED THAI BASIL AND ONIONS AND SMOKED CHILE—ROASTED PEANUTS

Seriously, what the heck is "Thai barbecue" anyway? Like a lot of the things that end up on our truck, Thai barbecue was just a part of my imagination that screamed, "We need to create a Thai-influenced barbecue sauce with fresh lemongrass, chiles, Thai basil, lime juice, and galangal!" I mean, it sounded really fun to me one night at three A.M. when I was dreaming up our special for the week, and it turned out to be one of our most popular specials in spring 2013.

By the time I got to making one for myself, we were sold out of the seitan ribs, so I had the sandwich with baked tempeh in place of the ribs. I liked it so much that way that I added it full-time to our menu. Now it's one of my favorite things to eat from our truck, and it works fantastically on our gluten-free millet flax bread. These seitan "ribs" can be used in many ways for other dishes, and they freeze well, if carefully wrapped, for up to two months. They really need the final sauce on them to be awesome, so resist the temptation to eat them when they are fried but not yet finished in the Thai barbecue sauce. Promise?
MAKES 3 SANDWICHES

For the pickled basil and onions
½ cup rice vinegar
⅓ cup apple cider vinegar
½ teaspoon sea salt
1 tablespoon brown mustard seeds
1 tablespoon evaporated cane juice
⅔ cup fresh Thai basil leaves
2 medium red onions, sliced

For the smoked chile—roasted peanuts
2 cups unsalted roasted peanuts
3 tablespoons agave nectar
3 tablespoons brown rice vinegar
1 tablespoon chipotle powder
1 teaspoon smoked paprika
½ teaspoon ground ginger
1 tablespoon extra-virgin olive oil
1 teaspoon sea salt

For the Thai barbecue sauce
1 cup freshly squeezed lime juice
1 fresh lemongrass stalk, trimmed (outer layers removed) and chopped into 4 pieces
1 tablespoon minced fresh galangal (or peeled fresh ginger)
¼ cup chopped fresh Thai basil leaves
½ cup chopped fresh cilantro leaves
1 medium habanero pepper, stemmed
1 teaspoon crushed red pepper flakes
3 tablespoons tamari
2 teaspoons ground coriander
½ cup tomato paste
1 cup extra-virgin olive oil

For the seitan ribs
½ block firm tofu
3 tablespoons tamari
½ medium onion, chopped
½ celery stalk, chopped
½ medium carrot, chopped
2 garlic cloves
½ cup vital wheat gluten
1 tablespoon paprika
1 teaspoon ground cumin
1 tablespoon Thai red curry paste
1 tablespoon ground coriander
1 cup canola oil, for frying

For assembly
Three 8- to 10-inch sections of wide baguette (from 2 whole baguettes)
Sriracha Mayonnaise (page 256)
2¼ cups arugula

1 **Pickle the onions:** In a small saucepan, bring the vinegars, salt, mustard seeds, and evaporated cane juice to a boil. Stir in the basil and onions. Allow the mixture to boil, then cover the pan, turn off the heat, and cool for 20 minutes. Transfer the onion mixture to a clean glass jar with a sealing lid, and refrigerate until ready to use. (The onions will keep well for several weeks.)

2 **Roast the peanuts:** Preheat the oven to 350°F. Lightly oil a rimmed baking sheet, and line with parchment paper. In a mixing bowl, thoroughly combine the peanuts, agave nectar, vinegar, chipotle powder, paprika, ginger, olive oil, and salt. Evenly spread the coated nuts onto the baking sheet and bake for 8 minutes, or until the nuts are roasted and mostly dry. Use immediately, or store at room temperature in an airtight container for up to 3 weeks.

3 **Make the Thai barbecue sauce:** Combine the lime juice, lemongrass, galangal, basil, cilantro, habanero, red pepper flakes, tamari, and coriander in a small saucepan over medium heat. Bring the ingredients to a boil, then cover the pot, turn off

the heat, and allow the mixture to cool for 20 minutes. Pour the mixture into a blender with the tomato paste and olive oil. Blend on high for 40 seconds to create a mostly smooth sauce. Use immediately, or refrigerate in an airtight container for up to 4 days, or freeze for up to a month.

4 **Make the seitan ribs:** In a food processor, puree the tofu fully. Add the tamari, onions, celery, carrot, and garlic and process until smooth.

5 In a medium bowl, combine the wheat gluten, paprika, cumin, curry paste, and coriander. Mix in the blended tofu and vegetables, kneading for a minute or so to form a thoroughly combined dough.

6 **Fry the ribs:** Heat the canola oil to approximately 355°F in a skillet or pan with high sides. On a cutting board, press the dough into a rectangle approximately 3½ by 7 inches. Slice the rectangle into 14 to 16 thin strips. In two batches, fry the strips of dough in the hot oil, turning as needed to thoroughly brown the outsides, about 5 minutes total. Remove the fried

strips to a paper-towel-lined plate just long enough to soak up any residual oil.

7 Place the seitan ribs in a pan over high heat. Once the seitan starts to sizzle, pour on 1 cup of the Thai barbecue sauce. Toss the seitan in the sauce while it cooks for about 2 minutes, or until the seitan is coated and seared thoroughly.

8 **Assemble the sandwiches:** Heat a pan or griddle over medium heat. Cut each baguette portion in half lengthwise. Toast the baguettes in the pan, cut side down. Spread 2 to 3 tablespoons of Sriracha mayonnaise on each baguette half. Place ¾ cup of the arugula on each bottom half of baguette, followed by 5 or 6 pieces of the seitan ribs. Sprinkle with about ¼ cup of the pickled onions, including some of the basil, and top with a liberal sprinkle of the roasted peanuts. Cover with the top half of baguette.

Lemongrass Five-Spice Seitan

WITH CURRIED CASHEWS AND SZECHUAN CHILE SAUCE

When we add new menu items, it means we have to take something off. But when we tried to take off the Lemongrass Five-Spice Seitan, rioting ensued. This ever-popular sandwich draws inspiration from all over Asia—Thai influences from the curried cashews and the lemongrass marinade, a hint of Japan in the wasabi mayonnaise, and Chinese flavors in the Szechuan chile sauce and five-spice powder. Served on a crisp French baguette, it is reminiscent of Vietnamese banh mi sandwiches.

The cashews are a mellow, Thai-inspired version of a classic Indian snack that is fried and tossed with hot chili powder, salt, and *hing* (a savory, sulfury asafetida powder). Instead of frying the nuts, we prepare them in a food dehydrator for a cleaner, brighter taste. If you can't wait two days for the cashews to be ready, you can bake them instead. They will still be wonderful, but the seasonings will be slightly muted.

MAKES THREE SANDWICHES

For the curried cashews
4 cups raw cashews
¼ cup umeboshi plum vinegar
2 ripe medium tomatoes, quartered
1 small red onion, peeled and quartered
½ bunch of fresh cilantro (leaves and stems)
1 whole jalapeño pepper, stem and seeds removed
1-inch piece of peeled fresh ginger
2 tablespoons extra-virgin olive oil
2 tablespoons sambar masala
1 teaspoon asafetida
4 teaspoons Thai red curry paste

For the lemongrass marinade
¼ cup extra-virgin olive oil
1 fresh lemongrass stalk, trimmed (outer layers removed) and coarsely chopped
2 tablespoons minced peeled fresh ginger
½ cup chopped fresh cilantro (leaves and stems)
2 tablespoons Thai red curry paste
1 tablespoon Chinese five-spice powder
¼ cup umeboshi plum vinegar

For the Szechuan chile sauce
⅓ cup toasted sesame oil
3 tablespoons crushed red pepper flakes
2 tablespoons black mustard seeds
1 tablespoon chipotle powder
½ teaspoon ground cloves
½ teaspoon ground ginger
3 tablespoons agave nectar
⅓ cup tomato paste

For the seitan
3 tablespoons extra-virgin olive oil
3¾ cups chopped seitan (about 2 pounds)

For assembly
Three 6- to 8-inch sections of wide baguette (about 2 whole baguettes)
Wasabi Mayonnaise (page 256)
3 cups arugula

1 **Prepare the cashews:** Place the cashews in a medium bowl. Place the vinegar, tomatoes, onion, cilantro, jalapeño, ginger, olive oil, sambar masala, asafetida, and red curry paste in a blender and blend them at high speed for 30 seconds. Pour the puree over the cashews. Mix briefly to distribute evenly. Allow the mixture to rest for 30 minutes.

recipe continues

For a dehydrator: Carefully spread the cashews and all the liquid on a single dehydrator tray with a Teflex sheet. Dehydrate at 112°F for 24 hours. Remove the Teflex sheet, placing the cashews directly on the dehydrator screen. Continue to dehydrate for 24 more hours. (These cashews can stay fresh for 2 months if stored in an airtight container.)

For an oven: Preheat the oven to 350°F. Spread the seasoned cashews on a parchment paper–lined rimmed baking sheet. Bake the cashews for 12 minutes, until the nuts are lightly golden and have absorbed most of the marinade.

2 Make the lemongrass marinade: Heat the olive oil in a small saucepan over medium heat. Add the lemongrass and ginger and sauté for 2 to 3 minutes, stirring, until the ginger is fragrant and golden. Add the cilantro, curry paste, five-spice powder, and plum vinegar with 1½ cups water and bring to a boil. Cover the pot and turn off the heat. Allow the ingredients to soften in the hot water for 15 minutes. Pour the mixture into a blender and blend at high speed for 45 seconds to form a smooth

marinade. Chill the marinade until ready to use. (Sealed and refrigerated, the marinade will last for up to 8 days.)

3 Make the chile sauce: Heat the sesame oil in a small saucepan over medium heat. Add the red pepper flakes, mustard seeds, chipotle powder, cloves, and ginger. Stir the spices in the oil until they become fragrant but not too dark, 40 to 60 seconds. Place the fried spices and oil into a blender along with the agave nectar, tomato paste, and 1 cup water. Blend on high speed for 45 seconds to form a smooth, emulsified sauce. Set aside.

4 Cook the seitan: Heat the olive oil in a large pan or cast-iron skillet over medium

heat. Add the chopped seitan and sauté for 4 to 6 minutes, until the seitan is seared and golden brown in spots. Pour ¾ cup of the lemongrass marinade onto the seitan and allow it to cook for another 2 minutes.

5 Assemble the sandwiches: Heat a pan or griddle over medium heat. Cut each baguette portion in half lengthwise. Toast the baguettes in the pan, cut side down. Spread 2 to 3 tablespoons of the wasabi mayonnaise on each baguette half. Place 1 cup of the arugula on each bottom half of baguette, followed by 1¼ cups of the cooked seitan and 2 tablespoons of the chile sauce. Sprinkle liberally with curried cashews and cover with the top half of baguette.

THE INTERNATIONAL BAGUETTE CONSPIRACY

Some nefarious person, who probably has a grumpy-looking cat on their lap, has intentionally planned for baguettes to be tricky to make our sandwiches on. Many baguettes, while wonderful for eating on their own, aren't great for making humongous sandwiches—they're simply not wide enough for all the yummy toppings. To fit a substantial amount of good ingredients, you will need to find baguettes that are at least three inches wide. I recommend also looking for baguettes with a thin crisp crust and soft interior, so that some of the extra sauce from the delectable fillings gets absorbed into the bread without making the crust soggy. Once you've found the perfect baguette, please tell those behind this baguette pandemic, so more bakeries everywhere will produce perfect baguettes for sandwich making!

KOREAN BARBECUE SEITAN

The Cinnamon Snail's Korean Barbecue Seitan is our take on the Asian-Mexican fusion cuisine pioneered by West Coast food trucks. In our version, a bubbly, crisp tortilla grilled with homemade chile butter is filled with kimchi and seitan in a smoked chile sauce. As a whole, this dish is designed to be eaten sort of like Ethiopian food. You rip off little pieces of the tortilla to eat the juicy filling as you go. This has become one of our signature dishes at the truck. Its flavors are bold and spicy, and it's a dish I always recommend to Snail virgins who can tolerate heat. Our KBBQ has claimed many a snailginity!

MAKES 4 SANDWICHES

For the chile butter
¼ cup vegan margarine (such as Earth Balance)
3 tablespoons coconut oil
2 teaspoons chipotle powder
2 teaspoons smoked paprika

For the Korean smoked chile seitan
¼ cup extra-virgin olive oil
3 cups chopped seitan (about 1½ pounds)
2 tablespoons tomato paste
1 tablespoon chipotle powder
1 tablespoon Korean ground chile (or crushed red pepper flakes)
2 tablespoons umeboshi plum vinegar

For assembly
Four 12-inch flour tortillas
Simple Marinated Kale (page 177)
2 cups baby arugula
1⅓ cups kimchi, homemade (see page 175) or store-bought
¼ cup sliced scallions, light green and white parts (optional)

1 **Make the chile butter:** In a saucepan over medium heat, warm the vegan margarine and coconut oil until all solids have melted. Whisk in the chipotle powder and smoked paprika. Pour the mixture into an airtight container and refrigerate, stirring every 10 minutes to ensure even distribution of the chile flavor, until the chile butter is solid.

2 **Make the seitan:** In a 9-inch skillet or sauté pan, heat the olive oil on medium high. Add the seitan and sauté, stirring, for about 7 minutes, until the seitan browns and the outside becomes seared. In a small bowl, whisk together the tomato paste, chipotle, ground chile, and vinegar along with ⅓ cup water. Stir the sauce into the pan to thoroughly coat the seitan.

3 **Assemble the sandwiches:** Spread chile butter evenly on both sides of a tortilla. Heat a large skillet or griddle over medium heat. Place the buttered tortilla on the pan, and wait for it to bubble up (about 30 seconds). Flip the tortilla and add ½ cup of the kale, ½ cup of the arugula, ⅓ cup of the kimchi, and ⅓ cup of the seitan. Top with scallions, if desired. Allow the tortilla to cook for another 40 to 60 seconds, or until the bottom is golden brown. Using two spatulas, transfer to a plate, folding the sides of the tortilla over at an angle to create a triangle, with one side open. Repeat for the remaining 3 servings.

PARKED!

OUR FIRST HOME IN HOBOKEN — SINATRA AND FIRST

For most of our first two years on the road, we mainly parked on Frank Sinatra Drive between First and Second in Hoboken. We were mostly safe from harassment there, and there were benches for our customers to enjoy their food and the amazing Manhattan skyline.

It was the best place to park—close to the commuter foot traffic at the train station, to Pier A Park, and to the couple of office buildings on Sinatra. Getting a spot there was always tough; we would watch and wait for a big spot with a "no standing" area or a fire hydrant. In all of Hoboken there were really only three or four spots that we could use, and we could wait up to three hours for one of those spots to open up. (We'd sell pastries out of the passenger side window with our hazards on while we waited to park.)

This all worked well for our first years out, but then the food truck trend really exploded. They all tried to park downtown and were harassed, and eventually they followed us onto Sinatra Drive. In no time at all, there were four or five trucks every day, fighting for the same parking spaces. Some of the local owners would park their own cars overnight on the street to save a spot. Pretty soon, it was almost impossible for us to find parking at our old spot.

At the same time, more of Hoboken's bar and grill owners started to complain that we were encroaching on their business. A couple of the food truck owners weren't helping: two of them got drunk in a Hoboken bar and bragged to the owners that they parked right in front and sold similar food cheaper. Business owners who had previously "put up" with us would now take pictures of the truck to prove we weren't parked within the yellow lines or that our meters weren't fed, and would call the parking authority to ticket us. We soon learned from our loyal customers at City Hall that the local bar owners were conspiring to change the vending ordinance in Hoboken, which would make it impossible for food trucks to continue operating.

The ordinance's author told us food vendors that her plan would work in favor of food trucks, to our relief. Yet when we received a draft of the ordinance, we saw it proposed an increase in our permit costs (to more than twenty times what we currently paid), much stricter parking regulations, a requirement that we be tracked by a GPS tracking device (so that the parking authority could ticket us more easily), and restrictions on how long we could park in one neighborhood. With each passing meeting with town officials, it became more clear that a severe change in Hoboken and nearby Jersey City was imminent.

We knew the ultimate path for survival would be to invest in a permit for New York City. It was a scary prospect, which would involve huge sums of cash and the underground permit market, and it seemed impossible to pull off. Yet our stint in Hoboken was just what we needed: It gave us the time to iron out our operation, to train a small staff, to refine our recipes, and to adjust to the constant struggle of street vending. By the time we were forced out of Hoboken into the big city, we were ready to take it on. Almost ready, at least.

Brown Sugar–Bourbon Glazed Seitan
WITH SMOKY ONIONS AND ANCHO CHILE AIOLI

In the summer of 2013, Maker's Mark contacted us about sponsoring a special promotion from our truck. They suggested we pick a food-related holiday and offer a special sandwich for the day using their bourbon. Most of the holidays were not suitable for us (National Cod Gumbo Day and International Haggis Day, for example), but we really liked the idea of Cow Appreciation Day. It sounded like a good fit: If you appreciate cows, you'll be delighted to not eat them. After coming up with this really yummy bourbon-glazed seitan, I did some research about Cow Appreciation Day. Turns out, it's the brainchild of marketing people for the super-hideously evil Chick-fil-A (the restaurant chain famous for its funding of groups seeking to ban gay marriage, suing a guy in Vermont who makes "Eat More Kale" stickers, and all kinds of other mean, weird things). Cow Appreciation Day is a social-media stunt to get their customers to stand in line in cow costumes for free chicken, but their factory-farmed birds have lived a full life of confinement and cruelty: Only in death can they possibly be paired with the word *free*. Chick-fil-A pulls out all the stops for this event . . . and yet on 2013's Cow Appreciation Day, the number-one trending image on Twitter regarding cow appreciation was a picture of our seitan special with the words, "Don't worry @chickfila we got this. Go back to your bigotry and factory farming." Win for veganism. And the best part? The special is really the bomb, and here's the recipe for it.
MAKES 3 SANDWICHES

For the smoky onions
⅓ cup loose Lapsang souchong tea leaves
¼ cup extra-virgin olive oil
¼ cup tamari
1 tablespoon dried oregano
2 tablespoons smoked paprika
3 tablespoons stone-ground mustard
4 medium onions, halved

For the aioli
2 dried ancho chiles
2 cups boiling water
2 tablespoons extra-virgin olive oil
3 tablespoons whole-grain French mustard
2 garlic cloves
2 tablespoons agave nectar
Grated zest and juice of 2 limes
1½ cups vegan mayonnaise

For the glazed seitan
6 tablespoons extra-virgin olive oil
½ cup minced onion
1 dried ancho chile, stem and seeds removed
⅓ cup raisins
2 tablespoons fresh thyme leaves
½ cup packed dark brown sugar
1 cup bourbon
¼ cup white miso paste
3 tablespoons molasses
¼ cup brown rice vinegar
2 cups sliced seitan

For assembly
Three 6- to 8-inch sections of wide baguette (about 2 whole baguettes)
1 cup loosely packed baby arugula

1 **Make the onions:** Preheat the oven to 250°F.

2 In a small saucepan, bring 1½ cups water to a boil. Add the tea leaves and turn off the heat, cover the pot, and let the tea cool and steep for 20 minutes. Strain the tea into a blender, and add the olive oil, tamari, oregano, paprika, and mustard. Blend on high speed for 1 minute to emulsify.

3 Place the onions, cut side down, in a 9-inch square baking dish. Pour the marinade over the onions and bake for 60 minutes, until most of the marinade has evaporated and soaked into the onions. Remove from the oven and allow the onions to cool fully. Slice the onions into thin strips. If not using immediately, store in an airtight container in the refrigerator for up to 4 days.

4 **Make the aioli:** Heat an outdoor grill, stovetop grill, or broiler. Place the ancho chiles in a shallow, heat-proof dish and pour the boiling water over them. Immediately place a cover over the dish to allow the chiles to rehydrate for 8 minutes.

5 In a medium bowl, combine the olive oil and mustard. Drain the excess water from the chiles and toss them in the mustard and oil.

6 Grill the chiles on the hot grill for 2 to 3 minutes on each side to get charred grill marks. Allow the chiles to cool on a plate, and remove the stems only.

7 Place the chiles in a food processor with the garlic, agave nectar, and lime zest and juice. Process the chiles for about 2 minutes, until they become a rough paste. Add the mayonnaise and process for 1 minute to incorporate thoroughly. (The aioli will last in the refrigerator for up to 5 days in an airtight container.)

8 **Make the seitan marinade:** Heat a saucepan with 2 tablespoons of the olive oil over medium heat. Add the onions and stir, sautéing until the onions become translucent, about 3 minutes. Add the ancho chile, raisins, thyme, and brown sugar. Continue stirring for 2 minutes, until the sugar dissolves. Stir in the bourbon, miso paste, molasses, rice vinegar, and 2½ cups water. Bring the mixture to a boil, then turn off the heat, cover, and allow the liquid to cool for 20 minutes. Place the ingredients in a high-speed blender, and blend for 40 seconds to form a smooth, thick marinade.

9 **Cook the seitan:** Heat a large skillet or griddle with the remaining ¼ cup olive oil over medium heat. Add the seitan and sauté for 6 to 7 minutes, stirring frequently, until the seitan is seared and has a browned appearance. Pour the marinade over the seitan, and continue to cook, stirring, for 4 minutes, allowing the sugars to caramelize and the seitan to absorb the flavors.

10 **Assemble the sandwiches:** Heat a pan or griddle over medium heat. Cut each baguette portion in half lengthwise. Toast the baguettes in the pan, cut side down. Spread 2 to 3 tablespoons of aioli on each baguette half. Place a liberal handful of baby arugula on each bottom half of baguette, followed by ⅔ cup of the hot glazed seitan. Sprinkle with ½ cup of the smoky onions and cover with the top half of baguette.

Bangin' Bao

Bao, short for *baozi*, are happy little stuffed and steamed Chinese buns. Sometimes they are smaller and more dumpling-like, but I prefer these sandwich-style ones, which are folded over and steamed. Why do I prefer this style? Well, because this way (A) you can split them open and stuff them way fuller with yummy exciting fillings without worrying about the buns bursting or leaking, and (B) you can stuff them at least partially with fresh herbs and microgreens that would otherwise perish in the hot steam. The assembly instructions will be the same for these variations, but here are three remarkably different fun fillings to try (and each filling makes enough for a full batch of finished buns).

MAKES 18 BAO BUNS

1 package active dry yeast
  (2¼ teaspoons)
4 cups all-purpose flour, plus more for
  kneading
¼ cup evaporated cane juice
3 tablespoons vegan margarine (such
  as Earth Balance)
½ cup cornstarch
¼ cup toasted sesame oil
Boiling water

1 In a large bowl, dissolve the yeast in 1 cup warm water. Once the yeast is dissolved, whisk 1 cup of the flour into the yeast mixture, and let it rest until it is spongy and active, about 15 minutes.

2 In a separate, heat-proof bowl, pour ½ cup hot water over the evaporated cane juice and margarine, allowing the cane juice and fat to melt as the water cools. When the hot water has cooled to between 90°F and 110°F, pour the cane juice mixture into the yeast mixture, along with the remaining 3 cups of flour and the cornstarch. Knead the dough together by hand for about 2 minutes to form a smooth ball. Cover with a clean towel and leave the dough in a warm spot for 1 hour, until the dough has just about doubled in size. Cut 18 small squares of parchment paper, and brush them lightly with the sesame oil. Set aside.

3 Punch down the risen dough and divide it into 18 equal pieces. On a lightly floured surface, roll each piece into an oval shape, about 3 inches wide by 4 inches long. Brush the top of each oval with sesame oil, and gently fold the ovals in half like tacos. Place each folded bun onto an oiled parchment square, and place onto 2 baking sheets. Place a pan of boiling water onto the floor of the oven (the oven should be off), place the sheet of buns on the oven rack, close the oven, and let the buns proofs for 30 minutes.

4 Keeping the parchment paper on the bottom of the buns, place the buns in a steamer, or in a wok fitted with a steam plate, with at least an inch between each bun. Steam for 10 minutes. Remove the hot buns from the steamer with tongs, and peel off the parchment. Fill with any of the recipes that follow.

/ VARIATIONS /

Sesame Bean Paste Bao Buns

3 cups drained cooked or canned red beans

¼ cup white miso paste

2 tablespoons Korean ground chile

1 tablespoon Chinese five-spice powder

2 tablespoons tomato paste

3 tablespoons toasted sesame oil

1 tablespoon molasses

¼ cup toasted black sesame seeds

¼ cup minced scallions, light green and white parts, for serving

½ cup microgreens or chopped pea shoots, for serving

1 Place the beans, miso paste, ground chile, five-spice powder, tomato paste, oil, molasses, and ⅓ cup water in a food processor. Puree the mixture for about 1 minute to form a smooth, fragrant paste.

Add the sesame seeds and pulse a few times to quickly distribute them in the paste.

2 Pry the hot steamed buns open with a knife, and spoon into each one a tablespoon of bean paste, a teaspoon of minced scallions, and a pinch of microgreens or chopped pea shoots.

recipe continues

Peking Seitan Bao Buns

3 tablespoons tamarind concentrate

¼ cup molasses

¼ cup rice vinegar

¼ cup agave nectar

2 tablespoons minced peeled fresh ginger

2 tablespoons tamari

1 tablespoon crushed red pepper flakes

3 tablespoons cornstarch

3 tablespoons toasted sesame oil

3 cups thinly sliced seitan (about 1½ pounds)

1 cup Wasabi Mayonnaise (page 256), for serving

2 cups baby arugula, for serving

¼ cup minced scallions, light green and white parts, for serving

¼ cup coarsely chopped fresh mint, for serving

½ cup rainbow microgreens, for serving

1 Place the tamarind concentrate, molasses, rice vinegar, agave nectar, ginger, tamari, red pepper flakes, cornstarch, and ⅓ cup water in a blender, and blend until smooth.

2 In a sauté pan, heat the sesame oil over medium heat. Sear the seitan in the hot sesame oil, flipping every 45 seconds or so for about 3 minutes or until the seitan is browned and has a firm texture. Pour the pureed sauce into the pan and let it simmer and thicken for about 2 minutes, stirring gently to coat the seitan.

3 Pry the hot buns open with a knife, and spread onto the inside of each a tablespoon of wasabi mayonnaise, 5 to 10 baby arugula leaves, about 3 tablespoons of seitan, a tablespoon of minced scallions, a pinch of chopped fresh mint leaves, and a pinch of microgreens.

Oyster Mushroom Bao Buns with Kimchi and Sriracha Mayonnaise

2 tablespoons toasted sesame oil

2 tablespoons brown mustard seeds

1 pound oyster mushrooms, cleaned and sliced

3 garlic cloves, thinly sliced

2 tablespoons Korean ground chile

2 tablespoons umeboshi plum vinegar

⅓ cup julienned carrots

⅓ cup shredded daikon radish

¼ cup coarsely chopped fresh cilantro leaves

2 tablespoons rice vinegar

2 teaspoons evaporated cane juice

½ teaspoon sea salt

1 cup Sriracha Mayonnaise (page 256), for serving

⅓ cup chopped kimchi, homemade (see page 175) or store-bought, for serving

1 Heat the sesame oil in a sauté pan over medium heat. Add the mustard seeds and when they begin to pop, add the mushrooms and garlic. Sauté for about 2 minutes, stirring frequently, until the mushrooms are just tender. Mix in the chile and plum vinegar and turn the heat off. Mix the carrots, daikon, cilantro, rice vinegar, evaporated cane juice, and salt in a medium bowl and set aside.

2 Pry the hot buns open with a knife, and spread onto the inside of each a tablespoon of Sriracha mayonnaise, 2 to 3 tablespoons of the mushrooms, 2 tablespoons of chopped kimchi, and a large pinch of the marinated carrots, daikon, and cilantro.

SAGE TEMPEH Sausage Sliders

WITH FRIED SAGE LEAVES AND LAVENDER-ROASTED SHALLOTS

Back in our days on the streets of Hoboken, I offered these cute mini sandwiches for our summer menu. It is really a pretty sophisticated slider recipe, what with all that elegant floral, herbal flavor in the shallots and the sage leaves. The mini tempeh sausages make for an AWESOME breakfast when pan-fried, too. To get the most appetizing, easy-to-demolish sliders, try to find nice soft vegan slider buns. If they are hard to find (often slider buns contain eggs), you can use a 1½-inch ring mold to cut small burger buns down to perfect size. Make sure to spread this sandwich with both the delicious Provençal-flavored Niçoise Olive Tapenade and the Truffled Cashew Cheese to take it to the next level.
MAKES 18 SLIDERS

For the fried sage leaves
1½ cups canola oil
36 sage leaves
1 teaspoon sea salt
4 teaspoons cornstarch

For the lavender-roasted shallots
1 tablespoon dried edible lavender flowers
¼ teaspoon food-grade lavender oil
2 tablespoons stone-ground mustard
3 tablespoons apple cider vinegar
2 tablespoons agave nectar
2 teaspoons liquid smoke
1 tablespoon tamari
3 tablespoons extra-virgin olive oil
7 shallots, peeled and quartered

For the sage tempeh sausage
One 8-ounce package of tempeh, crumbled
3 tablespoons white miso paste
2 tablespoons toasted sesame oil
¼ cup chopped fresh sage leaves
1 tablespoon fennel seeds
½ medium yellow onion, chopped
2 garlic cloves, minced
1 teaspoon crushed red pepper flakes
3 tablespoons brown rice syrup
⅓ cup wheat germ

For assembly
18 slider buns
⅓ cup extra-virgin olive oil
Niçoise Olive Tapenade (page 259)
3 cups baby arugula
Truffled Cashew Cheese (page 261)

1 **Fry the sage leaves:** Line a baking sheet with paper towels. In a large saucepan over medium-high heat, heat the canola oil to about 360°F. If you don't have a frying thermometer, check for heat by sprinkling a drop or two of water on the surface of the oil. If it violently sputters, the oil is ready.

2 In a medium bowl, combine the sage, salt, and cornstarch. Shake any excess cornstarch off the sage leaves and sprinkle the leaves into the hot oil. Fry for up to 2 minutes to obtain a light brown color. Remove the leaves with a slotted spoon to dry on the paper towels.

recipe continues

3 **Make the shallots:** Preheat the oven to 400°F. In a medium bowl, combine the lavender flowers, lavender oil, mustard, vinegar, agave nectar, liquid smoke, tamari, and olive oil. Toss the quartered shallots into the marinade. Pour the contents of the bowl evenly over a rimmed baking sheet. Bake for 10 minutes, then flip the shallots with a spatula. Continue roasting for another 7 to 10 minutes, until the shallots are soft and lightly caramelized. Remove the baking sheet from the oven and let the shallots cool. Coarsely chop the shallots and set aside.

4 **Make the sausage:** Reduce the oven temperature to 350°F. Line a rimmed baking sheet with parchment paper and lightly oil the paper.

5 Add the tempeh, miso paste, sesame oil, sage, fennel seeds, onions, garlic, red pepper flakes, brown rice syrup, and wheat germ to a food processor, and process for 90 seconds to form a mostly smooth paste. Using 2 to 3 tablespoons for each, shape the mixture into 18 equal balls. Roll the balls in your hands to smooth them, and flatten them into round disks, 1½ to 2 inches in diameter. Place the sliders onto the prepared baking sheet and bake them for about 15 minutes, until golden brown and thoroughly cooked, but not dried.

6 **Assemble the sandwiches:** Split the slider buns open, and rub or brush the insides of the buns lightly with the olive oil. Place the slider buns, cut sides down, into a skillet or griddle over high heat and toast for a couple of minutes to form a crunchy golden interior.

7 Spread about 1 tablespoon of the tapenade onto the bottom bun, followed by a small pile of the arugula, a warm tempeh slider patty, a few pieces of roasted shallot, and 2 fried sage leaves. Spread about 1 tablespoon of the cashew cheese on the cut sides of the top buns and cover the sandwiches with them. If the sandwiches are too tall, press them down and place a toothpick through each slider to hold it together.

Blue Corn and Hemp Seed-Crusted Tempeh

with chile coconut bacon and beer-simmered onions

Okay, so, coconut bacon? Yes indeed—it's not greasy and meaty like strips of pig-based bacon, but instead contributes a smoky, chewy bite of bacon-like bliss. If you want to turn this totally hooked-up sandwich into a great main course, ditch the bread and serve it over rice and beans and shaved radishes. I love slathering this sandwich with Chipotle Mayonnaise and Roasted Tomatillo Salsa Verde, and those toppings are just as good when added to it in bowl form.

MAKES 4 SANDWICHES

For the tempeh
One 8-ounce package of tempeh
½ cup all-purpose flour or gluten-free flour mix
½ cup unsweetened soy milk
2 teaspoons freshly squeezed lime juice
⅓ cup blue corn flour or cornmeal
1 cup ground blue corn tortilla chips
¼ cup hemp seeds
1 tablespoon paprika
2 tablespoons Cajun seasoning
3 tablespoons extra-virgin olive oil, plus more for oiling the baking sheet

For the chile coconut bacon
1 teaspoon chipotle powder
1 teaspoon liquid smoke
2 teaspoons extra-virgin olive oil
2 tablespoons agave nectar
1 tablespoon apple cider vinegar
1 teaspoon tamari
⅔ cup dried coconut chips

For the beer-simmered onions
1 tablespoon extra-virgin olive oil
1 large yellow onion, sliced
6 garlic cloves, sliced
½ teaspoon crushed red pepper flakes
½ teaspoon fresh thyme leaves
⅔ cup vegan beer of your choice
2 tablespoons pure maple syrup
2 teaspoons tamari

For assembly
8 slices spelt bread (we use Rudy's)
Chipotle Mayonnaise (page 256)
1 cup arugula
Roasted Tomatillo Salsa Verde (page 259), or store-bought salsa

1 **Prepare the tempeh:** Preheat the oven to 350°F. Line a baking sheet with parchment paper and lightly oil the paper.

2 Cut the slab of tempeh in half, forming two squares. Slice those two pieces in half horizontally, forming 4 thin squares.

3 Place the flour into a bowl; mix the soy milk and lime juice in a separate bowl. In a third bowl, mix the blue corn flour, ground corn chips, hemp seeds, paprika, and Cajun seasoning. Coat each piece of tempeh in the plain flour, then dredge through the soy-lime mixture to coat the surfaces, letting excess liquid drain off; finally, dredge the tempeh in the blue corn coating. Place each piece of tempeh onto the prepared baking sheet. Drizzle the tempeh with the olive oil. Bake the tempeh for 12 to 15 minutes, until the crust is crisp.

4 **Make the chile coconut bacon:** Preheat the oven to 350°F. Lightly oil a parchment-lined baking sheet. In a small bowl, combine the chipotle powder, liquid smoke, oil, agave nectar, vinegar, and tamari. Toss the coconut chips in the seasonings, then evenly spread them and any remaining liquid onto the prepared baking sheet. Bake for 11 to 14 minutes, until the bacon is dark brown and crispy.

5 **Cook the onions:** Heat the olive oil in a sauté pan over medium-high heat. Sauté the onions and garlic for 4 minutes, stirring frequently. Add the red pepper flakes, thyme, beer, maple syrup, and tamari and lower the heat to medium. Allow the onions and garlic to simmer in the liquid for 10 minutes, until soft and golden brown.

6 **Assemble the sandwiches:** Toast the bread for the sandwiches, and reheat the tempeh in the oven. Smear 2 tablespoons of the chipotle mayonnaise on each bottom slice of bread. Top with ¼ cup of arugula, 1 piece of crusted tempeh, 2 tablespoons of salsa, 2 tablespoons of the onions and garlic, and finally 2 tablespoons of chile coconut bacon. Spread 2 tablespoons chipotle mayonnaise onto each remaining piece of bread, and place them on top of the sandwiches.

Maple Barbecue Tempeh

WITH BEER-BATTERED PICKLES AND GARLIC CABBAGE SLAW

This is an example of how carried away I sometimes get with our sandwich specials on the truck. I mean, this is basically everything you would want to load your plate up with at a barbecue, sandwiched between two pieces of grilled baguette. Add a dollop of Habanero Aioli and a few pieces of Simple Marinated Kale, and you're all set. Summer block party on a bun.

MAKES 3 SANDWICHES

For the maple barbecue sauce
⅓ cup pure maple syrup
1 tablespoon molasses
¼ cup tomato paste
2 tablespoons apple cider vinegar
¼ teaspoon ground cloves
1 teaspoon ground coriander
½ teaspoon onion powder
½ teaspoon garlic powder
½ teaspoon liquid smoke
1 tablespoon tamari
¼ cup extra-virgin olive oil

For the tempeh
One 8-ounce package of tempeh
2 cups vegetable broth
¼ cup tamari
3 tablespoons stone-ground mustard
3 tablespoons extra-virgin olive oil

For the garlic cabbage slaw
8 garlic cloves
3 tablespoons extra-virgin olive oil
1 teaspoon dried oregano (or substitute
    1 tablespoon minced fresh oregano
    if available)

½ teaspoon sea salt
2 tablespoons agave nectar
3 tablespoons mirin
½ cup vegan mayonnaise
4 teaspoons grated lemon zest, plus
    2 tablespoons freshly squeezed
    lemon juice
2 cups shredded cabbage
1 teaspoon caraway seeds

For the beer-battered pickles
2 cups canola oil, for frying
1 cup all-purpose flour
1 tablespoon evaporated cane juice
¼ teaspoon sea salt
1 teaspoon fresh thyme leaves
1 teaspoon paprika
1 cup vegan beer of your choice
1½ cups sliced sour pickles, drained
⅓ cup cornstarch

For assembly
Three 8-inch sections of wide baguette
    (from one 24-inch-long baguette)
Habanero Aioli (page 257)
1 cup Simple Marinated Kale (page 177)

1 **Make the maple barbecue sauce:** Combine the maple syrup, molasses, tomato paste, vinegar, cloves, coriander, onion powder, garlic powder, liquid smoke, tamari, olive oil, and ¼ cup water in a blender, and blend at high speed for 40 seconds until smooth. (You will have about 1 cup of sauce.) Set aside, or store in an airtight container in the refrigerator for up to 5 days.

2 **Prepare the tempeh:** Cut the block of tempeh into 3 equal portions. Turn each portion on its side and cut in half so you have 6 thin cutlets.

3 In a small saucepan, combine the broth, tamari, mustard, and 1 tablespoon of the oil. Place the tempeh into the pan, submerging all of the pieces. Bring the mixture to a boil over high heat. Cover the pan, reduce the heat to a simmer, allowing the tempeh to soften and become moist, about 12 minutes. Carefully remove the tempeh from the liquid with a slotted spoon and allow it to cool.

4 Make the garlic cabbage slaw: Preheat the oven to 400°F. Line a small rimmed baking sheet with parchment paper. In a small bowl, combine the garlic, olive oil, oregano, and salt. Spread the garlic mixture on the prepared baking sheet and roast for 18 to 22 minutes, until the garlic is soft and golden brown.

5 Transfer the roasted garlic, oil, and oregano to a blender along with the agave nectar, mirin, mayonnaise, and lemon juice. Blend on high speed for 45 seconds, until the mixture forms a smooth puree. Place the shredded cabbage, lemon zest, and caraway seeds into a large bowl and, using your hands, massage the roasted garlic sauce thoroughly into the cabbage. Use immediately, or store in an airtight container in the refrigerator for up to 2 days.

6 Make the pickles: Heat the oil in a deep saucepan over medium-high heat to 355 to 370°F.

7 In a small bowl, whisk together the flour, evaporated cane juice, salt, thyme, paprika, and beer. In a separate bowl, toss the pickles with the cornstarch.

8 One at a time, submerge each pickle slice in the batter, and then transfer it to the hot oil. (Work quickly so that you can fry all slices in one batch without too much difference in cooking time.) Allow the pickles to fry for about 3½ minutes, until golden brown. Transfer them to a wire rack to cool, and then press them with a paper towel to pat dry. Use immediately.

9 Cook the tempeh: Heat the remaining 2 tablespoons of olive oil in a sauté pan over medium heat. Fry the pieces of drained tempeh for about 3 minutes on each side to sear. Pour the barbecue sauce into the pan, and carefully flip the tempeh in it to coat thoroughly.

10 Assemble the sandwiches: Heat a pan or griddle over medium heat. Cut each baguette portion in half lengthwise. Toast the baguettes in the pan, cut side down. Spread the habanero aioli on each baguette half. Place about ⅓ cup of the kale on each bottom half of baguette, followed by 2 pieces of tempeh, ⅔ cup of garlic cabbage slaw, 4 to 6 fried pickle slices, a drizzle of any remaining barbecue sauce, and the top piece of bread.

Gochujang Burger Deluxe

Often people get to the head of the line at our truck and ask for "that really yummy spicy one that I can't pronounce." *Go-chew-jung* is a Korean chile paste condiment made with sweet glutinous rice flour. It can be found in Asian food stores in plastic tubs, and it's dangerously addictive. We make our own version for the truck, and we spread it on juicy, chile-spiked seitan burger patties, topping them with our sautéed homemade kimchi, pickled leeks and daikon, and Black Sesame Gomasio. It just wouldn't be right if this didn't come on a bun slathered with Sriracha Mayonnaise and topped with crisp, fresh baby arugula.

MAKES 4 BURGERS

For the pickled vegetables
½ cup white vinegar
¼ cup apple cider vinegar
3 tablespoons brown rice syrup
1 tablespoon brown mustard seeds
½ teaspoon sea salt
6 inches of daikon radish, cut into long ¼-inch-wide strips
6 inches of leek, light green and white parts only, halved, washed well, and thinly sliced crosswise

For the gochujang
¼ cup agave nectar
3 tablespoons apple cider vinegar
⅓ cup Korean ground chile
⅓ cup glutinous rice flour
3 tablespoons soy flour
1 tablespoon all-purpose flour
½ teaspoon sea salt

For the burgers
1 pound seitan, chopped
½ cup chopped yellow onion
3 tablespoons ground coriander
1 tablespoon crushed red pepper flakes
2 tablespoons Korean ground chile
3 tablespoons tomato paste
3 tablespoons soy sauce
2 tablespoons extra-virgin olive oil
1 cup all-purpose flour

For assembly
1 tablespoon toasted sesame oil
1 cup kimchi, homemade (see page 175) or store-bought
2 tablespoons vegan margarine (such as Earth Balance)
4 burger buns
1 cup Sriracha Mayonnaise (page 256)
1 cup baby arugula
Black Sesame Gomasio (page 257)

1 Pickle the vegetables: Bring the white vinegar, cider vinegar, brown rice syrup, mustard seeds, salt, and ¾ cup water to a boil in a small pot over high heat. Stir the radish and leeks into the boiling liquid, cover the pot, and turn off the heat. Allow the vegetables to marinate in the covered pot for 10 minutes. Pour the pickled vegetables and brine into a glass jar and cool, without the lid, for at least 2 hours in the refrigerator. Use immediately, or store for up to 10 days, covered with a lid, in the refrigerator.

recipe continues

2 **Make the gochujang:** Bring the agave nectar, cider vinegar, and 1 cup water to a boil in a small saucepan over high heat. Place the Korean chile, rice flour, soy flour, all-purpose flour, and salt in a stand mixer fitted with the paddle attachment. Mix the ingredients at low-medium speed, while slowly pouring in the hot liquid ingredients. Continue to mix for about 2 minutes to form a sticky red paste. Allow the paste to cool, and use immediately; or store in an airtight container in the refrigerator for up to 2 weeks.

3 **Make the burgers:** Preheat the oven to 350°F. Line a rimmed baking sheet with parchment paper and lightly oil the paper.

4 Place the seitan, onions, coriander, red pepper flakes, Korean chile, tomato paste, soy sauce, and olive oil in a food processor and process for 2 minutes, or until the seitan and onions are in very small fragments. Place the ground mixture in a mixing bowl and thoroughly mix the flour in. Divide the mixture into 4 equal portions. With wet hands, roll the portions into balls and flatten them gently into smooth disks on the prepared baking sheet. Bake the burgers for 12 to 14 minutes, until the outsides of the burgers are firm but not dried out.

5 **Assemble the sandwiches:** Heat the sesame oil in a medium sauté pan over medium heat. Sauté the kimchi in the hot oil for 5 minutes, until hot and fragrant.

6 In a separate pan over medium heat, melt the margarine. Cook the burgers on one side for 2 minutes. Flip the burgers and cook for 2 minutes on the second side.

7 Split the burger buns and toast in a third pan, cut side down. Spread 2 tablespoons of the Sriracha mayonnaise onto the cut sides of each bun. Place ¼ cup of the arugula on the bottom half of each bun, followed by a burger. Spread 1 to 2 tablespoons of the gochujang on each patty, spoon on ¼ cup of the sautéed kimchi and 2 to 3 tablespoons of the pickled vegetables, and then add 1 tablespoon of the gomasio. Finish the burger with the top half of the bun.

ROSEMARY
HEMP SEED-
CRUSTED TOFU

CiNNamaiNS

151   Rosemary Hemp Seed–Crusted Tofu

153   Galangal Pea Pancakes

156   Pecan-Crusted Seitan

158   Red Bean–Scallion Pancakes

160   Live Szechuan String Bean Ramen

163   Raw Pizza

165   Pizza Toppings Galore

    165   Spinach and Pine Nuts

    165   Peppers, Mushrooms, and Basil

    165   Rosemary Faux-tato

    165   Balsamic Figs and Parsnips

166   Ginger Island Tofu

168   Jalapeño Roasted Corn–Stuffed Red Quinoa Croquettes

WHEN I FIRST STARTED RUNNING THE TRUCK, the menu was totally different. I thought it would be a cool thing to offer really tricked-out gourmet restaurant-style entrées from the truck. In fact, that's mostly what our menu was: We had only three sandwiches (Maple Mustard Tempeh, Creole Grilled Tofu, and Smoked Portobello Carpaccio), and the rest of our dishes were absurdly decadent, food sculpture masterpieces. The entrée thing was really cool—the only problem was that no one wants to eat that kind of meal from a paper plate in their lap. In addition, I couldn't really afford to offer that kind of food at prices that fit people's lunchtime budgets. It was just too labor intensive, and there were tons of expensive ingredients, like porcini mushrooms, truffle oil, and fancy exotic salts. It's kind of hilarious when I think back to my original vision/fantasy.

While these entrées don't make a ton of sense to try to put together and serve from a food truck, they make a TON of sense for you to serve your family for dinner. Some of these recipes are a bit complex, but all of them are well worth the effort. Now you can enjoy all of these really yummy creations without having to eat them in a paper box in your car.

ROSEMARY HEMP SEED–CRUSTED TOFU

WITH TARRAGON GARLIC BREAD PUDDING

This entrée was offered on the truck in the early days of the Cinnamon Snail. We served it with truffled mashed potatoes with marinated kale and French mustard dressing. It's a great entrée for a vegan Thanksgiving dinner, or for any other occasion calling for a hearty, savory centerpiece.

SERVES 6

For the tarragon garlic bread pudding

¼ cup extra-virgin olive oil

6 garlic cloves, minced

1 medium onion, chopped

3 tablespoons stone-ground mustard

3 tablespoons soy sauce (tamari or shoyu)

¼ cup chopped fresh tarragon leaves

2 tablespoons fennel seeds

2 tablespoons ground coriander

3 tablespoons brown sugar or Sucanat

Grated zest of 2 lemons

1 loaf soft spelt or whole wheat bread (we use Rudy's spelt bread), cut into large pieces

For the rosemary hemp seed–crusted tofu

¼ cup extra-virgin olive oil

¾ cup shelled hemp seeds

⅓ cup wheat germ

¼ cup chopped fresh rosemary

2 tablespoons dried thyme

2 tablespoons dried oregano

1 tablespoon sea salt

1¼ cups all-purpose flour

1½ cups unsweetened soy milk

2 tablespoons freshly squeezed lemon juice

2 tablespoons stone-ground mustard

Two 14-ounce blocks extra-firm tofu

Using Curdled Soy Milk

Sounds gross, right?!? Well, when I say "curdled" soy milk, I'm not talking about food gone bad, okay? When you introduce acid to soy milk, it instantly curdles and thickens. In this recipe, it is the lemon juice and mustard that are the source of acid used to curdle the soy milk. Depending on the recipe, you can curdle the soy milk with hot sauce, cider vinegar, balsamic, fig vinegar, et cetera. A lightly flavored acid (like rice vinegar, white vinegar, or lemon juice) makes a great substitute in recipes that call for buttermilk. It is also awesome for recipes like this, in which you want a thick liquid for dredging so that a lot of the breading sticks to the tofu.

1 Make the bread pudding: Preheat the oven to 350°F. Lightly oil a medium rectangular glass baking dish.

2 Heat 2 tablespoons of the olive oil in a small saucepan over medium heat. Add the garlic and onions and cook until the garlic becomes lightly golden. Add the mustard, soy sauce, tarragon, fennel seeds, coriander, brown sugar, lemon zest, and 1 cup water. Bring the mixture to a boil, then turn off the heat and let the mixture cool completely.

3 Add the bread pieces and the cooled onion mixture to a mixing bowl and toss together to coat and soak the bread evenly. Press the mixture into the prepared baking dish, and sprinkle with the remaining 2 tablespoons of olive oil. Cover with foil and bake for 40 minutes. Remove the foil, and bake for 12 more minutes to brown and crisp the top.

4 Prepare the tofu: Line a rimmed baking sheet with parchment paper and oil the paper with 2 tablespoons of the olive oil. Mix the hemp seeds, wheat germ, rosemary, thyme, oregano, salt, and ¾ cup of the flour in a small bowl.

5 Mix the soy milk, lemon juice, and mustard together in one flat-bottomed, wide bowl; the soy milk will curdle and thicken (see Note, page 151). Place the remaining ½ cup of flour in a separate bowl.

6 Slice each block of tofu horizontally into 3 thin, wide slices. Dredge each slice in the flour, then dip it in the curdled soy milk and gently toss it in the breading mixture. Carefully transfer each coated slice to the prepared baking tray, and drizzle the remaining 2 tablespoons of olive oil onto the tofu pieces. Bake the breaded tofu for 30 minutes, or until the slices are golden and crisp (rotate the pan once during baking).

7 Serve the tofu and bread pudding stacked on top of each other with your favorite greens as a base, or serve them alongside one another with other vegetable sides.

Galangal Pea Pancakes

WITH BASIL SEITAN AND FRIED KAFFIR LIME LEAVES

This is a mostly Thai-inspired entrée, with some subtle notes of Chinese influence. Something special happens when you borrow from several regional cooking styles and have them collide in one yummy dish. That's what makes me excited about Southeast Asian food in the first place. Food from Burma, for instance, incorporates stir-fries reminiscent of China, with a Thai-influenced curry and Indian spices. This is the sort of culinary get-together that really inspires me. This dish is a great example of that sort of cooking mentality, especially with a little watercress in between the layers for a bit of Western crunch. (To really bring in that final sweet flavor, add a drizzling of the Habanero Apricot Glaze on page 262.)

SERVES 4

For the fried lime leaves
- 1 cup canola, peanut, or safflower oil, for frying
- 20 fresh kaffir lime leaves, available at specialty food stores and some Asian food stores
- 3 tablespoons mirin
- ½ cup cornstarch
- 1 teaspoon sea salt

For the basil seitan
- 1 cup chopped fresh Thai basil leaves
- ½ cup chopped fresh cilantro leaves
- 1 fresh lemongrass stalk, trimmed (outer layers removed) and sliced
- 1 jalapeño pepper, stem and seeds removed
- 4 garlic cloves
- 1 tablespoon ground coriander
- ½ cup freshly squeezed lime juice
- ½ teaspoon sea salt
- ¼ cup toasted sesame oil
- 16 ounces seitan, sliced

For the galangal pea pancakes
- 1 cup unbleached all-purpose flour
- ¼ cup buckwheat flour
- 1 tablespoon baking powder
- 2 teaspoons baking soda
- 1 tablespoon ground coriander
- 1⅓ cups unsweetened soy milk
- 2 tablespoons toasted sesame oil
- 3 tablespoons soy sauce (shoyu or tamari)
- 1 cup cooked peas (fresh or frozen)
- 1½ inches fresh galangal or peeled fresh ginger, cut into julienned strips
- ¼ cup minced scallions, light green and white parts
- 2 tablespoons sesame seeds
- 2 tablespoons crushed red pepper flakes
- 2 cups blanched watercress or fresh arugula
- ¼ cup minced fresh cilantro (optional; for garnish)
- 2 minced fresh Thai chiles or one minced jalapeño (optional; for garnish)

1 **Fry the lime leaves:** Pour the oil into a pot or pan with high sides, and preheat to about 350°F. Slice the lime leaves into matchstick-thin strips. In a small bowl, toss the strips in the mirin. Remove the strips with tongs or a metal slotted spoon, and toss them in a bowl with the cornstarch and salt. Scatter the coated strips into the hot oil, and cook for about 60 seconds or until crisp. Dry the strips on a paper towel.

2 **Prepare the seitan marinade:** Preheat the oven to 400°F. Line a rimmed baking sheet with parchment paper.

recipe continues

3 Place the Thai basil, cilantro, lemongrass, jalapeño, garlic, coriander, lime juice, salt, and 1 cup water into a saucepan and bring to a boil. Cover the pot, turn off the heat, and allow the mixture to steep for 10 minutes. Place the mixture in a blender along with the sesame oil and blend on high speed for 40 seconds, until a fairly smooth marinade is formed.

4 **Dredge and bake the seitan:** Place the sliced seitan in a bowl. Pour the marinade over it and toss to coat the seitan thoroughly. Using a slotted spoon, lift the pieces of seitan out of the sauce and transfer them to the prepared pan, allowing space between them. Bake for 25 minutes, until the outsides of the pieces form a lightly browned skin.

5 **Make the pancake batter:** Whisk together the all-purpose flour, buckwheat flour, baking powder, baking soda, and coriander in a medium bowl until no lumps remain. Whisk in the soy milk, sesame oil, and soy sauce to form a smooth and somewhat thick batter. Fold in the peas, galangal, scallions, sesame seeds, and red pepper flakes.

6 **Fry the pancakes:** Using coconut or olive oil, lightly oil a skillet or griddle and set over medium heat. Spoon out small pancakes (2½ inches in diameter) using a scant ¼ cup of batter for each. When bubbles appear toward the center and the edges are slightly pulling up from the pan, flip the pancakes and continue cooking for about 2 minutes.

7 To serve, place a pancake in the center of each plate. Cover the pancake with a small pile of watercress and top with another pancake. Top the pancake stack with another small pile of watercress and 6 to 8 pieces of seitan. Garnish with the fried lime leaves and, if using, the minced cilantro and chiles.

Pecan-Crusted Seitan
WITH SMOKED MUSHROOM GRAVY AND FRIED PARSNIP MATCHSTICKS

The fried parsnips are the cherry on top of this hearty autumnal dinner. I can't think of anything better than this seitan on a bed of Horseradish Mashed Potatoes scooped up with a big forkful of Lemon-Garlic Swiss Chard. If you can, I really recommend making all of those elements together with this dish. The seitan achieves a wonderful texture from the mixture of wheat germ and panko (Japanese bread crumbs) in its crust. The gravy is pretty much the bomb, thanks largely to the smoked black tea, which lends a great smoky aroma and is a perfect complement to the mushrooms.

We like to make this with a round ring mold that is 3 to 4 inches tall and 3 to 4 inches in diameter for ideal presentation, but you can plate however you like.

SERVES 8

For the pecan-crusted seitan
2 cups coarsely ground pecans
¼ cup chopped fresh rosemary leaves
½ cup wheat germ
2¼ cups all-purpose flour
1 cup panko bread crumbs
1 tablespoon ground coriander
1 tablespoon sea salt
1½ cups unsweetened soy milk
2 tablespoons stone-ground mustard
16 ounces seitan, sliced into 2- or 3-inch-long, ½-inch-thick cutlets
⅓ cup extra-virgin olive oil, plus more for the baking sheet

For the smoked mushroom gravy
4½ cups vegetable broth
⅓ cup loose Lapsang souchong tea leaves
3 tablespoons extra-virgin olive oil
1 medium onion, finely chopped
16 shiitake mushrooms, thinly sliced
3 garlic cloves, thinly sliced
2 tablespoons minced fresh rosemary leaves
½ teaspoon freshly ground black pepper
2 tablespoons tamari
3 tablespoons cornstarch

For the fried parsnip matchsticks
2 medium parsnips
2 cups canola, vegetable, peanut, or safflower oil, for frying
1 tablespoon evaporated cane juice
1 teaspoon sea salt
1 tablespoon coarsely chopped fresh rosemary leaves

For assembly
Horseradish Mashed Potatoes (page 182) or other mashed potatoes
Lemon-Garlic Swiss Chard (page 187) or other cooked greens
Minced fresh flat-leaf parsley (optional; for garnish)

1 **Prepare the seitan:** Preheat the oven to 350°F. Line a rimmed baking sheet with parchment paper and lightly oil the paper.

2 In a medium bowl, combine the pecans, rosemary, wheat germ, ¼ cup of the flour, the panko, coriander, and salt. In a separate wide, shallow bowl, beat the soy milk and mustard together with a fork; the milk will curdle. In a third bowl, place the remaining 2 cups of flour.

3 Working with 1 seitan cutlet at a time, toss a cutlet in the bowl with the plain flour. Lift out, shaking off the excess flour. Submerge the cutlet in the curdled soy milk and lift out, allowing excess liquid to drip back into the bowl. Toss the cutlet in the pecan mixture and place it onto the prepared baking sheet. Drizzle the breaded cutlets liberally with the olive oil. Bake for 14 to 17 minutes to obtain a crisp, golden crust.

4 **Make the gravy:** In a large saucepan over high heat, bring the vegetable broth to a boil. Stir in the tea leaves, cover the pot, and turn off the heat. Allow the tea to steep for 8 minutes.

5 Heat the olive oil in a large sauté pan over medium heat. Sauté the onions in the hot oil for 3 minutes, or until softened and translucent. Stir in the mushrooms, garlic, rosemary, and pepper. Continue to sauté, stirring, for 4 minutes, until the garlic and onions are thoroughly cooked.

6 Strain the tea-infused broth into the sauté pan, discarding the tea leaves. Raise the heat to high. In a small bowl, whisk the tamari and cornstarch with ½ cup water to thoroughly disperse the cornstarch. Once the mushroom mixture has come to a boil, stir in the cornstarch slurry and cook until a thick gravy forms, about 90 seconds. Use immediately, or store in an airtight container in the refrigerator for up to 4 days.

7 **Make the parsnip matchsticks:** Carefully cut the parsnips into julienned strips. (The ideal way to do this evenly is with a mandoline with a julienne attachment. Otherwise, cut julienne strips by hand.)

8 In a medium pot over medium-high heat, heat the oil to 340° to 360°F. Slowly sprinkle the parsnip matchsticks into the hot oil. (Dropping large amounts in all at once will cause the oil to bubble violently and possibly overflow.) Fry the parsnips for about 2 minutes, until they become golden brown. Remove the parsnips from the hot oil using tongs or a slotted spoon and drain them on paper towels. Place the warm parsnips into a mixing bowl with the evaporated cane juice, salt, and rosemary, and toss them to evenly coat the pieces.

9 **Assemble the plates:** Working with one plate at a time, place a ring mold in the center of the plate. Fill with about ½ cup of the mashed potatoes, and top with about ⅓ cup of the Swiss chard. Invert and remove the ring mold, and stack 2 seitan cutlets on top of the greens. Ladle ½ cup of the gravy onto the seitan and around the plate. Place a small pile of the fried parsnips on top of the seitan. Garnish the plate with minced parsley, if you like.

Red Bean–Scallion Pancakes

WITH THAI BASIL TOFU STRIPS AND TAMARIND PLUM SAUCE

This was one of the entrées we featured in the beginning of our second season. We would prepare the pancakes using a fancy form, so that we could stack them in a ring mold perfectly with greens and kimchi. We garnished the top of the entrée with fresh Thai basil leaves and with curried cashews (see page 127).

SERVES 4

For the tamarind plum sauce
½ cup pitted and chopped prunes, soaked in 2 cups warm water for at least 1 hour
3 tablespoons tamarind concentrate
3 tablespoons agave nectar
2 tablespoons tamari
2 tablespoons molasses
2 tablespoons freshly squeezed lime juice
1 teaspoon ground coriander
½ teaspoon freshly ground black pepper

For the Thai basil tofu strips
⅓ cup chopped fresh Thai basil leaves, plus more for garnish
2 tablespoons chopped fresh cilantro leaves
3 tablespoons soy sauce
3 tablespoons toasted sesame oil
3 tablespoons Thai red curry paste
2 tablespoons rice vinegar
2 tablespoons dry sweetener (sugar, Sucanat, or evaporated cane juice)
One 14-ounce block extra-firm tofu

For the red bean–scallion pancakes
1 cup all-purpose flour
¼ cup buckwheat flour
1 tablespoon baking powder
2 teaspoons baking soda
1 tablespoon ground coriander
1⅔ cups unsweetened soy milk
2 tablespoons toasted sesame oil
3 tablespoons soy sauce (shoyu or tamari)
½ cup rinsed cooked red beans
¼ cup minced scallions, light green and white parts
2 tablespoons sesame seeds
2 teaspoons crushed red pepper flakes
¼ cup coconut oil, for the pan
2 cups blanched watercress or fresh arugula
2 cups kimchi, homemade (see page 175) or store-bought
Curried cashews (see page 132), for garnish
Black sesame seeds (optional; for garnish)

1 **Make the tamarind plum sauce:** Place the prunes, soaking water, tamarind concentrate, agave nectar, tamari, molasses, lime juice, coriander, and pepper in a blender and blend on high speed for 30 seconds, until the mixture forms a smooth puree. Place the puree in a small saucepan and bring to a boil. Lower the heat and simmer, uncovered, for 20 minutes. Cool and store the sauce in an airtight container in the refrigerator for up to 6 days.

2 **Make the tofu marinade:** Preheat the oven to 400°F. Line a rimmed baking sheet with parchment paper and lightly oil the paper.

3 Place the Thai basil, cilantro, soy sauce, sesame oil, curry paste, vinegar, and sweetener in a blender and blend on high until smooth and emulsified. Cut the tofu into strips approximately ½ inch wide by ½ inch thick and 2 inches long. Gently toss the tofu with the marinade in a small mixing bowl to coat all sides.

4 Bake the tofu strips: Transfer the strips to the prepared baking sheet and bake for 30 minutes, turning once, until the strips are crispy on the outside and have absorbed the bulk of the marinade. Transfer the strips to a wire rack to cool. If not immediately using, the cooled strips can be kept in an airtight container for 3 or 4 days.

5 Make the pancake batter: Whisk together the all-purpose flour, buckwheat flour, baking powder, baking soda, and coriander in a small bowl until no lumps remain. Whisk in the soy milk, sesame oil, and soy sauce until you create a smooth, somewhat thick batter. Fold in the beans, scallions, sesame seeds, and red pepper flakes.

6 Fry the pancakes: Using some of the coconut oil, lightly grease a skillet or griddle and set over medium heat. Spoon out small pancakes (about 2½ inches in diameter) using a scant ¼ cup of batter for each. When bubbles appear toward the center and the edges are slightly pulling up from the pan, flip the pancakes and continue cooking for another 2 minutes.

7 To serve, place 1 pancake on each plate, and drizzle with the tamarind plum sauce. Top each pancake with ½ cup of the greens and ½ cup of the kimchi. Layer another pancake on top and add several pieces of the Thai basil tofu. Drizzle over the top with another spoonful of the sauce and garnish with the basil leaves, curried cashews, and black sesame seeds (if using).

Thai Basil

You can find Thai basil at Asian food stores, or get organic seeds and grow your own. Thai basil has pointier, smaller leaves and a distinctly less sweet flavor than the more familiar Italian basil. If you're in a jam, though, don't worry about substituting regular fresh basil. The flavor will be different, but your dish will still be powered by the fantastic essence of basil!

Live Szechuan String Bean Ramen WITH

Ginger-Basil Shiitake Mushroom Caps

This raw recipe requires some time and a dehydrator, but not a whole lot of work, to put together a balanced, nourishing meal. The kelp noodles are made from seaweed, and they make a nice alternative to flour-based noodles. You can find the kelp noodles at large health food stores. Otherwise, you could also make this dish using spiralized squash as the noodle portion of the recipe.

SERVES 3 (GF)

For the string beans
½ pound string beans, stems removed, halved crosswise
1 leek, light green and white parts only, trimmed to 4 inches, halved lengthwise, washed well, and very thinly sliced
1 teaspoon minced peeled fresh ginger
½ small Thai chile, or ⅓ medium habanero pepper, minced
1 tablespoon freshly squeezed lime juice
2 tablespoons extra-virgin olive oil
2 tablespoons nama shoyu (raw soy sauce)
2 tablespoons agave nectar
2 tablespoons sesame seeds (preferably black sesame, but white is fine, too)

For the shiitake mushroom caps
15 shiitake mushroom caps
2 teaspoons finely minced peeled fresh ginger
1 teaspoon Korean ground chile (or crushed red pepper flakes)
¼ cup coarsely chopped fresh Thai basil leaves
2 tablespoons minced fresh cilantro leaves
2 tablespoons extra-virgin olive oil
1 tablespoon umeboshi plum vinegar
2 tablespoons pure maple syrup

For the ramen broth
¼ cup chopped fresh cilantro leaves
½ medium jalapeño pepper, stem and seeds removed
1 garlic clove
1 celery stalk
1 teaspoon Chinese five-spice powder
2 tablespoons nama shoyu
1 tablespoon agave nectar
1 cup kelp noodles, rinsed
3 tablespoons minced scallion, light green and white parts
3 tablespoons sesame seeds
3 tablespoons microgreens (optional; for garnish)

1 **Prepare the string beans:** Mix together the beans, leeks, ginger, chile, lime juice, olive oil, nama shoyu, agave nectar, and sesame seeds in a small bowl. Evenly lay the beans out onto a Teflex-lined dehydrator tray, and dehydrate at 110°F for 5 hours.

2 **Prepare the mushroom caps:** Mix together the mushroom caps, ginger, chile, basil, cilantro, olive oil, plum vinegar, and maple syrup in a small bowl. Evenly lay the mushrooms onto a Teflex-lined dehydrator tray, and dehydrate at 110°F for 3 hours.

3 **Make the ramen broth:** Place the cilantro, jalapeño, garlic, celery, five-spice powder, shoyu, and agave nectar in a blender with 1¼ cups warm water. Blend at high speed for 45 seconds.

4 In a bowl, combine the kelp noodles and dehydrated string beans. Evenly distribute the string beans and noodles into 3 bowls. Pour the blended broth evenly into each bowl over the noodles and string beans (about ⅔ cup broth in each bowl). Place 5 dehydrated mushroom caps around the top of each heap of noodles. Garnish each bowl with 1 tablespoon each of scallions, sesame seeds, and microgreens (if using).

Raw Pizza

WITH SUN-DRIED TOMATO SAUCE, CASHEW CHEESE, OLIVES, AND ONIONS

I have tried raw pizzas at all kinds of vegan restaurants, and I'm disappointed by what I usually get: a measly plate of raw crackers garnished with pizza-themed toppings. But a few years before we started the truck, one of my private cooking clients (an angel named Gene) brought me a couple of slices of raw pizza he had made. It was doughy, with just the right texture and flavor, and was made with plenty of good olive oil. Gene shared his recipe with me, I tweaked it over the years, and the result is one of my favorite things we offer on the Cinnamon Snail. I often enjoy a slice with a salad and some sliced jalapeños as my lunch while I drive the truck home.

This recipe takes about a full day to complete. To enjoy raw pizza more often without it taking forever, multiply the recipe several times over. Portion the cheese and sauce into single-pizza containers, and freeze them. When the crusts have been dehydrated, wrap or place them in an airtight container to freeze for future use. Whenever you want a raw pizza, thaw out a crust, a container of sauce, and a container of cheese, and proceed to the final step of this recipe for an easy, fast raw pizza.

Pizza is a great canvas for any toppings you love. The toppings are best "baked on," so add your favorite veggies before the pizza's final four-hour dehydration time. You'll find a whole bunch of yummy ideas for raw pizza toppings on page 165.

MAKES ONE 12 BY 10-INCH PIZZA (GF)

Food Dehydrators

Food dehydrators use a fan blowing warm air over food to evaporate the moisture. They are great for preserving fruits, making kale chips, or preparing raw foods, where you want to completely dry the food without degrading its nutrients with excessive heat.

For the pizza crust
1 cup sunflower seeds
¼ cup extra-virgin olive oil, plus more for kneading the dough
1 celery stalk, chopped
1 medium tomato, chopped
1 medium onion, half chopped, half thinly sliced (for topping)
1 teaspoon dried oregano
3 tablespoons nama shoyu
1½ cups yellow flax meal
⅓ cup chopped olives, for topping

For the cashew cheese
1½ cups cashews, soaked in water for at least 30 minutes
⅔ cup extra-virgin olive oil
1 tablespoon umeboshi plum vinegar
½ teaspoon asafetida
2 teaspoons dried oregano
1 teaspoon dried thyme
½ teaspoon crushed red pepper flakes

For the sun-dried tomato sauce
⅔ cup unsulfured sun-dried tomatoes
1 medium beefsteak tomato, diced
2 garlic cloves
3 tablespoons extra-virgin olive oil
3 tablespoons chopped fresh basil leaves
2 teaspoons dried oregano
1 teaspoon fennel seeds
1 tablespoon agave nectar
1 tablespoon nama shoyu or tamari

1 Make the pizza dough: In a food processor, process the sunflower seeds for 60 seconds into a coarse flour. Add the olive oil, celery, tomato, chopped onions, oregano, and shoyu. Continue processing while slowly adding 1¼ cups water over the course of about a minute to achieve a mostly smooth puree. Place the yellow flax meal into a mixing bowl, and add the contents of the food processor to it. Knead the ingredients together by hand to form a smooth dough.

2 With lightly oiled hands, press out the dough onto a Teflex-lined food dehydrator tray. Form a perfect rectangle 10 inches wide by 12 inches long, about ½ inch high. Smooth the edges and top of the rectangle with lightly oiled hands. Dehydrate at 108°F for 5 hours. Remove the tray from the dehydrator and place an upside-down dehydrator tray on top of the crust. Carefully flip the crust over onto the new dehydrator tray, peeling off the original sheet of Teflex from the dough. Dehydrate for another 3 hours on the second side.

3 Complete the pizza with the toppings in the steps below, or wrap it well in plastic wrap and store the crust in the refrigerator for up to 5 days, or freeze for up to a month.

4 Make the cashew cheese: Drain the cashews and transfer them to a blender along with the olive oil, plum vinegar, asafetida, oregano, thyme, red pepper flakes, and 3 tablespoons cold water. Blend on high speed for 60 seconds, until it forms a smooth, thick puree. You may need to stop occasionally to scrape down the sides of the blender with a spatula, to ensure that everything is thoroughly incorporated. Use immediately, or store in an airtight container in the refrigerator for up to 4 days.

5 Make the sun-dried tomato sauce: Soak the sun-dried tomatoes in 1½ cups water for at least 3 hours (or overnight). Drain the sun-dried tomatoes over a bowl, reserving the soaking water, and place them in a food processor. Add the diced tomato, garlic, olive oil, basil, oregano, fennel seeds, agave nectar, and shoyu to the food processor and pulse together, slowly adding back in the reserved soaking water as the tomatoes break down. Continue to process for 3 minutes, until you have a smooth, thick, dark red tomato sauce.

6 To assemble the pizza, spread up to 2 cups of the cashew cheese onto the pizza crust, and ladle up to 2 cups of the sun-dried tomato sauce over the top of that. Arrange the sliced onions and olives on top of the pizza. Dehydrate at 108°F for four hours, until the onions have shriveled slightly and the sauce has darkened but not become too dry. Serve warm from the dehydrator, or cool and store in an airtight container in the refrigerator for up to 4 days.

Pizza toppings Galore

Of course you can also get buck-wild silly on your raw pizza . . . Bothered by the mundane status of onions and olives? Want to send an onion a letter in the mail telling it that its status is delinquent?!? DON'T DO THAT.

Instead, you can be a happy-clappy person and replace the onions and olives on top of the raw pizza in the recipe on page 163 with a few of these life-altering combinations. Like the onions and olives, these toppings should all be added to the top of the pizza before its final four-hour dehydration time.

Spinach and Pine Nuts (GF)

2 cups chopped baby spinach
¼ cup pine nuts
1 tablespoon chopped fresh rosemary
4 teaspoons freshly squeezed lemon juice
1 tablespoon agave nectar
2 tablespoons extra-virgin olive oil
¼ teaspoon sea salt

In a medium bowl, massage together the spinach, pine nuts, rosemary, lemon juice, agave nectar, olive oil, and salt so that the spinach wilts slightly.

Peppers, Mushrooms, and Basil (GF)

⅔ cup thinly sliced red bell pepper
⅔ cup chopped oyster or portobello mushrooms
¼ cup chopped fresh basil leaves
2 garlic cloves, minced
1 tablespoon umeboshi plum vinegar
2 tablespoons balsamic vinegar
1 tablespoon extra-virgin olive oil
1 tablespoon truffle oil
½ teaspoon freshly ground black pepper

Combine the bell pepper, mushrooms, basil, garlic, plum vinegar, balsamic vinegar, olive oil, truffle oil, and black pepper in a mixing bowl and allow to sit for 20 to 30 minutes for the mushrooms to soak up the marinade. Squeeze handfuls of the topping to tenderize the mushrooms and peppers more before using them.

Rosemary Faux-Tato (GF)

4 teaspoons coarsely chopped fresh rosemary leaves
Grated zest and juice of 1 lemon
2 tablespoons smoked paprika
1 teaspoon dried thyme
1 teaspoon dried oregano
1 tablespoon agave nectar
1 tablespoon nama shoyu
3 tablespoons extra-virgin olive oil
1 medium jicama, peeled

In a small bowl, combine the rosemary, lemon zest and juice, paprika, thyme, oregano, agave nectar, shoyu, and olive oil. Slice the jicama into paperthin slices with a mandoline or vegetable peeler. Toss the jicama slices in the seasonings.

Balsamic Figs and Parsnips (GF)

3 tablespoons balsamic vinegar
2 tablespoons pure maple syrup
2 tablespoons extra-virgin olive oil
1 teaspoon black mustard seeds
1 teaspoon fennel seeds
¼ teaspoon sea salt
½ cup julienned parsnips
8 fresh figs, cut into quarters

In a medium bowl, combine the balsamic vinegar, maple syrup, olive oil, mustard seeds, fennel seeds, and salt. Toss the parsnips and figs in the dressing. When topping the pizza, make sure to distribute any remaining dressing evenly over the surface of the pizza.

Ginger Island Tofu WITH
Coconut Mashed Yams and Fried Ginger

The components of this entrée are all inspired by different Caribbean flavors. Any of the building blocks to this dish hold their own, but together, the entrée has a great range of flavors, textures, and colors and just the right amount of heat. If you can't stand the heat, cut the spice with a scoop of Grilled Mango Salsa. It's best to make this meal in the summer, because you are going to put your grill to work for it.

SERVES 4 (GF)

For the ginger island tofu
3 tablespoons coconut oil
1 tablespoon brown mustard seeds
2 tablespoons minced peeled fresh ginger
2 garlic cloves
½ medium habanero pepper (use less if you don't like spice), stem and seeds removed
¼ cup chopped fresh cilantro leaves
1 teaspoon ground cloves
1 teaspoon ground allspice
½ teaspoon ground nutmeg
3 tablespoons tamarind concentrate
3 tablespoons tamari
⅓ cup pure maple syrup
¼ cup molasses
¼ cup freshly squeezed lime juice
One 14-ounce block extra-firm tofu, drained

For the coconut mashed yams
3 pounds yams, peeled and quartered
2 tablespoons coconut oil
1 tablespoon minced peeled fresh ginger
¼ teaspoon ground cloves
2 teaspoons ground cinnamon
2 tablespoons Sucanat
One 13.5-ounce can coconut milk
Sea salt

For the fried ginger
¼-pound piece of fresh ginger, peeled
1 tablespoon cornstarch
1 cup canola oil
½ teaspoon ground cinnamon
½ teaspoon Mexican chili powder
1 teaspoon evaporated cane juice
½ teaspoon sea salt

For assembly
2 cups baby spinach
Grilled Mango Salsa (page 260) or other sweet salsa
¼ cup micro radish greens
¼ cup thinly sliced scallions, light green and white parts

1 **Prepare the tofu:** Preheat an outdoor grill, stovetop grill, or grill pan.

2 In a saucepan over medium heat, heat the coconut oil. Add the mustard seeds and wait for the seeds to pop and sputter in the pan. Add the ginger, garlic, habanero, and cilantro. Sauté the mixture for about 4 minutes, stirring, until the cilantro wilts and the garlic becomes lightly golden. Add the cloves, allspice, and nutmeg, continuing to stir for 2 more minutes. Add the tamarind, tamari, maple syrup, molasses, and lime juice and continue to cook until the mixture is bubbling. Turn off the flame and allow to cool for 15 minutes. Transfer the mixture to a blender and blend on high speed for 40 seconds to form a mostly smooth marinade.

3 Cut the tofu horizontally into 4 thin rectangular slices and place them in a baking dish. Pour about half of the marinade over the tofu slices, and allow the slices to soak up the marinade for 10 minutes.

4 Remove the tofu from the marinade, allowing excess liquid to drip down into the baking dish. Grill the tofu for about 3 minutes on each side to achieve dark grill marks. Place the grilled slices of tofu on a cutting board and cut the tofu into thin strips. Return the strips of tofu to the baking dish and pour the remaining marinade over the tofu.

5 **Prepare the yams:** Place the yams in a large pot with enough water to cover. Bring to a boil over high heat and cook for about 8 minutes until the yams can be cut into easily with the side of a fork. Drain the yams in a colander.

6 In a small saucepan over medium heat, melt the coconut oil. Add the ginger and sauté for about 3 minutes, until the ginger becomes golden. Stir

in the cloves, cinnamon, and Sucanat, and continue cooking until the Sucanat melts and begins to caramelize. Add the coconut milk, raise the heat to high, and bring to a boil. Place the cooked yams into a food processor and begin processing, while slowly pouring in the contents of the saucepan through the feed tube. Continue until a smooth puree forms. Salt to taste.

7 **Fry the ginger:** Using a vegetable peeler, peel the ginger into very thin strips. Toss the ginger strips in the cornstarch to dry excess moisture from the surface of the slices.

8 Heat the canola oil in a saucepan (preferably one with high sides) over medium-high heat to about 360°F. If you don't have a thermometer, you can check the heat of the oil by dipping a single piece of ginger into the hot oil. If it bubbles around the ginger rapidly, it's ready to go! Sprinkle the ginger into the hot oil, making sure the oil doesn't bubble up over the sides. Stir the ginger slices a few times as they cook over the course of 1½ to 2 minutes, to

become golden brown and crisp. Using a slotted spoon, remove and drain the ginger slices on a paper-towel-lined plate.

9 In a medium bowl, combine the cinnamon, chili powder, evaporated cane juice, and salt. Toss the ginger slices in the seasonings. Use immediately, or store for up to a week in a paper-towel-lined container in the refrigerator.

10 **Assemble the plates:** Place a 3-inch ring mold in the center of each dinner plate. Fill with about ⅓ cup of the hot mashed yams, then press on top of it about ½ cup of the baby spinach leaves, one quarter of the tofu strips, and ⅓ to ½ cup of the salsa. Pour about 2 tablespoons of the remaining tofu marinade onto the plate around the ring mold. Remove the mold and garnish the tofu with 4 or 5 pieces of the fried ginger and 1 tablespoon each of the microgreens and scallions.

Jalapeño Roasted Corn-Stuffed Red Quinoa Croquettes

WITH CAJUN FRIED SWEET POTATOES AND CASHEW MORNAY SAUCE

Mornay sauce is a form of béchamel (a French white sauce made with lots of butter and flour) that's normally prepared with some melted cheese. In this entrée we use tangy cashew cream, black salt, and asafetida in the sauce to provide a similar cheesy richness. The recipe calls for starting with room-temperature oil to fry the sweet potatoes. This simulates the Belgian "low-and-then-high-temperature" frying method, which yields soft, tender insides and crisp, nicely textured outsides. The cashew mornay sauce is heavenly over the lightly spiced sweet potatoes, and it would make a pretty amazing poutine-type side dish on its own. Along with the hearty quinoa croquette, adding some dark greens to the dish, like Bourbon-Blanched Mustard Greens or Lemon-Garlic Swiss Chard, makes for a VERY flavorful and nutritionally complete meal.

SERVES 6

For the croquettes

Raw kernels from 2 ears yellow corn, or about 1¾ cups frozen corn kernels, thawed

3 garlic cloves, minced

3 tablespoons mirin

1 tablespoon smoked paprika

2 teaspoons ground cumin

5 tablespoons tamari

10 tablespoons extra-virgin olive oil, plus more for greasing the pan

1 medium jalapeño pepper, seeded and minced

2 scallions, light green and white parts, minced

1½ cups red quinoa

1 shallot, minced

2 celery stalks, minced

1 medium carrot, minced

2 teaspoons dried thyme

2 teaspoons ground coriander

1 tablespoon Mexican chili powder

1 teaspoon crushed red pepper flakes

For the cashew mornay sauce

1 cup cashew pieces, soaked in water for 30 to 60 minutes

3 garlic cloves

2 tablespoons tahini

2 tablespoons umeboshi plum vinegar

2 tablespoons freshly squeezed lemon juice

2 tablespoons evaporated cane juice

2 teaspoons fennel seeds

1 teaspoon dried oregano

¼ cup vegan margarine (such as Earth Balance)

3 tablespoons all-purpose flour

1 teaspoon asafetida

1 teaspoon fine black salt (or sea salt, if you can't get the sulfuric-smelling black stuff)

For the Cajun fried sweet potatoes

2 large sweet potatoes

2½ cups canola oil

2 tablespoons Cajun seasoning

2 teaspoons garlic powder

2 teaspoons smoked paprika

2 teaspoons grated orange zest and 1 tablespoon freshly squeezed orange juice

Sea salt

For assembly

Bourbon-Blanched Mustard Greens (page 187), Lemon-Garlic Swiss Chard (page 187), or other cooked greens, warmed

½ cup minced fresh chives or thinly sliced scallions, light green and white parts (for garnish)

½ cup micro jalapeño greens or micro radish greens (optional; for garnish)

1 **Make the croquette filling:** Preheat the oven to 350°F.

2 In a medium bowl, combine the corn with the garlic, mirin, paprika, cumin, 2 tablespoons of the tamari, and 3 tablespoons of the olive oil. Place the mixture into a small baking dish and roast for 17 minutes, until the corn is lightly browned. Mix in the jalapeño and scallions, and allow to cool.

3 **Make the croquette mixture:** Place the quinoa, shallots, celery, carrot, thyme, coriander, chili powder, red pepper flakes, and 2½ cups water into a 2-quart pot with a lid. Place the pot

over medium-high heat, and bring to a boil. Lower the heat to a simmer, cover, and cook for 12 to 15 minutes, until the water has been fully absorbed and the quinoa is fully cooked.

4 Remove half of the cooked quinoa and place it in a food processor with the remaining 3 tablespoons of tamari and ¼ cup of the olive oil. Puree the quinoa for about 2 minutes, until completely smooth. Briefly pulse the whole quinoa into the pureed quinoa in the food processor, just to evenly distribute. Allow the mixture to cool to room temperature, about 30 minutes.

5 **Form and bake the croquettes:** Liberally oil 6 cups in a large muffin or cupcake pan with the remaining 3 tablespoons of olive oil.

6 Place ⅓ cup of the quinoa mixture into each oiled cup in the pan. Press the filling into the molds, so that you create bottoms and sides to the croquettes with cavities

recipe continues

in the centers for filling. Place 3 tablespoons of the roasted corn filling into each croquette. With wet hands, flatten a 3- to 4-tablespoon disk of quinoa mixture between your hands. Press the disk into one of the molds, pressing it against the sides of the croquette to seal the filling inside.

7 Bake the croquettes for 18 minutes, then remove from the oven. Allow the croquettes to cool for 8 minutes before carefully inserting a paring knife around the sides of each mold to help separate the croquettes from the pan. Place a lightly oiled baking sheet upside down on top of the muffin pan. Flip the pan and sheet together, and lightly rap them on a table to loosen the croquettes from the pan, so that they transfer onto the baking sheet. Bake for an additional 6 minutes to crisp the sides and tops of the croquettes.

8 Make the cashew mornay sauce: Drain and rinse the soaked cashews. Place the cashews, garlic, tahini, plum vinegar, lemon juice, evaporated cane juice, fennel seeds, oregano, and 1½ cups water into a high-speed blender, and blend on high for 60 seconds to make a smooth, liquidy cream.

9 Melt the margarine in a saucepan over medium heat. Once the margarine is hot, whisk in the flour and continue stirring until the flour becomes lightly browned. Whisk in the cashew cream along with the asafetida and black salt. Continue cooking for a couple of minutes until the sauce starts to bubble and thicken slightly. Keep warm until ready to serve.

10 Prepare the sweet potatoes: Cut the sweet potatoes into shoestrings. Place the shoestring potatoes into a wide pot with the canola oil to cover.

11 Place the pot onto a burner and turn the heat to high. The oil will slowly come to a boil, allowing the middle of the sweet potatoes to become tender while the outsides develop a well-textured crust. Meanwhile, in a small bowl combine the Cajun seasoning, garlic powder, paprika, orange zest and juice, and salt. After about 13 minutes, or when the sweet potatoes are thoroughly cooked to your taste inside and out, remove them from the hot oil with a slotted spoon or spider, and let them drain on a cooling rack. Blot the remaining oil off with paper towels. Place the still-hot fried sweet potatoes in a bowl, and toss with the mixture of seasonings.

12 Assemble the plates: Place a small pile of the warm greens in the center of each plate. Top with a quinoa croquette, a generous pile of hot fried sweet potatoes, and ¼ cup of the warm mornay sauce. Garnish with 2 tablespoons of chives or scallions, and sprinkle with microgreens if using.

BASIC NAPA CABBAGE
AND RADISH KIMCHI

Veggies and Sides

175 Kimchi

   175 Basic Napa Cabbage and Radish Kimchi

   176 Spicy Kimchi with Mustard Greens and Carrot

177 Simple Marinated Kale

177 Lemon-Soy Watercress

178 Raw Maple Miso Brussels Sprouts

180 Maple-Roasted Kabocha

182 Horseradish Mashed Potatoes

187 Lemon-Garlic Swiss Chard

187 Bourbon-Blanched Mustard Greens

NYC ATE OUR TRUCK ALIVE,

LEAVING ONLY THE BUMPER

In 2012, we had just moved into our own commissary kitchen in central New Jersey when we took the Cinnamon Snail to New York City. We finally had our own walk-in refrigeration space, commercial dishwasher, giant mixers, space to do serious production. Sean's lovely sister, Michelle, was our entire prep crew . . .

For our first day on the streets of NYC in the spring, we hit the Flatiron District in Manhattan, and hit Midtown later that week. There were still just two people on the truck: either I or a really wonderful cook named Sydney worked the grill, and Sean worked the window. The days were epic, and we were NOT PREPARED ONE BIT. Suddenly, we were serving almost as much food in a single afternoon as we had served in four days. New York City was ready for us, but we didn't have nearly enough staff.

Not only did it become a mad dash to hire some more talented, passionate vegans, but we had to change how we prepared things. If we needed to caramelize fifty pounds of onions regularly, we had to get some equipment that could slice onions effortlessly. We were still employing the same methods of prep we had used before, but it was clear that we needed to have tools that could handle massive volume. Once we needed to start blending sauces in thirty batches or more, it made sense to upgrade to giant industrial blenders. Our prep crew grew from one person a few days a week to a small army working together on huge lists of giant-size recipes.

As you make some of the recipes at home and think, "Wow, forming those burgers was a breeze," just remember that for us, forming three thousand of anything takes a lot of time and effort. One wrong move on a giant batch can yield tons of unusable food. I had to start tweaking the recipes so that they still came out the way I loved them, but on a giant scale. After working in massive volumes for a few years, writing this book meant reverse engineering many of our recipes to still work properly on home kitchen equipment in batches small enough to make sense for the home cook.

Kimchi

I can't even put into words my deep love of kimchi. Kimchi is a Korean fermented condiment, frequently made with napa cabbage and radishes. Hundreds of years ago, the idea was that salted veggies were buried in clay pots after the fall harvest in Korea. The salting would kill off the bulk of "bad bacteria" and resist mold, and the insulation of the earth and clay pots would keep the veggies above freezing temperatures, allowing them to ferment slowly. Kimchi is great for your digestive flora, and it's a mouthwatering ingredient to cook with. You will find it all over our menu on the truck, and either recipe below can be used to make the many recipes featured in this book that call for kimchi. If you are lazy, vegan kimchi can be found now in many health food stores, but the homemade stuff is better, fresher, and less expensive.

Basic Napa Cabbage and Radish Kimchi (GF)

MAKES ABOUT ½ GALLON

This is the basic kimchi recipe we use in a lot of recipes on the truck. We also like to include watermelon radishes or other heirloom radishes in the mix, but I kept the recipe here a little simpler, so that the kimchi ingredients will be easier for the average home cook to get his or her hands on.

1 head of napa cabbage, any wilted outer leaves discarded

1 daikon radish, peeled and cut into short strips

8 red radishes, scrubbed and sliced thin

½ cup plus 1 teaspoon sea salt

1 tablespoon minced peeled fresh ginger

¼ cup chopped onion

3 garlic cloves

2 teaspoons evaporated cane juice

⅓ cup Korean ground chile

1 Core and coarsely chop the cabbage. In a bowl, toss together the cabbage, daikon, and red radishes.

2 In a gallon jar (or other large nonreactive container), combine the ½ cup salt with 4 cups water. Pack the cabbage and radishes into the jar, cover it, and allow to sit out at room temperature in the brine for 5 hours. Drain and rinse the brined vegetables in a colander with cool water.

3 In a food processor, process the ginger, onions, garlic, evaporated cane juice, Korean ground chile, the remaining teaspoon of salt, and

3 tablespoons water to form a bright red, smooth paste. In a bowl, massage the chile paste into the drained vegetables to coat all sides.

4 Press the chile-coated vegetables into a ½-gallon glass jar, and really tamp them down to remove extra air. Cover the jar and let it ferment at room temperatures between 60 and 78°F for 3 days. At this point, open the jar and press the kimchi down again to remove air bubbles. Allow the kimchi to ripen for at least 4 more days under refrigeration before use. (The kimchi should stay good for a few weeks under refrigeration.)

recipe continues

Spicy Kimchi with Mustard Greens and Carrot (GF)

MAKES ABOUT ½ GALLON

The mustard greens lend a fantastic bitter flavor to this spicy kimchi. If you are feeling wimpy, cut back a little on (or even omit) the crushed red pepper flakes in the recipe.

1 head of napa cabbage, any wilted
   outer leaves discarded
8 red radishes, thinly sliced
2 carrots, thinly sliced (with a wavy
   vegetable cutter if available)
1 head of mustard greens, coarsely
   chopped
½ cup plus ½ teaspoon sea salt
1 tablespoon minced peeled fresh
   ginger
⅓ cup chopped scallions, light green
   and white parts
1 teaspoon evaporated cane juice
¼ cup Korean ground chile
3 tablespoons crushed red pepper
   flakes

1 Core and coarsely chop the cabbage. In a bowl, toss together the cabbage, red radishes, carrots, and mustard greens.

2 In a gallon jar (or other large nonreactive container), combine the ½ cup salt with 4 cups water. Pack the cabbage, radishes, carrots, and greens into the jar and let them sit out at room temperature in the brine for 5 hours. Drain and rinse the brined vegetables in a colander with cool water.

3 In a food processor, process the ginger, scallions, evaporated cane juice, Korean ground chile, red pepper flakes, the remaining ½ teaspoon of salt, and 3 tablespoons water until you have a bright red, smooth paste. In a bowl, massage the chile paste into the drained vegetables to coat all sides.

4 Press the chile-coated vegetables into a ½-gallon glass jar, and really tamp them down to remove extra air. Cover the jar and let it ferment at room temperatures between 60 and 78°F for 3 days. At this point, open the jar and press the kimchi down again to remove air bubbles. Allow the kimchi to ripen for at least 4 more days under refrigeration before use. (The kimchi should stay good for a few weeks under refrigeration.)

Simple Marinated Kale

You are up to no good. This super-simple kale allows you to sneak raw, dark leafy greens into everything you feed your family! The trick to getting the texture just like cooked greens is to really squeeze the marinade into the kale as you massage it with your hands. The acid from the plum vinegar will penetrate the greens and help soften them and make them easy to eat and digest, while still retaining all of their enzymes and nutrients—which would otherwise degrade a little from being cooked.

MAKES ABOUT 3 CUPS (GF)

1 bunch of curly, lacinato, or red kale
3 tablespoons extra-virgin olive oil
1 tablespoon umeboshi plum vinegar
1 teaspoon dried thyme
½ teaspoon freshly ground black pepper

Thoroughly submerge the kale in water, then rinse and drain the leaves. Remove the bottom couple inches of thick stems, and slice the greens into 1-inch-wide ribbons. Place the kale ribbons into a mixing bowl with the olive oil, vinegar, thyme, and pepper. Using your hands, squeeze and massage the greens until they are tender and you no longer see any dry-looking kale. Use immediately, or store in an airtight container in the refrigerator for up to 2 days.

Lemon-Soy Watercress

I love the fresh crunch and mild flavor of watercress. It lends itself really well to some of our entrées, especially as a topping to the Red Bean–Scallion Pancakes (page 158), to bring contrast in flavor and texture and to make the dishes more nutritionally complete.

MAKES ABOUT 2 CUPS (GF)

2 bunches of watercress
2 tablespoons extra-virgin olive oil
2 teaspoons mustard seeds
Juice of 1 lemon
2 teaspoons tamari

Chop only the roots off of the watercress, leaving the stems intact, and rinse the leaves in cold water. In a sauté pan, heat the olive oil over medium heat. Add the mustard seeds and let them pop in the hot oil. Add the watercress and sauté for about a minute, until the leaves start to wilt. Stir the lemon juice and tamari into the watercress and turn the heat off. Serve immediately.

Raw Maple Miso Brussels Sprouts

This might be one of the easiest Brussels sprouts recipes ever, and it's such a lovely way to have them uncooked. They get really nicely glazed from the marinade, and the outsides get crispy while the insides become tender. If you don't have a dehydrator, you could roast the Brussels sprouts in olive oil for about 12 minutes at 350°F, toss them in the marinade, and return them to the oven for an additional 8 to 10 minutes to let the coating caramelize and permeate the sprouts.

MAKES 3 CUPS (GF)

¼ cup white miso paste
¼ cup pure maple syrup
2 tablespoons toasted sesame oil
1 tablespoon crushed red pepper flakes
½ teaspoon ground cloves
20 Brussels sprouts (about ½ pound)

1 Mix the miso, maple syrup, sesame oil, red pepper flakes, and cloves with 3 tablespoons water in a mixing bowl, using a small whisk or a fork. Cut the stem ends off of the Brussels sprouts and cut the heads in half lengthwise. Place all the Brussels sprouts in the marinade and mix thoroughly, so that the insides of the Brussels sprouts are permeated with marinade.

2 Place the Brussels sprouts on dehydrator screens (not lined with Teflex sheets), and dehydrate for 10 to 14 hours at 110°F. The crispier you want the final product, the more time you should leave it dehydrating. Serve warm from the dehydrator, or store in an airtight container in the refrigerator for up to 3 days.

Maple-Roasted Kabocha

Kabocha is a fantastic winter squash, with a flavor somewhere between acorn squash and pumpkin. The pretty, bumpy outer skin is perfectly fine to eat once cooked, so go ahead and use the whole thing. If you can't find kabocha, substitute acorn squash (discard the skins).

MAKES ABOUT 3 CUPS (GF)

3 tablespoons tamari
1 teaspoon liquid smoke
¼ cup pure maple syrup
¼ cup toasted sesame oil
½ teaspoon ground nutmeg
2 teaspoons ground cumin
2 teaspoons ground coriander
½ medium-size (about 3 pounds) Kabocha squash, cut into very thin 3- to 4-inch strips

1 Preheat the oven to 350°F. Line a rimmed baking sheet with parchment paper and lightly oil the paper.

2 Combine the tamari, liquid smoke, maple syrup, sesame oil, nutmeg, cumin, and coriander in a mixing bowl, then turn the slices of squash in the bowl to coat them evenly in the mixture. Evenly lay out the squash slices on the prepared baking sheet. Bake the squash for 15 to 18 minutes, until golden brown. Use immediately, or store in an airtight container in the refrigerator for up to 3 days.

 Street Vegan

SUPERHEROES TO THE FOOD TRUCKS

The Street Vendor Project was started by Sean Basinski, who sold burritos on the street while putting himself through law school. In his years as a vendor, Sean became aware of the marginalized legal status of street vendors.

Food vending has always been a way for new immigrants, and for people with very little upfront capital, to provide income for their families. A high percentage of New York's vendors don't speak English as their first language, and many don't fully understand their rights and the complexity of the law. At the same time, the permit process for vendors is broken. Since the early '80s there has been a black market for permits and licenses, and so it's no longer possible to obtain a permit through the city. In addition, it's not uncommon for thousand-dollar tickets to be issued for violations as minor as being a foot too close to the crosswalk, or having your vendor's photo ID accidentally tucked *inside* of a jacket on a cold day.

Sean started the Street Vendor Project as an advocacy group to help vendors fight bogus tickets, understand their rights, and settle disputes. It also lobbies for changes in the current laws affecting vendors. We meet monthly to work together with hot dog vendors, handbag merchants, and street artists alike, with the goal of creating solutions for the problems we all face. I have been moved to tears at hearing the plight that some vendors faces. I am so grateful to Sean, Matt, Lei Bai, Osama, James, Derrick, and all of the hard-working volunteers who fight for our right to provide a modest income for our families. I don't get to attend monthly meetings so frequently now, and I miss sharing stories and building friendships and solidarity, face to face, with so many good people who organize under the SVP flag. I still get involved whenever I can with actions and demonstrations, and it's always like returning home. The other vendors remember me dragging my kids with me to the meetings as babies, and they always ask about them. SVP is my street food freedom fighter family, and I love that we are fighting for our rights together.

horseradish MaSHeD Potatoes

Eating raw fresh horseradish is sort of like eating a small stick of dynamite: The heat is strong, but just in your head, and only for a moment. Cooking the horseradish mellows it out a lot and allows it to bring a fantastic flavor to boring old mashed potatoes. If you really love the flavor of horseradish, consider adding a couple of teaspoons of fresh, finely grated horseradish to the finished mashed potatoes as well, and you will get both the cooked and fresh dimension of flavor in there.

MAKES ABOUT 5 CUPS (GF)

3 pounds russet potatoes, peeled and quartered
¼ cup extra-virgin olive oil
⅔ cup grated fresh horseradish
3 tablespoons minced fresh dill
1 cup vegetable broth
1 cup unsweetened soy milk
Sea salt

1 Place the potatoes in a large pot with enough water to cover and bring the pot to a boil over high heat. Continue to boil, covered, until the potatoes are soft, about 10 minutes.

2 Meanwhile, heat the olive oil in a saucepan over medium heat. Add the horseradish and sauté, stirring, for about 3 minutes to soften the horseradish. Add the dill, broth, and soy milk and bring to a boil. Lower the heat to medium low and simmer for 8 minutes.

3 Drain the potatoes into a colander, then return them to their original (now empty) pot. Add the simmered horseradish mixture and mash thoroughly with a potato masher until smooth. Add salt to taste. Serve immediately.

READING THE RIOT ACT OF FOOD TRUCKS

Getting tickets is part of our daily expenses in New York City: we always get at least one, namely for "vending merchandise from a metered location." No time was this more true than in 2011, when the love affair between food trucks and New York really exploded.

People loved having a rotating variety of interesting food options in neighborhoods with limited lunch spots. Take Midtown, for example, where there are few independent restaurants but hundreds of thousands of hungry office workers. It makes sense for everyone that street vendors come to these areas. Unfortunately, the folks unhappy about this arrangement are the business improvement districts (BIDs) that represent the big chain businesses, and they wield all the power.

With the bogus argument that food trucks take away from sales at McDonald's, the BIDs came together to get food trucks out of their areas. Their lawyers dug up a turn-of-the-century law prohibiting the sale of merchandise in front of parking meters, a law so old that it refers to vendors as "Hawkers, Hucksters, and Peddlers." (I secretly love thinking of us with those snazzy antiquated titles.) The BID lawyers had the courts change the legal definition of "merchandise" in New York State to include "food." Food trucks were now only allowed to operate in commercial (nonmetered) parking spaces. And do you know how many NON-METERED COMMERCIAL spaces there are in Manhattan? That's right, none. So in one quick legal move, the BIDs made it virtually illegal to sell food from a food truck in New York.

Most days, we *just* get a ticket, but enforcement is random and inconsistent. Parking cops just give you a ticket, but the Health Department shuts you down and gives you a full inspection. Regular police or special vending police can shut you down in the middle of lunch, hit you with thousand-dollar fines, and even tow you to the impound lot. If truck employees are working without a special vending photo ID, then things can get really serious. Sometimes people get taken away in handcuffs just for not having their ID on them. It all depends on what kind of cop you get, and what kind of mood he is in.

DID YOU KNOW? FOOD TRUCKS ARE UNFAIR COMPETITION TO RESTAURANTS!

Here's a little questionnaire for restaurateurs who feel threatened by the invasion of food trucks:

- *Does your restaurant get flat tires?*

- *Does the generator that powers your refrigerators sometimes die, needing to be repaired (closing your place for days), causing you to have to toss all your food?*

- *Does your restaurant occasionally need its transmission replaced?*

- *How many parking tickets does your restaurant get, even when it's legally parked?*

- *Do you have other restaurant owners call the police or health department on you, simply because they are angry that you are on "their block"?*

- *Do your customers have to eat their food on a paper plate on their lap?*

- *When it's freezing rain, do your customers wait in the rain for their food?*

- *When you get to your restaurant, do you often find that someone else moved his business into the place where you usually operate?*

- *Does it take you three hours driving around in circles while paying your staff to do the same with you, just to open for business again?*

So in short, restaurants and food trucks are completely different businesses. Food trucks are required to rent commercial kitchens to take in deliveries, store ingredients, do prep work, and pay all the same taxes and insurance that restaurants do. We are inspected by health departments *way* more frequently than restaurants are, and have to ensure the same level of food safety. And then we have all the challenges of being an actual vehicle, a mode of transportation, as the cherry on top. So, to the restaurateurs who worry about the unfair advantages food trucks have over them—go for it! Shut your restaurant down and run a food truck instead. You will surely have an easier, more profitable life.

But I suppose the one real bonus of the draconian vending laws and criminalization of food trucks is that there aren't corporate chain food trucks all over New York City. If the day comes when Starbucks coffee carts and McDonald's burger trucks line the streets, and do so without the same struggles as us, it will be the death knell of New York street food.

Right now New York street food culture resembles the 1980s graffiti and break-dancing scene. It's underground, and the party is alive and fresh, as long as you're willing to bend rules and be innovative to survive. If the laws change and the climate allows corporate giants to flourish, it will become much like what graffiti and break-dancing have become—a commodified ghost of an art form, like break-dancing for a Gap ad. While I wish our industry weren't criminalized, I also celebrate every day that street food remains a guerrilla movement, out of reach of the Colonel's claws or the Hamburgler's swindling schemes.

LEMON-GARLIC Swiss Chard

Swiss chard is a watery dark leafy green with a mild flavor like spinach. The lemon and garlic in this simple recipe make it similar to Greek *horta* (steamed or broiled dandelion greens); and it pairs nicely with Mediterranean flavors, or makes a great veggie side to go with heavier meals, like Thanksgiving.

MAKES ABOUT 4 CUPS (GF)

3 tablespoons extra-virgin olive oil
1 tablespoon brown or black mustard seeds
2 bunches (9 to 12 large leaves) of Swiss chard, sliced into ½-inch ribbons
Grated zest and juice of 3 lemons
4 garlic cloves, minced or mashed into a paste
½ teaspoon sea salt
2 tablespoons mirin

In a deep pan or wide pot, heat the olive oil over medium heat. Add the mustard seeds to the hot oil and wait for the seeds to start to pop (about 50 seconds). Add the Swiss chard and stir to coat it with the hot oil. Immediately stir in the lemon zest and juice, garlic, salt, and mirin. Put a lid over the pan and allow the chard to steam for 2 minutes. Remove from the heat and serve

---

bouRBON-BlaNcHED MustArd GREENS

A splash of oaky bourbon makes these spicy mustard greens a great component of Southern-style entrées and sandwiches. They really complete the meal with our Jalapeño Roasted Corn–Stuffed Red Quinoa Croquettes with Cajun Fried Sweet Potatoes and Cashew Mornay Sauce (page 168).

MAKES 3 CUPS (GF)

¼ cup bourbon
1 cup vegetable broth
3 tablespoons tamari
2 tablespoons rice vinegar
2 bunches of mustard greens (10 to 12 leaves), coarsely chopped
2 tablespoons extra-virgin olive oil
1 tablespoon minced fresh dill
Sea salt

1 Place the bourbon, broth, tamari, and vinegar into a 4-quart pot. Cover the pot, place it over high heat, and bring the mixture to a boil. Place the chopped mustard greens into the pot, and stir the greens into the broth to ensure that all parts of the greens have been in contact with the hot liquid. Cover the pot again, turn off the heat, and let the greens steep in the hot liquid for 3 minutes.

2 Remove the cooked greens with a slotted spoon and transfer them to a bowl, leaving behind most of the cooking liquid. Toss the greens with the olive oil, dill, and salt to taste.

ROASTED MANDARIN-
CHOCOLATE GANACHE
TART

DESSErts

191 Pop Tarts 'n' Pop Hearts

    192 Strawberry-Rhubarb Filling

    192 Peanut Butter–Chocolate Ganache

    192 Lavender-Raspberry Filling

193 Roasted Mandarin–Chocolate Ganache Tart

194 Macadamia–White Chocolate Twinkies

196 Gooey Salted-Caramel Pecan Turtle Bars

198 Raspberry Coconut Frou Frous

199 Raw Chocolate Pudding

201 Lavender–Vanilla Bean Crème Brûlée

202 Mint Matlock Took All His Clothes Off

203 Pine Nut Friendlies

204 Mini Peanut Butter–Chocolate Cheesecakes

207 Live Pumpkinish Pie

208 Rum-Glazed Pecan Cookies

210 Rum Pumpkin Chiffon Pie

211 Raw Raspberry–Chocolate Fudge Tart

213 Chocolate Sambuca Cookies

214 Raw Brownies

    215 Jalapeño Raw Brownies

217 Raw Lemon-Blueberry Cheesecake

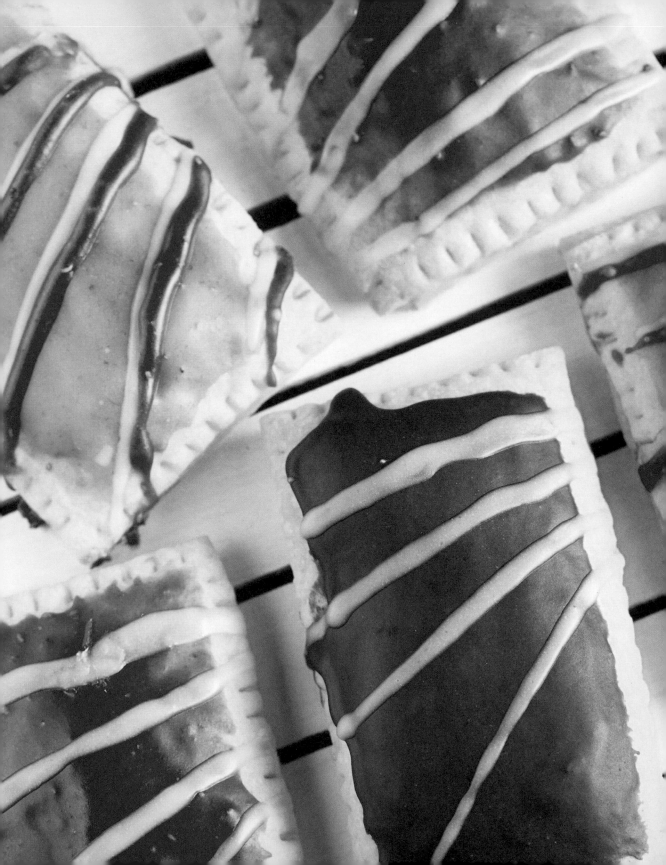

Pop Tarts 'N' Hearts

There is something just totally trashy and yet decadent about Pop-Tarts, which makes them a lovely canvas for a gourmet vegan makeover. I mean, if you nail the flaky pie-crusty outside just right, then the outside and inside of the pastries make a fantastic landing place for a myriad of flavors. Included here are our recipes for a great basic crust, plus a few fillings that can be paired with decorative glazes. (Each variation makes enough filling for ten pop tarts.) Make pop tarts in rectangular shapes, or use a heart-shaped cookie cutter to make pop hearts instead. These are perfect treats for Valentine's Day, so much better than those chalky heart-shaped candies that break my heart with lameness.

MAKES 10

1 teaspoon apple cider vinegar
2 teaspoons egg replacer powder
2⅔ cups all-purpose flour
½ teaspoon sea salt
1 cup vegan margarine (such as Earth Balance)
1 tablespoon coconut oil, for greasing the baking sheet
1½ cups of your desired filling (see suggestions on page 192)
2 cups of your desired glaze (see suggestions on page 192)

1 In the bowl of a stand mixer fitted with the paddle attachment, mix together the cider vinegar and egg replacer with ½ cup cold water until foamy. Add the flour, salt, and margarine, and continue mixing on low speed just until a dough is formed. Allow the dough to sit for 15 minutes before rolling out, in order for the flour to become fully hydrated.

2 Preheat the oven to 350°F. Line a baking sheet with parchment paper and grease the paper lightly with coconut oil.

3 Roll out the dough to form a large rectangle about ⅛ to ¼ inch thick. Cut the dough into 6 by 3-inch rectangles. Reroll the scraps as you go, and keep cutting until you have 20 rectangles. Spread 2 tablespoons of the filling in the center of half of the rectangles; top with the other half of the rectangles, and crimp the edges of each tart together thoroughly with the tines of a fork. Prick the center of each tart a few times with a fork to allow steam to escape during baking, just enough to prevent the pop tarts from bursting. Place each tart on the prepared baking sheet, leaving about ½ inch between each pastry.

4 Bake the pop tarts for 12 minutes, until golden brown around the edges. Cool the pop tarts on a wire cooling rack. Brush each tart with the desired glaze that best suits the filling. Allow the main glaze to set on each pop tart for at least 5 minutes before striping with any additional decorative glaze.

recipe continues

Strawberry-Rhubarb Filling

1 tablespoon extra-virgin olive oil
2 cups stemmed and chopped fresh
    strawberries
1 rhubarb stalk, peeled and diced
2 tablespoons freshly squeezed lime
    juice
¼ cup evaporated cane juice
2 tablespoons cornstarch

1 Warm the olive oil in a saucepan over medium heat. Add the strawberries and rhubarb and sauté, stirring, for 4 minutes. Add the lime juice and evaporated cane juice, and continue to cook, stirring, for 2 minutes. Blend the cornstarch with 3 tablespoons water in a small bowl. Pour the cornstarch slurry into the fruit and stir to combine. Turn off the heat and allow the filling to cool before using in the pop tarts. Chill until ready to use, up to 3 days.

2 Suggested glazes for frosting and decorating: Fresh Cranberry Glaze (page 231) or Lemongrass Mango Glaze (page 231) with stripes of Vanilla Glaze (page 230)

Peanut Butter–Chocolate Ganache

2 cups vegan dark chocolate chips
1 cup unsweetened soy milk
1 cup smooth peanut butter
½ teaspoon coarse sea salt

1 Pour the chocolate chips into a heat-proof mixing bowl.

2 Bring the soy milk to a rolling boil in a saucepan set over medium heat. Pour the hot soy milk over the chocolate chips, and whisk rapidly for 2 minutes, until absolutely all the chocolate has melted. Chill the ganache for 2 hours.

3 Combine the ganache, peanut butter, and salt in a medium bowl, and swirl together with a spoon to create ribbons of peanut butter throughout the ganache. Chill until ready to use, up to 4 days.

4 Suggested glazes for frosting and decorating: chocolate glaze (see page 248) with stripes of Vanilla Glaze (page 230)

Lavender-Raspberry Filling

3 cups frozen raspberries
2 teaspoons dried lavender flowers
2 teaspoons grated lemon zest
⅓ cup agave nectar
2 tablespoons cornstarch

1 Combine the raspberries, lavender, lemon zest, and agave nectar in a saucepan set over medium heat. Cook for 6 minutes, stirring, until all the raspberries are thawed and breaking down.

2 Blend the cornstarch with 3 tablespoons water in a small bowl, and pour the slurry over the cooking raspberries. Continue to cook, stirring, for 2 minutes, then turn off the heat and allow the filling to cool. Chill until ready to use, up to 4 days.

3 Suggested glazes for frosting and decorating: Fresh Cranberry Glaze (page 231) or Lemongrass Mango Glaze (page 231) with stripes of Vanilla Glaze (page 230)

Roasted Mandarin-Chocolate Ganache Tart

Packed into a thin crust made of ground chocolate cookies, this lightly spiced, rich chocolate tart is topped with contrasting sweet-bitter mandarin orange slices, lightly caramelized from being roasted with their rinds on. **MAKES ONE 9-INCH TART**

For the mandarin topping
¼ cup pure maple syrup
¼ teaspoon sea salt
1 tablespoon extra-virgin olive oil, plus more for greasing the pan
½ teaspoon pure vanilla extract
4 mandarin oranges, skin scrubbed clean

For the crust
Olive oil, for greasing the pan
1½ cups ground vegan chocolate sandwich cookies (I prefer Newman-O's)
½ teaspoon ground cloves
3 tablespoons melted coconut oil

For the chocolate ganache filling
⅔ cup coconut milk
⅓ cup freshly squeezed orange juice
2 cups vegan chocolate chips
¼ teaspoon ground cardamom
⅛ teaspoon ground cloves
½ teaspoon ground cinnamon

1 **Make the mandarin topping:** Preheat the oven to 350°F. Line a rimmed baking sheet with parchment paper and lightly grease the paper with olive oil.

2 In a medium bowl, mix together the maple syrup, salt, olive oil, and vanilla. Using a serrated knife, without peeling, cut each mandarin into about 10 thin round slices; discard any seeds. Toss the mandarin slices into the bowl and stir to coat.

3 Arrange the mandarin slices on the prepared baking sheet and bake for 10 minutes, until lightly caramelized. Remove and transfer the warm mandarin slices to a cooling rack (so that they don't stick to the parchment paper while cooling).

4 **Make the crust:** Lightly oil a 9-inch pie pan or fluted metal tart pan with a removable bottom. Combine the ground cookies, cloves, and coconut oil in a small bowl. Evenly distribute the moistened crumbs around the pan. With wet hands, firmly press the crumbs to form a thin crust that evenly covers the bottom and sides of the pan.

5 **Make the chocolate ganache filling:** Bring the coconut milk and orange juice to a boil in a 2-quart saucepan over medium heat.

6 Combine the chocolate chips, cardamom, cloves, and cinnamon in a medium, heat-proof bowl. Pour the boiling liquid into the bowl of chocolate and whisk rapidly for about 3 minutes, until the mixture is completely smooth and all of the chocolate is fully melted.

7 Pour the warm chocolate ganache into the prepared crust. Chill the tart for 30 minutes to partially firm the ganache. Arrange the mandarin slices on the surface of the ganache in a neat circular pattern. Chill the tart for at least 5 more hours before serving, so that the ganache sets up firmly and becomes sliceable.

Macadamia-White Chocolate Twinkies

These were one of the sweets we featured at the 2012 Vendy Awards that helped win us the People's Choice award. It's a classy rendition of the ultimate not-all-that-classy dessert. Like so many things that inspire what I do with the Cinnamon Snail, these Twinkies are a balancing act between the elegance of the yummy refined flavors and the complete chaos of dripping white chocolate glaze and chunky candied macadamia nuts.

MAKES 12

For the candied macadamia topping

Coconut oil, for the baking sheet

1 cup coarsely chopped macadamia nuts

3 tablespoons pure maple syrup

3 tablespoons evaporated cane juice

½ teaspoon ground cardamom

½ teaspoon pure vanilla extract

¼ teaspoon sea salt

1 tablespoon extra-virgin olive oil

For the white chocolate glaze

2½ cups vegan powdered sugar

¼ cup unsweetened soy milk

2 tablespoons melted cacao butter

1½ teaspoons chocolate extract

For the filling

1 cup macadamia nuts

1 cup coconut milk

1½ cups evaporated cane juice

2 tablespoons all-purpose flour

1 teaspoon sea salt

1 tablespoon chocolate extract

1 cup melted cacao butter

½ cup melted non-hydrogenated vegetable shortening

For the batter

2¼ cups all-purpose flour

2 teaspoons baking powder

½ teaspoon baking soda

½ teaspoon sea salt

1 cup evaporated cane juice

½ cup canola oil

1½ cups unsweetened soy milk

2 teaspoons apple cider vinegar

1 teaspoon pure vanilla extract

1 tablespoon chocolate extract

1 **Make the topping:** Preheat the oven to 350°F. Line a rimmed baking sheet with parchment paper and lightly oil the paper with coconut oil.

2 Combine the nuts, maple syrup, evaporated cane juice, cardamom, vanilla, salt, and olive oil in a mixing bowl. Spread the mixture evenly on the prepared baking sheet. Bake for 10 minutes, stirring at the halfway point, until the nuts are golden and dry. Remove the nuts from the oven, and allow them to cool fully before packing into an airtight container. (The candied macadamias can be stored in an airtight container at room temperature for up to a month.)

3 **Make the glaze:** Whip the powdered sugar, soy milk, cacao butter, and chocolate extract together in a mixer for 2 minutes, until thoroughly combined. Use the glaze at room temperature. The glaze will keep in an airtight container in the refrigerator for up to 3 weeks.

4 **Make the filling:** Combine the macadamia nuts and coconut milk in an airtight container and allow to soak for 1 hour.

5 Place the soaked nuts and the milk into a high-speed blender and blend on high for 60 seconds to form a smooth puree. Place the nut mixture, along with the evaporated cane juice, flour, salt, chocolate extract, cacao butter, and shortening into the bowl of a stand mixer fitted with the paddle attachment, and mix on medium speed for 30 minutes, stopping occasionally to scrape down the sides of the mixer, to ensure that everything is fully incorporated. The extensive mixing time will force the fats and liquids to emulsify, producing a creamy filling. Use a rubber spatula to transfer the filling into a pastry bag fitted with a long, thin filling tip (or you can load the filling into a plastic bag and cut off a corner of the bag to make a small piping tip). Set aside, covered, at room temperature until the Twinkies are ready for filling.

6 **Make the batter:** In a medium bowl, sift together the flour, baking powder, baking soda, salt, and evaporated cane juice. In a large bowl, combine the oil, soy milk, cider vinegar, vanilla, and chocolate extract. Whisk the wet ingredients into the dry ingredients until a smooth batter forms.

7 **Shape the Twinkies:** Lightly oil two Twinkie or canoe pans. Pour ¼ cup batter into each form. Bake the Twinkies for about 9 minutes, until they are golden and a toothpick comes out clean when inserted into the center of the cake. (Do not overbake, or your Twinkies will be dry and will make children cry.) Remove the pan from the oven. Allow the Twinkies to set in the pans for 5 minutes, then transfer the Twinkies to a wire rack to cool fully.

8 **Fill the Twinkies:** Using a serrated knife, cut any excess cake from the flat bottom of each Twinkie, so that they stand neatly and evenly. Inject the filling from the bottom of each Twinkie in 3 separate places, in order to evenly fill each Twinkie with as much filling as it can take. Brush the tops of the Twinkies with the white chocolate glaze, and sprinkle liberally with the candied macadamia pieces while the glaze is still wet.

Gooey Salted-Caramel Pecan Turtle Bars

Think of these as your secret weapon for cookie exchange parties (yes, they exist, and you should have them often). Better than any boring cookie, these bring together a great variety of textures and flavors; and yes, the fact that "turtle" rhymes with "girdle" will make them a hit among every crowd, even burlesque Republican rappers.

MAKES 20

Coconut oil, for greasing the pan

1½ cups vegan margarine (such as Earth Balance)

1⅔ cups all-purpose flour

½ cup cornstarch

¾ cup vegan powdered sugar

2 teaspoons pure vanilla extract

1¾ cups evaporated cane juice

¼ cup agave nectar

1 teaspoon molasses

1 cup coconut milk

1½ teaspoon very coarse sea salt, or fleur de sel

2 cups toasted pecan pieces

½ cup vegan chocolate chips

1 Preheat the oven to 350°F. Lightly oil a 9 by 13-inch rectangular tall-sided baking pan.

2 Beat 1¼ cups of the margarine at medium speed in a mixer fitted with the paddle attachment for 30 seconds, to remove any lumps. Add the flour, cornstarch, powdered sugar, and 1 teaspoon of the vanilla and mix together for 60 seconds until a smooth dough forms. Press the dough into an even layer in the prepared baking pan. Bake the crust for 20 minutes, until lightly golden brown.

3 Combine the evaporated cane juice, agave nectar, molasses, the remaining ¼ cup of margarine, and the remaining teaspoon of vanilla with ¼ cup water in a tall pot. Cook over medium heat, stirring occasionally, until the evaporated cane juice melts.

Once the mixture starts to bubble rapidly, stir in the coconut milk. Using a candy thermometer, wait until the caramel reaches a temperature of 240°F (about 15 minutes), then turn off the heat.

4 Immediately pour the hot caramel over the baked shortbread crust, and sprinkle on the coarse salt, toasted pecans, and chocolate chips. Allow the hot caramel to melt the chocolate chips, and then, if desired, marble the topping by gently dragging a metal spoon through the caramel and chocolate (be careful not to scrape into the crust). Allow the topping to cool to room temperature before cutting the tray of turtle bars into whatever shape and size you prefer.

Raspberry Coconut Frou Frous

These are easy mini cakes, which we first served from our stand at the Red Bank farmer's market years before we started the truck. Very occasionally, when the weather is cool enough for them to not melt in our display case, we bring them back on the truck, and our long-standing customers go pretty bonkers. Unlike fondant or marzipan-wrapped treats, or chocolate-glazed petit fours, these have a coconut frosting, and the edges are coated in toasted coconut. You don't have to be patient or have super-duper cake decorating skills. Any old fool can make these and have them look adorable.

MAKES 16

For the cakes

2¼ cups all-purpose flour

2 teaspoons baking powder

½ teaspoon baking soda

½ teaspoon sea salt

1 cup evaporated cane juice

½ cup canola oil, plus extra for greasing the pan

1½ cups unsweetened soy milk

2 teaspoons apple cider vinegar

1 teaspoon pure vanilla extract

½ teaspoon coconut extract

⅔ cup fresh or frozen raspberries

⅓ cup shredded coconut

For the coconut frosting

1¼ cups evaporated cane juice

1½ cups coconut milk

2 tablespoons all-purpose flour

1 teaspoon sea salt

1 tablespoon coconut extract

⅔ cup melted coconut oil

⅔ cup melted non-hydrogenated vegetable shortening

For assembly

1 cup toasted shredded coconut

16 fresh raspberries

1 Preheat the oven to 350°F. Lightly oil 16 medium-size muffin pan molds with canola oil.

2 **Make the cakes:** In a medium bowl, whisk together the flour, baking powder, baking soda, salt, and evaporated cane juice. Make a well in the center of the dry ingredients, and pour in the oil, soy milk, vinegar, vanilla, and coconut extract. Whisk together the dry and wet ingredients until smooth, and then fold in the raspberries and shredded coconut.

3 Portion out ¼ cup of batter into each oiled muffin tin mold. Bake the cakes for about 14 minutes, until golden and just cooked through. Allow the cakes to cool partially in the muffin pan for about 8 minutes, and then carefully trim off any cake that has risen above the top edge of the pan, using a serrated knife (this will allow all the little cakes to sit flat, upside down on their "top" side, when removed from the pan). Remove the cakes from the pan, and allow them to cool to room temperature.

4 **Make the frosting:** Whisking frequently, bring the evaporated cane juice, coconut milk, and flour to a boil in a medium saucepan set over medium heat. Once the mixture starts bubbling, remove the pan from the heat and allow the mixture to cool for 30 minutes.

5 In the bowl of a stand mixer fitted with the paddle attachment, mix the coconut with the salt, coconut extract, coconut oil, and shortening on medium speed for 30 minutes, stopping occasionally to scrape down the sides of the mixer, to ensure that everything is fully incorporated. The extensive mixing time will force the fats and liquids to emulsify, producing a creamy frosting.

6 **Assemble the cakes:** Place all of the cakes upside down on a work surface (sitting on their trimmed flat top sides). Using a small offset spatula, evenly ice the sides and tops of the little cakes. Coat the sides in the toasted coconut, and place a raspberry in the center of the tops. Chill the little baby cakes for at least an hour before serving.

Raw Chocolate Pudding

This pudding is an absolute staple in my home. We also serve it on the truck, because it's rich and decadent but leaves you feeling awesome. This is unbelievably easy to throw together, taking about as much time as it takes to make a smoothie.

SERVES 4 (GF)

2 cups cashew pieces, soaked in water
    for 30 minutes
⅔ cup pure maple syrup
¼ cup cacao powder
¼ teaspoon sea salt
2 teaspoons cacao nibs

1 Drain the soaked cashews and rinse them under cold water. Place the cashews, maple syrup, cacao powder, and salt with ⅔ cup water in a high-speed blender and blend on high until completely smooth, about 90 seconds.

2 Portion the pudding into 4 ramekins, half-pint glass jars, or short glasses. Garnish each serving with ½ teaspoon of the cacao nibs. Chill the puddings for at least 2 hours before serving. (If storing for longer, cover the puddings, and keep under refrigeration for up to 5 days.)

Lavender-Vanilla Bean Crème Brûlée

Crème brûlée was always one of my favorite desserts. There's no reason that is has to be something you eat only on the rare occasions you find a restaurant that offers a vegan one. The lavender in this dessert comes from both dried lavender flowers and lavender essential oil. Hate lavender? Replace the lavender with finely minced orange zest, saffron, crushed pistachios, rosewater, or any other fun fancy ingredient you love. The custard is thickened by the magical power of agar-agar, a sea vegetable that has gelatin-like thickening powers.

This dessert requires the use of a blowtorch. Miniature butane torches for making crème brûlée are available at any good restaurant- or cooking-supply shop, or (like us) you can use a real industrial blowtorch, the kind used for sweating pipes.

SERVES 8 (GF)

6 cups coconut milk

⅓ cup plus ½ cup evaporated cane juice

¼ cup pure maple syrup

¼ teaspoon vanilla beans, scraped from the inside of vanilla bean pods

1¼ teaspoons fresh or dried lavender flowers

⅛ teaspoon food-grade lavender oil

1 teaspoon sea salt

1½ teaspoons agar-agar powder

1 In a saucepan over medium heat, whisk together the coconut milk, the ⅓ cup of evaporated cane juice, the maple syrup, vanilla beans, lavender flowers, lavender oil, and salt. Whisking occasionally, bring the mixture to a boil, then add the agar-agar and lower the heat to a simmer. Cook for 5 minutes, to let the custard thicken. Evenly divide the hot custard into 8 ramekins (about ⅔ cup in each). Chill the ramekins for at least 3 hours and up to 2 days to set.

2 To serve, working with one serving at a time, evenly sprinkle 1 tablespoon of the remaining evaporated cane juice over the surface of each custard, trying to avoid getting sugar onto the rim of the ramekin itself. With a butane torch, flame the surface, using constant circular motions, to form a brown caramelized surface.

Mint Matlock Took all His Clothes Off

When people ask us what's in this cookie, the only honest answer is that hidden inside is an elderly detective gentleman without trousers, who could jump out at you. (I could tell you that there are cacao nibs, chocolate chips, and mint—but boy would you be in for a surprise when the detective jumps out in his birthday suit . . .)

MAKES 16 COOKIES

3 tablespoons unsweetened soy milk

2 teaspoons egg replacer powder

¼ cup coconut oil

1¼ cups evaporated cane juice

2 teaspoons mint extract

½ teaspoon pure vanilla extract

1¼ cups all-purpose flour

⅓ cup Dutch-process cocoa powder

½ teaspoon baking powder

½ cup vegan chocolate chips, coarsely chopped

3 tablespoons cacao nibs

1 Preheat the oven to 350°F. Line 2 baking sheets with parchment paper.

2 In the bowl of a stand mixer fitted with the paddle attachment, beat together the soy milk and egg replacer powder at medium speed. Stop the mixer, and add the coconut oil, evaporated cane juice, mint extract, and vanilla extract. Continue mixing at medium speed for 2 minutes, until the evaporated cane juice and coconut oil are thoroughly creamed. Stop the mixer and add the flour, cocoa, and baking powder. Mix again for about 60 seconds, just until a firm dough forms. Add the chopped chocolate chips and cacao nibs, and mix for 60 seconds more until evenly distributed in the dough.

3 Using about 2 tablespoons of dough per cookie, scoop out the dough and press flat between your palms. Place each cookie staggered on the baking sheets, about 2 inches apart. Bake the cookies for 11 to 13 minutes, until they have risen and the edges are pulling up slightly from the pan. Allow the cookies to cool partially on the sheet pans, about 3 minutes, then transfer them to cool completely on a wire rack.

PINE NUT FRIENDLIES

One of my fondest cookie memories goes back to a really cold day around the time our first daughter, Idil, was born. We were snowed in, and I was working on music all day (I used to do that a lot before the truck came into our lives). I was so entranced with what I was doing that I didn't even notice what Joey (Ms. Snail) was doing in the kitchen. All of a sudden, she appeared with a giant plate of these perfect pine nut cookies, still a little warm. Whenever Joey makes these, I eat an embarrassing number of them. I always feel bad that I forget to share them, but damn it, they are too good.

MAKES 16

½ cup vegan margarine (such as Earth Balance)

2 tablespoons evaporated cane juice

1 teaspoon pure vanilla extract

1 cup all-purpose flour

¾ cup coarsely chopped pine nuts

¼ teaspoon sea salt

½ cup vegan powdered sugar

1 Preheat the oven to 350°F. Line a baking sheet with parchment paper.

2 Working by hand or in the bowl of a stand mixer fitted with the paddle attachment, thoroughly combine the margarine, evaporated cane juice, vanilla, flour, pine nuts, and salt with 1 teaspoon water. Divide the dough into 16 small balls (approximately 2 teaspoons each). Roll the balls into perfect circles and place them on the prepared sheet pan, at least 1 inch apart.

3 Bake the cookies for 16 to 18 minutes, until lightly brown. Spread the powdered sugar on a wide plate or bowl. Allow the cookies to cool partially for 5 minutes, then toss the cookies in the powdered sugar to coat all sides evenly. Serve warm, if possible—though they will still be splendid when cooled.

MiNi PeaNut ButteR— Chocolate CheeSeCaKes

When we first started the truck, these were in the display case really often. We served them on pretty little gold foil paper saucers. To make bite-size cheesecakes, look for a miniature cheesecake pan with a removable bottom that holds up to a dozen minis. (We use the ones made by Nordic Ware.) Besides making mini cheesecakes with this recipe, we hijack the filling and repurpose it for Peanut Butter–Chocolate Cheesecake Donuts (page 240).

MAKES 12

For the crust

Canola oil or coconut oil, for greasing the pan

1 cup ground vegan chocolate sandwich cookies (we use Newman-O's)

2 tablespoons vegan margarine (such as Earth Balance), melted

For the filling

1 cup tofu cream cheese

½ block extra-firm tofu

½ cup peanut butter

1 cup evaporated cane juice

2 tablespoons rice vinegar

3 tablespoons coconut milk

¼ teaspoon sea salt

2 tablespoons cacao nibs, plus more for garnish

¾ cup chocolate ganache (see page 248)

1 Preheat the oven to 250°F. Lightly oil the cheesecake molds with canola oil or coconut oil.

2 Make the crust: In a large bowl, combine the ground chocolate cookies and the margarine with 2 tablespoons water, and stir until well combined.

3 Make the filling: Blend the tofu cream cheese, tofu, peanut butter, evaporated cane juice, vinegar, coconut milk, salt, and cacao nibs in a food processor until the cacao nibs have broken down into tiny bits and the mixture is free of lumps.

4 Using a wet finger, press 1 tablespoon of crust into the bottom of each mold in the prepared pan. Place 2 tablespoons of the filling into each mold, pressing it level with a wet finger or wet spoon.

5 Bake the cakes for 45 minutes, until the cheesecakes appear puffed and the tops are lightly browned and have developed a skin. Remove from the oven.

6 While the cheesecakes are still warm, place 1 tablespoon of the chocolate ganache in the center of each cheesecake, and top with a sprinkling of cacao nibs. Once the cheesecakes reach room temperature, carefully remove them from the molds, and chill for at least 2 hours. Use immediately, or store in an airtight container in the refrigerator for up to 4 days.

LIVE PUMPKINISH PIE WITH CINNAMON COCONUT CREAM

Just because you are trying to treat your body like a temple instead of a garbage disposal doesn't mean you can't have a really yummy Thanksgiving. This "pumpkin" pie doesn't actually contain pumpkin, but instead gets its pumpkin pie status from carrot juice, sweet potatoes, and the spices that are typical in pumpkin pie. (No gluten, soy, turkeys, or Pilgrims are contained in this pie either.)

MAKES ONE 9-INCH PIE (GF)

1 pecan crust (see page 217)
2⅔ cups cashew pieces
1½ cups carrot juice
½ cup shredded peeled sweet potato
⅔ cup coconut oil
⅓ cup agave nectar
2 teaspoons ground cinnamon, plus more for garnish
½ teaspoon ground nutmeg
¼ teaspoon ground allspice
¼ teaspoon ground cloves
½ teaspoon sea salt
Cinnamon Coconut Cream (recipe follows, for garnish)
Shredded coconut (optional; for garnish)

1 Prepare the crust and set aside.

2 Place the cashew pieces in a medium bowl and cover them with the carrot juice. Allow the cashews to soak in the carrot juice for 30 minutes.

3 Place the soaked cashews and carrot juice into a high-speed blender, add the sweet potato, coconut oil, agave nectar, cinnamon, nutmeg, allspice, cloves, and salt, and blend for 90 seconds to form a smooth, loose filling. Scrape the filling into the crust, and smooth the top with a warm, wet offset spatula. Chill the pie for at least 12 hours before serving it; the center of the pie should feel firm to the touch.

4 Plate each slice with 1 to 2 tablespoons of the coconut cream, if using, and garnish with a dusting of cinnamon and with shredded coconut, if desired.

Cinnamon Coconut Cream

MAKES 1½ CUPS

1½ cups coarsely chopped fresh young Thai coconut meat (see page 56)
¼ cup coconut water
1 tablespoon coconut oil
3 tablespoons pure maple syrup
½ teaspoon ground cinnamon
⅛ teaspoon ground cloves
½ teaspoon pure vanilla extract
¼ teaspoon sea salt

Add the coconut meat, coconut water, coconut oil, maple syrup, cinnamon, cloves, vanilla, and salt to a high-speed blender and blend on high for 60 seconds to form a very smooth off-white cream. Chill the cream for at least 1 hour before using. Store in an airtight container in the refrigerator for up to 3 days.

Rum-Glazed Pecan Cookies

Spiced rum, pecans, and maple make these little round cookies hard to stop eating, and then Santa exploded because he ate too many, and now everyone has to celebrate Hanukkah—'nuff said.

MAKES ABOUT 24

For the cookies
⅔ cup canola oil, plus more for greasing the baking sheets
1 cup evaporated cane juice
¼ cup pure maple syrup
1 tablespoon finely ground flax seeds
½ teaspoon pure vanilla extract
1 teaspoon coconut extract
2 cups all-purpose flour
½ teaspoon baking soda
½ teaspoon sea salt
1¼ cups chopped pecan pieces

For the rum glaze
1½ cups vegan powdered sugar
2 tablespoons spiced rum
2 tablespoons pure maple syrup
½ teaspoon ground cinnamon, plus more for garnish if desired
½ teaspoon sea salt

1 **Make the cookies:** Preheat the oven to 350°F. Line 2 baking sheets with parchment paper and lightly oil the paper.

2 In the bowl of a stand mixer fitted with the paddle attachment, mix the oil, evaporated cane juice, maple syrup, ground flax seeds, vanilla extract, and coconut extract on medium speed for 2 minutes, or until completely creamed. Add the flour, baking soda, salt, and pecans and continue mixing for 1 to 2 minutes, until a loose dough is formed.

3 Drop heaping tablespoons of the dough onto the prepared baking sheets, leaving 2 inches of space between each cookie. Bake the cookies for 14 minutes, until the edges start to brown and slightly lift away from the pan. Let the cookies cool on the pans for 3 to 5 minutes, then carefully transfer to a wire cooling rack. Let cool completely.

4 **Make the glaze:** Combine the powdered sugar, rum, maple syrup, cinnamon, and salt in a medium bowl, whisking to form a smooth, thick, lump-free glaze. Warm the glaze in a double boiler, or by placing the bowl over a pan of simmering water. (Warming it will make it thinner to work with, but will still allow it to set up nicely into an icing.)

5 Brush about 1½ teaspoons of glaze neatly over the surface of each cookie. Lightly sprinkle with cinnamon before the glaze fully dries, if desired.

RUM PUMPKIN CHIFFON PIE

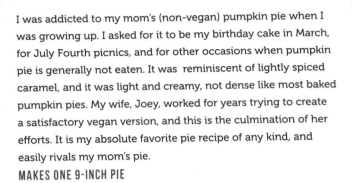

I was addicted to my mom's (non-vegan) pumpkin pie when I was growing up. I asked for it to be my birthday cake in March, for July Fourth picnics, and for other occasions when pumpkin pie is generally not eaten. It was reminiscent of lightly spiced caramel, and it was light and creamy, not dense like most baked pumpkin pies. My wife, Joey, worked for years trying to create a satisfactory vegan version, and this is the culmination of her efforts. It is my absolute favorite pie recipe of any kind, and easily rivals my mom's pie.

MAKES ONE 9-INCH PIE

For the crust
1¼ cups ground vegan gingersnap cookies

3 tablespoons melted vegan margarine (such as Earth Balance), plus more for greasing the pan

For the filling
½ cup cashew pieces, soaked in water for 30 minutes

One 13.5-ounce can coconut milk

1 tablespoon molasses

½ cup vegan cream cheese

½ teaspoon sea salt

½ teaspoon ground cinnamon

½ teaspoon ground nutmeg

2 tablespoons agar-agar powder

One 13.5-ounce can pumpkin puree

1 cup evaporated cane juice

2 tablespoons rum

For assembly
3 tablespoons toasted shredded coconut

Vegan whipped cream (optional; for serving)

1 **Make the crust:** Lightly grease a 9-inch pie pan with vegan margarine.

2 In a small bowl, mix together the gingersnaps, margarine, and 1 tablespoon warm water. Evenly distribute the moistened ground gingersnaps around the pan. With wet hands, firmly press the crumbs to form a thin crust that evenly covers the entire bottom and sides of the pan.

3 **Make the filling:** Drain and rinse the cashew pieces in a colander. Add them to a high-speed blender along with the coconut milk, molasses, vegan cream cheese, salt, cinnamon, nutmeg, and agar-agar. Blend on high for 45 seconds, until all cashew pieces are fully broken down and the resulting puree is smooth. Add the pumpkin puree and continue blending on high for another 30 seconds, until thoroughly incorporated.

4 Scrape the pumpkin mixture into a 2- to 4-quart pot along with the evaporated cane juice and, whisking frequently, bring the mixture to a boil. Once the mixture is letting out large bubbles, lower the heat to a simmer and continue to cook for 6 minutes, stirring frequently with a whisk, until thickened. Turn off the heat and whisk the rum into the warm filling.

5 **Assemble the pie:** Pour the warm pie filling into the crust, and rap the pan against a work surface a couple of times, to release any air bubbles from the filling and settle it evenly into the crust. Sprinkle the toasted coconut evenly over the surface of the pie. Chill the pie for at least 5 hours, or overnight if possible. Serve cold with dollops of vegan whipped cream, if desired.

Raw Raspberry-Chocolate Fudge Tart

Let this be the return of ecstatic raspberry and chocolate-dripping slices of bliss. This recipe dates back to before we started the truck; I started making it when I worked at Down to Earth, a vegan restaurant in Red Bank. Later, I served it to private cooking clients and sometimes offered it at our stand at the Red Bank farmer's market. Now it's yours to serve chilled as a decadent dessert that is also fantastic for you. Make it in the height of raspberry season, so you can serve each slice with fresh berries.

MAKES ONE 9-INCH TART (GF)

For the raspberry sauce
2 cups fresh raspberries
Grated zest and juice of 1 medium orange
2 tablespoons pure maple syrup
¼ teaspoon sea salt

For the chocolate-almond crust
1¾ cups raw almonds
¼ cup cacao powder
¼ teaspoon sea salt
1 teaspoon pure vanilla extract
3 tablespoons agave nectar
1 tablespoon melted coconut oil, plus more for greasing the pan

For the raspberry-chocolate filling
2⅔ cups cashew pieces, soaked in water for 30 minutes
⅔ cup agave nectar
1¼ cups coconut oil
1 cup cacao powder
⅔ cup fresh raspberries, plus more for garnish
1 teaspoon pure vanilla extract
¼ teaspoon sea salt
¼ cup cacao nibs (optional; for garnish)

1 Make the raspberry sauce: Place the raspberries, orange zest and juice, maple syrup, and salt into a blender, and blend on high speed for 45 seconds. If you prefer a very smooth sauce, strain the sauce through a fine-mesh strainer. Store in an airtight container in the refrigerator for up to 4 days. (You'll have about 1¼ cups of sauce.)

2 Make the chocolate-almond crust: Lightly grease the bottom and sides of a 9-inch springform pan with coconut oil. Process the almonds, cacao powder, and salt in a food processor for 90 seconds to form a medium-fine almond meal. Add the vanilla, agave nectar, and coconut oil, and continue processing for 45 seconds to form a slightly gritty brown dough. Using wet hands, press the crust into the springform pan, covering the bottom and sides with a very thin layer of smooth crust. Chill the crust for at least 30 minutes in the freezer, before pouring in the filling.

3 Make the raspberry-chocolate filling: Drain the cashews, and place them in a blender along with the agave nectar, coconut oil, cacao powder, raspberries, vanilla, salt, and 1 cup water. Blend for 60 seconds. Scrape down the sides of the blender and blend on high speed for an additional 60 seconds, until completely smooth. Pour the pie filling into the crust, and refrigerate overnight. (The center of the tart should be firm to the touch.) Store the pie covered in the refrigerator for up to 6 days.

4 Plate each slice with 2 tablespoons of the raspberry sauce, scatter with fresh raspberries, and garnish with cacao nibs, if desired.

Chocolate Sambuca Cookies

These small cookies are especially nice to serve around the holidays. The fragrant anise-like qualities of the Sambuca are a lovely complement to the chocolate. The cookies are a bit like traditional crinkly Christmas cookies, but with a way more exciting flavor.

MAKES ABOUT 24

2 cups vegan chocolate chips

¼ cup plus 1 tablespoon coconut oil

2 tablespoons egg replacer powder

2 tablespoons evaporated cane juice

½ cup Sambuca

1¼ cups all-purpose flour

1 tablespoon baking powder

½ teaspoon sea salt

1¼ cups vegan powdered sugar

1 In a double boiler (or a small heat-proof bowl set over a simmering pot of water), melt the chocolate chips and ¼ cup coconut oil, stirring until all the chips are fully melted and the mixture is free of lumps. Once the chocolate mixture has fully melted, whisk into it the egg replacer powder, evaporated cane juice, and Sambuca.

2 In a medium bowl, whisk together the flour, baking powder, and salt. Pour the chocolate mixture into the flour mixture, and thoroughly mix, forming a very thin dough. Place the dough into a container and chill for 3 hours, until it sets up and stiffens.

3 When ready to bake the cookies, preheat the oven to 350°F. Line 2 baking sheets with parchment paper and lightly grease the paper with the remaining tablespoon coconut oil.

4 Place the powdered sugar in a small bowl. Portion out 24 to 26 balls of dough, each a heaping tablespoonful. Roll the portions of dough into perfect balls, and toss them one by one in the powdered sugar to coat them thoroughly. Arrange the balls, staggered 2 inches apart, on the prepared baking sheets. Bake for 10 to 12 minutes, until the surfaces show cracks. Allow the cookies to set for 4 minutes, then transfer to a wire rack and cool to room temperature.

RAW BROWNIES

These totally yummy dark chocolate brownies are thick and rich, and they have a fudgy top. I like to eat them straight up, pulse them into raw chocolate milk shakes, or crumble them on top of vegan ice cream sundaes. They're also a perfect travel snack, given that they are made out of healthy, nourishing ingredients; and they keep well, even at room temperature, because they have been made in a food dehydrator and not baked.

MAKES TWENTY-SEVEN 1 BY 3-INCH BROWNIES (GF)

For the brownie base

4 cups shredded coconut

6 cups cashew pieces

1⅓ cups agave nectar

⅔ cup cacao powder

¼ cup cacao nibs

1½ teaspoons sea salt

4 teaspoons pure vanilla extract

For the topping

⅔ cup agave nectar

½ cup cacao powder

½ teaspoon sea salt

2 tablespoons coconut oil

3 tablespoons cacao nibs

1 **Make the brownie base:** Place the shredded coconut in a food processor and process for 6 minutes, until it gives off its oil and becomes soft and doughy in appearance. Transfer to a mixing bowl.

2 Place the cashews in the food processor and grind them as fine as possible. (You may need to use a rubber spatula to scrape coarse pieces off the sides of the container, to achieve a consistently fine meal.) Add the cashew meal and the agave nectar, cacao powder, cacao nibs, salt, and vanilla to the bowl containing the coconut. Mix thoroughly, until the entire mixture is equally brown in color. On a dehydrator tray covered with a Teflex sheet, form the dough into a 1-inch-thick 9 by 9-inch square. Use wet hands to smooth the top and straighten the edges. Dehydrate the brownie base for 6 hours at 112°F.

3 **Make the topping:** Place the agave nectar, cacao powder, salt, and coconut oil in a small mixing bowl. Thoroughly mix the ingredients together with a fork.

4 Remove the brownie base from the dehydrator. Place a dehydrator tray (without the Teflex sheet) upside down on top of the brownie base. Carefully flip the brownie onto the new tray, and remove the original tray and Teflex sheet. Using an offset spatula, spread the topping evenly over the brownie. Sprinkle evenly with cacao nibs, and return the brownie to the dehydrator for 6 more hours. Cut the brownie into 3 rows and cut each row into nine 1 by 3-inch bars, or into whatever size you prefer.

Street Vegan

/ VARIATION /

Jalapeño Raw Brownies GF

One of my favorite snacks came about on the drive home from Midtown in the truck. I sliced fresh jalapeño and put slices of it on our raw chocolate brownies, and the heat and sweet were pretty addictive. So we started doing trays of brownies with sliced jalapeños dehydrated right onto the tops. SO. FREAKING. YUMMY. Chocolate loves spice.

If you want to try this, just remove the stems from a couple of jalapeños, and scatter thin slices onto the tops of the brownies before you dehydrate the topping. The denser the jalapeños on top, the more heat. I like to put enough on that just about every bite has a piece of jalapeño on it.

Raw Lemon-Blueberry Cheesecake

There's something really wonderful about relying on the natural richness of nuts to form a thick, creamy cheesecake. This one, in a lightly spiced pecan crust, gets its cheesecake-like tang from the lemon zest and juice and is topped with an easy-to-make blueberry sauce.

MAKES ONE 9-INCH CHEESECAKE (GF)

For the pecan crust
1½ teaspoons olive oil, for greasing the pan
½ cup pitted dates, soaked for 10 minutes in water and drained
2 tablespoons coconut oil
½ teaspoon ground cinnamon, plus extra for garnish if desired
¼ teaspoon ground nutmeg
¼ teaspoon sea salt
1⅓ cups pecan pieces

For the filling
2½ cups cashew pieces, soaked in water for 1 hour
½ cup coconut oil
⅔ cup pure maple syrup
1 teaspoon pure vanilla extract
Grated zest and juice of 2 lemons
1½ teaspoons umeboshi plum vinegar

For the blueberry sauce
1½ cups frozen blueberries
2 tablespoons pure maple syrup
Grated zest and juice of 1 lemon, plus extra grated zest for garnish
1 cup fresh blueberries, plus extra for garnish

1 **Make the crust:** Lightly grease a 9-inch pie pan with the olive oil.

2 Process the drained dates, coconut oil, cinnamon, nutmeg, and salt in a food processor for 60 seconds, until fairly smooth. Add the pecan pieces and process for about 90 seconds, until a coarse dough is formed. (Don't overprocess, or you will end up with the consistency of a nut butter.) With wet hands, press the dough into the oiled pie pan, forming a thin, even crust.

3 **Make the filling:** Drain the soaked cashews, and rinse them under cold water. Place the cashews and the coconut oil, maple syrup, vanilla, lemon zest and juice, and vinegar into a high-speed blender. Blend on high speed for 90 seconds, until completely smooth. (You may need to stop the blender a couple of times while blending, to incorporate any bits of cashew clinging to the sides of the pitcher.) Scrape the cheesecake filling into the crust, and smooth it down with a warm, wet offset spatula. Chill the cheesecake for 24 hours before serving; the center of the cheesecake should feel firm to the touch.

4 **Make the blueberry sauce:** Place the frozen blueberries, maple syrup, lemon zest, and lemon juice into a high-speed blender, and allow the blueberries to thaw for 30 minutes. Once the berries have thawed, blend on high speed for 45 seconds to form a smooth, thin sauce. Add the fresh berries to the blender, and pulse once or twice to evenly distribute them. Store the sauce in an airtight container in the refrigerator for up to 3 days.

5 When ready to serve, plate each slice of cheesecake with 2 tablespoons of the blueberry sauce and garnish with a sprinkle of cinnamon (if using), a few blueberries, and fresh lemon zest.

THE COVETED VENDY AWARDS are what Chef Mario Batali calls "the Oscars of street food." When I was building our truck, being involved in the Vendy Awards was one of my greatest hopes and dreams. We turned out to be the only vendor ever nominated four years in a row, taking home several awesome awards and turning on street meat enthusiasts to bold yummy vegan street food. The event is one of the best-coordinated "foodie" events of the summer: Assembled together on Governors Island, all of the nominated food trucks prepare a selection of signature items for a crowd of a couple thousand hungry, happy foodies.

We always bring out our secret-weapon menu items and debut new innovative desserts and donuts. Here are our menus from the Vendy Awards, along with some epic, behind-the-scenes madness from each year.

THE 2010 *Vendy* AWARDS

Our menu for the day:

Porcini-Crusted Tempeh, with Garlic Greens, Truffled Mashed Potatoes, and White Wine–French Mustard Dressing

Ginger Island Tofu with Coconut Mashed Yams and Fried Ginger (page 166), served with greens, Grilled Mango Salsa (page 260), and spiced pecans (see page 34)

Flaky Spinach Pie (page 92)

Chocolate Ganache–Stuffed S'mores Donuts (page 248)

We'd been warned that, if we missed our ferry, we would not be able to get onto the island to compete, and sure enough, we got on the road later than expected. Racing to get there, we had to stop for gas. It was like a Nascar pit stop: super-fast, and the pressure was ON. But then I got back into the driver's seat and turned the key . . . No click. No ANYTHING. NOTHING. I could hear my heart falling out of my shirt and rolling away from the gas station in defeat. I called everyone I knew who knew anything about cars. But it was five A.M., and no one picked up.

Our team hovered over the engine block, scratching our heads and being extremely stressed, when an angel in the body of a mechanic pulled up. He did some stuff under the truck, and in a couple of minutes, had us started. I'm pretty sure I drove the truck about two hundred miles per hour that morning to get us to the ferry JUST in time.

THE 2011 *Vendy* AWARDS

Our menu for the day:

Red Bean–Tomato Tart with Habanero Whisky Sauce

Lemongrass Five-Spice Seitan (page 127)

Vanilla-Bourbon Crème Brûlée Donuts (page 246) made with Maker's Mark bourbon

Imagine hand-torching almost two thousand crème brûlée donuts, all while serving a killer plate of hot food to each person in an endless line. That's right: It's a pretty crazy process. Anthony was responsible for torching the donuts one by one ALL DAY, and after a few hours, he had entered some kind of sugar-torching hypnotic trance state. His pupils had transformed into swirling crème brûlée spirals . . . I doubt he will ever be the same again.

Our team was ON POINT that day—we were prepared, organized, relaxed, and totally blown away to take home the Maker's Mark Vendy Award. We used our acceptance speech as the official announcement that we would soon be serving New York City. Very exciting times.

THE 2012 *Vendy* AWARDS

Our menu for the day:

SWEETS: Roasted Chestnut Cake Donuts with Chamomile Glaze (page 237), Fresh Fig Pancakes with Chamomile–Blood Orange Syrup (page 30) served with Pine Nut Butter (page 255), and Macadamia–White Chocolate Twinkies (page 194)

SAVORIES: Gochujang Burger Deluxe (page 145); Smoked Mushroom Carpaccio over Greens, with Horseradish Mashed Potatoes (page 182), Fried Caperberries, and Spicy French Mustard Dressing

In 2012, we offered a "sweets plate" and a "savory plate," and everyone who came to our window wanted both. (We were no longer just the weird Jersey vegan truck with the yummy donuts.)

What's it like preparing sixteen hundred macadamia–white chocolate Twinkies, you ask? Well, they can only be made in novelty pans, eight at a time. Each pan takes about two minutes to fill, nine minutes to bake, eight minutes to cool, five minutes to remove and trim, five minutes to fill the cakes, and two minutes to glaze and pack them up. THERE! Eight Twinkies down, 1,592 to go!

We were among a small number of vendors nominated for the main category—after being in the Best Rookie and Best of New Jersey categories in years past, it was like being nominated for best picture. The main category is decided in two different ways: The panel of judges (mostly celebrity food people and Brooklyn rappers) decide who gets the Vendy Cup (it's like a thrift-store version of the Stanley Cup), and the general attendees vote for their favorite, the "People's Choice." So when we were awarded the 2012 Vendy People's Choice Award, it meant a great deal to us—that street food connoisseurs, at an event largely focused on "street meat," decided that our vegan organic food was the best in the city! In my opinion, the award was a win for animals, and for vegan cuisine's power to change mainstream culture.

We returned to the kitchen super-late but feeling victorious and exhausted. Our cleaning guy flaked out that night, so Michelle, our friend Doris, and I stayed up late into the night cleaning up, so we could be back out kicking ass the next day at the Red Bank farmer's market.

THE 2013 *Vendy* AWARDS

Our menu for the day:

Korean Barbecue Seitan (page 130) with homemade kimchi (see page 175), marinated greens, and smoked chile sauce (see page 130)

Lemon-Caper Grilled Oyster Mushrooms, with Parsnip Sage Bread Pudding, Fried Artichokes, and Roasted Chestnut Cream

Thai Barbecue Tempeh Tacos with Smoked Chile–Roasted Peanuts (see page 124), Pickled Thai Basil and Onions (see page 124), and Sriracha Mayonnaise (page 256)

Fresh Cranberry–Glazed Cake Donuts (see page 231)

Norberweiberberweiberhydrafab Donuts (White Chocolate–Glazed, Bourbon Hazelnut Ganache–Stuffed Donuts Dusted with Dirty Blonde Streusel)

In 2013, the Vendys' organizers said that we had received thousands of nominations, more than all the other vendors combined. We hustled hard and served a lot of gorgeous food, but this time, it wasn't enough to sway the judges for the cup. But we were proud to receive the Vendy HERO Award in recognition of our work in the aftermath of Hurricane Sandy.

While the Cinnamon Snail was safely parked in Red Bank, Hurricane Sandy crushed New Jersey and New York hard. We were not affected too badly, but we had friends who lost their homes to fire and flooding. Some neighborhoods in Queens and Staten Island looked like a bomb had fallen on them, and for months they were largely ignored by federal and state aid programs. Without immediate attention from disaster relief groups, or access to power or gas, some families burned debris to stay warm during the blizzard that came just a week after Sandy.

Once gas became available to us again, we knew what we had to do. We served up free hot meals in the worst-hit neighborhoods, and set up charging stations for people's phones. We didn't have much money or resources for outreach like this, but we figured we could go out a couple of times to help, to make sure all our food was being put to use for hungry people. Perhaps more nourishing to them than our hot food was the feeling that people cared, and the world hadn't forgotten them.

Then something magical happened: our fans set up a PayPal fund and donated like crazy to keep us going. Even weeks later, our customers were still donating to make sure we were able to provide food for those in need. People are really so good to each other, and have so much love. The outreach we were able to do was supported by others from all over the planet.

THE 2014 *Vendy* AWARDS

Our menu for the day:

Sage Tempeh Sausage Sliders with Fried Sage Leaves and Lavender-Roasted Shallots (page 137) with Niçoise Olive Tapenade (page 259) and Truffled Cashew Cheese (page 261)

Korean Barbecue Seitan Tacos (see page 130)

Beer-Battered Buffalo Cauliflower with Roasted Habanero Sauce, Pickles, Arugula, and Roasted Garlic–Dill Ranch Sauce

Vanilla-Bourbon Crème Brûlée Donuts (page 246)

After being nominated FIVE YEARS IN A ROW, at long last we were awarded with the coveted Vendy Cup. Standing on the stage in great suspense with the other nominees, I caught a glimpse of the piece of paper being handed to the MC. I thought I read "Cinnamon Snail" but really couldn't believe my eyes—until I heard them speak our name. I had dreamed of this day long before starting the truck, and 2014 had been a tough year—with a truck impounded and a hustle to raise $80,000 from our fans to buy a new truck. To tell the truth, there had been moments when I wasn't sure we'd even make it to the Vendys this year. Yet as we hoisted the glittering cup high, we felt like every broken generator and every parking ticket had finally paid off at last.

DONUTS

229   Master Raised Dough

230   Playing Dress-Up with Glazes and Toppings

    230   Vanilla, Coconut–Thai Basil

    231   Fresh Cranberry, Lemongrass Mango, Coffee Ice Cream Sundae

233   Cinnamon Snails

234   Chocolate Cake Donuts

235   Mexican Hot Chocolate–Glazed Twists

236   Roasted Chestnut Cake Donuts

238   Black Tea Twists

240   Peanut Butter–Chocolate Cheesecake Donuts and Snails

241   Donut Shop–Style Fritters

242   Suggested Fillings and Flavors for Fritters

    242   Bing Cherry Fritters, Plum Chestnut Fritters

    243   Cinnamon Apple Fritters, Blueberry–Pine Nut Fritters

245   Lavender Pear Fritters

246   Vanilla-Bourbon Crème Brûlée Donuts

248   Chocolate Ganache–Stuffed S'mores Donuts

WHAT HAPPENED TO DONUTS? I remember growing up and getting natural, fresh, warm donuts, made by a friendly, chubby man you could watch in the window. Now what? The rise of the industrial donut revolution, led by national and international franchise chains, has left its loveless mark on donut history.

Donut chains are some of the biggest individual consumers of factory-farmed eggs, and the industry standard is to fry donuts in hydrogenated frying shortening (because when it cools it solidifies, and the donuts *appear* to be less greasy). The loving dough-forming ritual has been reduced to a mechanical, automated system, where no love or friendliness could possibly be infused. It's as if there is an international plot to turn magical soft circles of doughy goodness into bad-time profit-driven death-circles.

As neighborhoods fell under the crushing foot of the corporate donut empire, the loving mom-and-pop donut shops became an endangered species. The last shops closed their doors, unable to keep up with the efficiency of factory equipment, the low cost of awful ingredients, and the onslaught of corporate marketing. It almost brings a tear to my eye when I think of the crappy factory-produced donuts in their brightly colored pastry-box coffins . . . The modern incarnation of the donut is, indeed, in a depressing condition. Will anyone fight back to save this classic American pastry from a seemingly bitter fate? We need a new generation of donut warriors to gather on the battlefield and fight for the survival of donut art!

The Cinnamon Snail is part of a growing army of traditional handmade-donut makers, striking back at the onslaught of commercial donut crappyness. We start with all organic ingredients, locally grown and milled flours, and fresh yeast, and we fry in organic oil. Instead of artificial colors and flavors, we produce our glazes with things like fresh berries, lavender flowers, lemon zest, and fair-trade cocoa. There is hope yet for the future of donuts. We are confident that one day, the trend of industrially produced donuts and chain stores will fade away, a faint memory of a bad dream. It's time to wake up and smell the coffee and the freshly made donuts!

It's natural to want to think about donut making in scientific terms, and there are a lot of subtle variables that can really make or break the quality of your finished donuts. That being said, I *don't* like to think about donuts in scientific terms. In fact, I really like to think of them as a result of some special kind of magic. You can't deny that there is some kind of alchemy occurring that transforms simple mundane ingredients into cloudlike orgasmic glazed happy-puffs. Donut making is beyond simple recipes; rather it is a foray into the pastry spirit world, where we can ride with our ancestors along rivers of steaming chocolate glaze.

UNIVERSAL DONUT MAGIC ATLAS:

THESE ARE THE VARIABLES YOU NEED TO BE AWARE OF, TO PERFECT AND TROUBLESHOOT YOUR DONUTS

FLOUR POWER

As your donuts rise, the leavening agents (yeast, baking powder, or baking soda) excrete tiny bubbles of gas as they get hot and interact with acids. The bubbles are held in by the elasticity of the dough, made from the protein (gluten) in the flour. The more gluten in the flour, the more it will be able to stretch around the growing gas bubbles (good thing), but it will also result in a chewier, tougher mouth-feel (bad thing). For my donuts, I recommend unbleached all-purpose flour, which has a medium amount of gluten.

A TIME TO SALT

In our recipes for yeast-raised donuts, salt is almost always added to the dough after the first rise. A small amount of salt is important to the overall flavor of the donut, but salt also makes it harder for the yeast to ferment the dough. By adding the salt later, we can use less yeast and still get the same amount of leavening.

WORK THAT GLUTEN

The gluten in the dough becomes more active when you work it—so work it, it's worth it! Yeast-raised doughs perform better when you knead them long enough to excite the gluten (usually just a few minutes). This helps make the dough puff up and keeps it from deflating during handling.

Cake donuts (leavened with baking soda and baking powder) are the opposite, especially when you plan to use a donut dropper (see page 226) to shape them. The cake donut batter gets gloopy and stringy from too much mixing and then drops unevenly, creating badly shaped donuts with a breadier mouthfeel. For cake donuts, I recommend mixing them only enough to thoroughly combine the ingredients.

BENCH TIME

With cake donuts, let the dough rest for at least twenty to thirty minutes before dropping the donuts into hot oil. The resting time allows the liquid ingredients to hydrate the flour, making the dough silky and more workable; and produce nicely formed donuts. We routinely make cake donut dough in large batches in advance, so go ahead, pop some into your freezer. Then you can easily make donuts for me to eat if I sleep over at your house unannounced.

THE BENCH ITSELF!

If you start making donuts regularly, you should have a nice work surface to roll and form the donuts on. I work on a thick, sturdy wooden butcher block—take good care of it, and it will reward you as your favorite donut-making assistant. You will of course be able to roll on any surface, but if you have stainless-steel countertops, the dough slides around a lot as you work. To remedy that, get a thick piece of canvas to put on your

table. Lightly floured, the canvas surface will provide just enough traction to prevent the dough from sliding all around.

DROPPING DONUTS LIKE THEY'RE HOT

The cutter we use for filled donuts is a three-inch donut cutter, and for normal ring-shaped donuts, we use a three-inch cutter with a three-quarter-inch hole in the middle. Wait, you don't have a cutter?!? It's okay, just use a glass or biscuit cutter with a similar diameter.

For cake donuts, you can roll and cut the dough (for a more traditional crusty donut) or drop the dough into the hot oil with a donut dropper (for a smoother cake-like donut). I prefer the dropped cake donuts, which absorb less oil and have a more appealing shape. It's not necessarily feasible for everyone to own a donut dropper if you're not making donuts frequently (we hope you aren't— at least for your waistline's sake). All of the cake donut recipes here create loose dough more suitable for a donut dropper, but if you want to make them as roll-and-cut donuts, reduce the amount of liquid just enough to get a rollable, thicker dough.

GOT SOMETHING TO PROOF?

Proofing can really make or break the end result of your yeast-leavened donuts. Once you've let the yeast ferment throughout the body of the dough, you form the donuts and give them a final chance to rise. This stage really determines how airy and pillowy your donuts are going to get. Proofing should be done in a warm, humid environment to allow the donuts to puff up, without developing a skin from contact with the cool, dry air. (That skin would prevent the donuts from expanding fully and will also become a thin crust, boo.)

In our kitchen, we use a big proofing cabinet that surrounds our rising donuts with thick, moist air. At home you can use your oven as a makeshift proofer: Just keep the oven off, and place a pan of steaming water on the bottom of the oven. Place the donuts on baking sheets (perforated ones are best, but regular ones can work, too). Place the sheets of proofing donuts on the oven racks above the steaming water, and keep the oven closed (don't even peek). At average room temperature, proofing takes about thirty minutes, but if your house is very hot, it could be as short as eighteen minutes. If your house is very, very cold, TURN ON THE HEAT, silly!

FINE-TUNING (AND TIMING) YOUR FRYING

You want to have your donuts sitting in oil for the least amount of time possible: the longer the frying time, the more fat they are going to absorb. I recommend a temperature of 365°F for the recipes in this book. If you do not have a thermostatic fryer, use a deep-frying thermometer and a watchful eye to regulate the temperature. Thicker donuts like our twists, filled donuts, or fritters take longer than regular donuts because they contain more dough, and you want to be sure the core gets thoroughly cooked. Always check one donut (let's call it the sacrificial donut) for doneness by pulling it apart and making sure the inside is fully cooked.

STORING DONUTS: DON'T

No. Just no. Eat them while they are fresh and awesome. Don't even try to save donuts to eat the next day. Ever had a day-old bagel? Day-old donuts are even worse. DON'T. DO. IT. Got leftover fresh donuts? Make your neighbors, mail carrier, tollbooth attendant, and everyone you know happy. (As far as storing them for a few hours, though, a paper or cardboard box is best. Do not store donuts in airtight containers or under refrigeration.)

PASTRY CRIMES

When I first got the Cinnamon Snail running, I ran the truck in Hoboken. Hoboken had some annoying parking laws that made it tough for food trucks (for example, moving the truck after EVERY sale), and when the police chose to enforce the laws, it made operating very difficult.

One slow Sunday morning, a policeman came and made me move the truck. Within five minutes of finding a new spot, he was back and already getting irritated. He gave me a ticket and told me that he could keep writing me tickets all day if I kept moving and serving people. It was a bummer, so I started packing up. But packing up a commercial kitchen on wheels takes time, and he was back within ten minutes, really mad now that I wasn't gone yet. He felt like I was being a smart-ass when I asked him to clarify the law a little to me, because it seemed really unclear. The officer gave me two more tickets and followed me as I drove out of town. I didn't leave town immediately, though: Instead, I boxed up all of my pastries and went to the police precinct and gave them to the police to enjoy (I make a regular habit out of doing this, even to this day).

A couple of days went by, and I felt like Hoboken was going to be a volatile place to operate in; and I didn't know what to expect as far as police harassment was concerned. I had been left with such a bad taste in my mouth about this police officer, so I decided to go to the police station to talk to him. I let the officer know that I was sorry if it had seemed like I was giving him a hard time the day he ticketed me. I was super-friendly, and immediately I could feel the tension clear. He told me how bad he had felt when he had returned to the station and helped eat the donuts I had given them.

At a later date, I was serving food on the Hoboken waterfront, and I saw a cop car pull up to the truck. Immediately my heart sank, figuring I was in for more ticketing and problems. The officer who had ticketed me previously came and stood on our line. He bragged to our other customers about how good our donuts were, and when his turn at the window came, he ordered some pastries with a smile. I started to see him more often at our truck, and I watched his choices evolve from pastries into tofu sandwiches and spinach pies. Every week, he would bring new policemen to the truck with him. I talked with him on slow days about his rough childhood and his difficult life, as I served him vegan food on Hoboken's scenic waterfront.

These are the customers of ours who drive me the most to continue running our truck. I watch them over time growing and evolving toward peace, driven in some small part by the influence of our food.

master raised dough

This dough forms the base to a very wide variety of donuts we prepare, as well as our Cinnamon Snails (page 233). Take donuts made with this dough and use any glaze on them that you find in this book. (This recipe is followed by a handful of our favorite glazes.) Or use new creative glazes and toppings to make your own fun variations. Since the dough gets rolled and cut (rather than dropped through a depositor), you can work some additions straight into the dough. Try kneading in chopped plums and fresh lavender, ribbons of caramel and ground dark chocolate, or ground pistachios and sliced fresh rose petals. Enjoy finding new ways to enhance this versatile, tried and tested dough.

MAKES ENOUGH DOUGH FOR 30 DONUTS

2 cups unsweetened soy milk

½ cup canola oil, plus more for frying the donuts

4½ teaspoons active dry yeast

½ cup evaporated cane juice

4½ cups all-purpose flour, plus extra for the work surface

½ teaspoon sea salt

½ teaspoon baking powder

½ teaspoon baking soda

1 In a large pot over low heat, warm the soy milk and canola oil to 95°F. Pour the warmed soy milk and oil into a large bowl. Sprinkle on the yeast, and sprinkle the evaporated cane juice on top of the yeast. Allow the yeast to activate for 5 minutes, until it foams up. Add the flour and knead together on a floured work surface for about 90 seconds to form a smooth dough. Place the dough in a medium bowl and allow the dough to rest, covered, for 1 hour, until the dough has just about doubled in size. (If the room temperature is cool, allow for slightly more time.)

2 Transfer the dough onto a floured work surface, and for 3 minutes, knead in the salt, baking powder, and baking soda. If you are using this dough to make one of the recipes in this book for filled donuts, cinnamon snails, or fritters, stop here!

3 To make plain raised donuts: Lightly dust a baking sheet with flour. Roll the dough out into a ½-inch thickness on a lightly floured surface. Cut with a 2½ - to 3-inch donut cutter and transfer the circles of dough to the floured baking sheet. Reroll any scraps to use up all the dough to form more donuts. Place the donuts in a proofer for 25 minutes, until they have puffed up (or use your home proofing technique, see page 226). At this point, the sides will be rounded (rather than straight from when they were first cut) and the donuts will have increased in size.

4 Fill a deep fryer or a deep-sided frying pan with 2 to 3 inches of canola oil and heat the oil to 360°F. Working in batches to prevent crowding, fry the proofed donuts for 2½ to 3 minutes on each side. Check the first donut with a knife to ensure that the center has cooked through perfectly (it should be risen and no longer doughy, without the outside being overcooked).

5 Drain and cool the donuts on a baking sheet lined with paper towels. Finish with any glaze and topping you like.

Playing dress-up WITH Glazes and Toppings

Don't just send your donuts to the ball wearing ordinary mothball-scented pajamas! Here are some ways you can dress up your donuts, to make them extra fun and exciting. Let the glazes inspire you, and try different combos, different herbs, extracts, or fruit to make your own flavors. (Each of these glazes makes enough for about 3 dozen donuts.)

Vanilla (GF)

This is the white glaze we use on our Vanilla-Bourbon Crème Brûlée Donuts (page 246), Cinnamon Snails (page 233), plain glazed donuts, and so many other yummy treats. This is a nice, simple recipe that you can tweak into any kooky glaze idea you fancy by adding flavors to it, or by changing the liquid (try replacing the soy milk with an equal amount of apple cider, flavorful tea, coconut milk, or whatever you love the most).

¾ cup unsweetened soy milk
1¼ teaspoons pure vanilla extract, or ½ teaspoon vanilla beans
6 cups vegan powdered sugar

In the bowl of a stand mixer fitted with the whisk attachment, combine the soy milk, vanilla, and powdered sugar and whisk until smooth. Use immediately, or store in an airtight container in the refrigerator for up to 3 weeks. Before using, gently warm in a double boiler to just above room temperature.

Coconut–Thai Basil (GF)

Seems like an unlikely combo, but the coconut milk and fresh Thai basil in the glaze, and the giant flakes of toasted coconut, make for a donut with really delicious aromas, textures, and flavors.

¼ cup chopped fresh Thai basil leaves
½ cup coconut milk
1 star anise seed (not the whole star, just 1 individual point)
½ teaspoon coconut extract
6 cups vegan powdered sugar
½ cup toasted coconut chips (in big flake pieces, not dried shreds)

Place the Thai basil, coconut milk, star anise, and coconut extract in a small saucepan and bring to a boil over medium heat. Turn the heat off, and allow the mixture to cool to room temperature. Blend the cooled liquid in a blender for 40 seconds on high, then pour the pureed liquid into the bowl of a stand mixer fitted with the paddle attachment and add the powdered sugar. Mix for 3 minutes at low speed to form a smooth, light green glaze. Use immediately, or store in an airtight container in the refrigerator for up to 3 weeks. Before using, gently warm in a double boiler to just above room temperature.

To finish the donuts, dip them neatly in the coconut–Thai basil glaze and top with toasted coconut chips. To make them look just like the ones we serve on the truck, drizzle each donut with about 2 teaspoons Vanilla Glaze (at left) to create a pretty contrast between the white and green glazes.

Fresh Cranberry (GF)

During the fall and winter, when cranberries are available, we coat apple cider donuts with this awesome glaze. It's one of my favorites of all the donuts we offer! You can use this glaze on raised donuts or on Cinnamon Snails (page 233; try sprinkling dried cranberries on the dough before rolling the snails) to focus on two distinctly fall-winter flavors.

1 medium orange, cut into quarters, seeds removed
2/3 cup fresh cranberries
1/2 teaspoon ground nutmeg
1/2 teaspoon minced peeled fresh ginger
1/4 teaspoon sea salt
10 cups vegan powdered sugar

In a saucepan over high heat, bring the orange slices (peel and all), cranberries, nutmeg, ginger, and salt to a boil with 3/4 cup water. Once the mixture has come to a boil, cover the pan and turn off the heat. Allow to cool for 30 minutes. Blend the mixture in a blender for 40 seconds on high speed. Pour the pureed liquid into the bowl of a stand mixer fitted with a paddle attachment and add the powdered sugar. Mix for 3 minutes, until you have a gorgeous purple-red glaze with specks of citrus and cranberry skin. Use immediately, or store in an airtight container in the refrigerator for up to 3 weeks. Before using, gently warm in a double boiler to just above room temperature.

Lemongrass Mango

This exciting and fragrant glaze tops one of our summertime donuts. You can replace the mangos with an equal amount of any other fruit, such as chopped peaches, pitted lychees, or Asian pears.

1/2 cup freshly squeezed lime juice
1 fresh lemongrass stalk, trimmed (outer layers removed) and chopped into 6 to 8 pieces
1 cup chopped mango (fresh or frozen)
2 tablespoons agave nectar
1/4 teaspoon ground cardamom
8 cups vegan powdered sugar

In a saucepan over high heat, heat the lime juice, lemongrass, mango, agave nectar, and cardamom. Once the mixture comes to a boil, cover the pan and turn off the heat. Allow to cool for 30 minutes. Blend the cooled liquid in a blender for 60 seconds on high speed. Pour the pureed liquid into the bowl of a stand mixer fitted with the paddle attachment and add the powdered sugar. Mix for 3 minutes, until the glaze is smooth and free of lumps.

Coffee Ice Cream Sundae

We debuted these donuts in late spring 2013. We thought the glaze and topping were perfect for Chocolate Cake Donuts (page 234), but these enhancements could rock pretty hard on raised donuts, too.

3/4 cup strong black coffee, cooled
1 tablespoon agave nectar
1/2 cup Dutch-process cocoa powder
7 cups vegan powdered sugar
8 sugar cones (ice cream cones), smashed
1/3 cup chopped vegan dark chocolate chips
3 tablespoons crushed espresso beans
1 cup chocolate glaze (see page 248)

In the bowl of a stand mixer fitted with the paddle attachment, combine the coffee, agave nectar, cocoa, and powdered sugar and mix on medium speed for 3 minutes, until a smooth, thick glaze forms. In a separate bowl, combine the smashed cones, chopped chocolate chips, and crushed espresso beans.

To glaze the donuts, warm the chocolate glaze over a double boiler to 100°F. Dip the donuts in the coffee glaze, top liberally with the cone-chocolate-coffee topping, and finish with a light drizzle of chocolate glaze.

Cinnamon Snails

These are our classic breakfast buns and the buns for which our truck is named. Cinnamon buns have a spiral, snail-shell shape to them, which is why some people call them cinnamon snails. People ask us so frequently about the truck's name. The truth is, we used to make these pastries for the farmer's market before we started the truck, and we thought the name was cute. That's pretty much the whole story . . . But then a Sasquatch snatched up all the puppies, and we had to save the day by riding on a giant cybernetic snail dousing the bad-guy Sasquatch with cinnamon, until he stopped being mean and did a lot of giggling, and we all ate cupcakes, and yayyyy!

MAKES 12

Vegetable oil, for greasing the pan
All-purpose flour, for rolling the dough
1 batch of Master Raised Dough
     (page 229)
½ cup melted vegan margarine (such as
     Earth Balance)
¼ cup evaporated cane juice
¼ cup ground cinnamon
2½ cups Vanilla Glaze (page 230)

1 Line a baking sheet with parchment paper and lightly oil the paper with vegetable oil.

2 On a floured work surface, roll the dough out into a rectangle ½ inch thick by 16 inches wide by 20 inches long. Brush the surface of the rectangle with the melted margarine. Sprinkle the evaporated cane juice and cinnamon evenly over the surface of the rectangle. Starting at the edge closest to you, evenly roll up the rectangle into a cylinder approximately 3½ inches in diameter.

3 Cut the roll crosswise into ¾-inch-thick slices. Place the slices at least 1½ inches apart on the baking sheet and allow to proof in a warm, humid environment for 15 to 30 minutes, until they have puffed to almost twice their original height.

4 Preheat the oven to 350°F.

5 Bake the proofed buns for 15 to 18 minutes, until lightly golden brown and no longer doughy to the touch. While still warm, brush the buns with 3 to 4 tablespoons of glaze apiece. Cinnamon snails are best if served warm and fresh from the oven, but they can be gently brought back to life if reheated in a toaster oven or in a covered skillet over low heat.

Chocolate Cake DONUTS

These donuts are like devil's food cake: rich, moist, dense, and sinfully chocolaty. There's a small amount of coffee in the batter, which helps accentuate the deep chocolate flavor without being noticeably coffee-ish. (If you have an aversion to coffee, you can substitute an equal amount of water.) Ms. Snail and I think chocolate cake donuts with Vanilla Glaze (page 230) are one of the yummiest desserts of any kind. If the simple pleasures in life sound too boring to you, though, you can glaze them with chocolate glaze (see page 248), coat them with ground chocolate cookies, and drizzle them with melted chocolate. (Note: This recipe requires a donut dropper to make.)

MAKES 24

2 tablespoons canola oil, plus more for frying the donuts

1 cup unsweetened soy milk

1 teaspoon apple cider vinegar

1 teaspoon pure vanilla extract

½ cup black coffee, cooled

¼ cup agave nectar

½ cup evaporated cane juice

2 cups all-purpose flour

1¼ cups Dutch-process cocoa powder

½ teaspoon baking powder

½ teaspoon baking soda

½ teaspoon sea salt

1 In the bowl of a stand mixer fitted with the paddle attachment, mix together the oil, soy milk, vinegar, vanilla, coffee, and agave nectar. Stop the mixer and add the evaporated cane juice, flour, cocoa, baking powder, baking soda, and salt. Mix on medium speed for 2 minutes to combine thoroughly into a smooth, thin dough.

2 Fill a deep fryer or a deep-sided frying pan with 2 to 3 inches of canola oil and heat the oil to 360°F. Fill a donut dropper with the batter and drop 3-inch donuts into the hot oil, working in batches to prevent crowding. Flip the donuts after about 90 seconds of frying, when bubbles appear throughout the uncooked side and when the sides of the donuts are becoming golden brown. Flip the donuts and fry for an additional 2 minutes on the second side. Remove the donuts from the oil and drain them on paper towels.

3 After the donuts are cool to the touch, glaze them and top them as desired and set them on a wire cooling rack for at least 8 minutes before serving.

Mexican Hot Chocolate-Glazed Twists

This is a lot of people's favorite donut that we offer on the truck daily. It's exactly like it sounds: chocolaty soft donut twisted with cinnamon and just a little heat. We use a mixture of cayenne, Mexican chili powder, and chipotle powder to provide a flavorful kick with just the right amount of bite.

MAKES 20

For the chocolate raised dough

4¼ cups unsweetened soy milk
1 cup canola oil, plus more for frying
5 teaspoons active dry yeast
1 cup evaporated cane juice
7 cups all-purpose flour, plus extra for the work surface
3 cups cocoa powder, sifted
1 teaspoon ground nutmeg
1 tablespoon sea salt
¼ cup ground cinnamon
¼ cup mixed chili powders (cayenne, Mexican chili powder, and chipotle powder)

For the Mexican hot chocolate glaze

1 cup cocoa powder, sifted
6 cups vegan powdered sugar
¾ cup unsweetened soy milk
2 teaspoons ground cinnamon
1 teaspoon mild chili powder

1 **Make the dough:** In a large pot over low heat, warm 4 cups of the soy milk with the canola oil just until warm to the touch. Sprinkle on the yeast, and sprinkle the evaporated cane juice on top of the yeast. Allow the yeast to activate for 5 minutes, until it foams up. Add the flour, cocoa, and nutmeg and knead together on a floured work surface for about 3 minutes to form a smooth dough. Place the dough in a medium bowl and allow to rest, covered, for 1 hour, until the dough has just about doubled in size. Transfer the dough to a floured work surface, and knead in the salt.

2 Roll the dough into a 10 by 20-inch rectangle, ½ inch thick. Brush the surface of the dough with the remaining ¼ cup soy milk and sprinkle it evenly with half of the cinnamon and half of the chili powder mix. Fold the rectangle in half the shorter way, and cut it into 1-inch-wide by 5-inch-long strips.

3 Lightly flour a baking sheet. Twist the strips 3 turns as you transfer them onto the baking sheet, pressing the ends down so the twists do not unravel. Place the sheet in a proofer for 25 minutes (or use your oven to proof, see page 226).

4 **Make the glaze:** In the bowl of a stand mixer fitted with a whisk attachment, beat together the cocoa powder, powdered sugar, soy milk, cinnamon, and chili powder until smooth. Keep the glaze warm in a double boiler.

5 Fill a deep fryer or a deep-sided pan with 2 to 3 inches of canola oil and heat the oil to 360°F. Working in batches, fry the proofed twists for 2 to 3 minutes on each side, cooking the insides without the outside getting too well done. Check the first twist with a knife to ensure that the center has cooked through. Twists take a little longer to fry than normal donuts due to their thickness. Transfer the finished twists to a cooling rack.

6 Dip both sides of the cooled twists in the warm glaze. Allow the glaze to set for 5 minutes. Dust with the remaining cinnamon and chili powder on both sides. Drizzle with glaze for a pretty finish.

Roasted Chestnut Cake Donuts
WITH CHAMOMILE GLAZE

There is something so laid-back and comforting about both chestnuts and chamomile: Both evoke such warm feelings, and their subtle flavors play really nicely together. We made these for the 2012 Vendy Awards, the year we won the People's Choice award. In addition to the chamomile glaze, we also drizzle these with a little Meyer Lemon Glaze (see page 245) for fun.
MAKES 30

For the chamomile glaze
5 cups vegan powdered sugar
½ cup strong chamomile tea, cooled
3 tablespoons agave nectar
1 teaspoon grated lemon zest
½ teaspoon sea salt

For the donuts
2 cups roasted chestnut meats
2¾ cups unsweetened soy milk
1 tablespoon apple cider vinegar
3 tablespoons egg replacer powder
¼ cup vegan margarine (such as Earth Balance)
1¼ cups evaporated cane juice
1 cup chestnut flour
2¾ cups all-purpose flour
2 teaspoons baking powder
2 teaspoons baking soda
¾ teaspoon sea salt
½ teaspoon ground nutmeg
Canola oil, for frying
3 tablespoons grated citrus zest (lemon, grapefruit, or orange), for garnish

1 **Make the chamomile glaze:** In the bowl of a stand mixer fitted with the whisk attachment, beat together the powdered sugar, tea, agave nectar, lemon zest, and salt until smooth.

2 **Make the donuts:** Blend the chestnuts, soy milk, vinegar, and egg replacer powder in a blender on high speed for 45 seconds. If the chestnuts haven't broken down completely, run for an additional 45 seconds to form a smooth puree.

3 In the bowl of a stand mixer fitted with the paddle attachment, cream together the margarine and evaporated cane juice. Add the chestnut puree and continue mixing for 2 minutes, until thoroughly combined. Stop the mixer and add the chestnut flour, all-purpose flour, baking powder, baking soda, salt, and nutmeg. Mix on medium speed for 2 minutes to combine into a smooth, thin dough.

4 Fill a deep fryer or a deep-sided frying pan with 2 to 3 inches of canola oil and heat the oil to 360°F. Using a donut dropper and working in batches to prevent crowding, drop 3-inch donuts into the oil. Flip the donuts after about 2 minutes of frying, when bubbles appear throughout the uncooked side and the sides of the donuts are becoming golden brown. Flip the donuts and fry for an additional 2 minutes on the second side. Remove the donuts from the oil and drain them on paper towels. Dip one side of the donuts into the chamomile glaze and garnish with the citrus zest.

BlacK Tea Twists

These are a fantastic donut to accompany tea. We made them for the first time when we were a finalist on Food Network's *Donut Showdown*, as part of a challenge to make three unique, Bollywood-inspired donuts. The other donuts we did were toasted pistachio custard donuts (with individual colored mandalas on each one), and also Medhu Vada (the savory South Indian donuts with spicy sambar, pickled lime, and curry leaves). Out of the three these twists were really a hit with the judges, and I love them a lot, too.

MAKES 24

For the tamarind-plum glaze
1 ripe plum, pitted and chopped
2 tablespoons unsweetened soy milk
1 tablespoon tamarind concentrate
1 tablespoon brown rice syrup
3 cups vegan powdered sugar

For the cardamom glaze
4 cups vegan powdered sugar
½ cup unsweetened soy milk
1 tablespoon agave nectar
¾ teaspoon ground cardamom
2 teaspoons rosewater

For the twists
4 cups mild black tea, cooled
Grated zest of 2 oranges
1 cup melted coconut oil
2½ teaspoons (one packet) active dry yeast
1 cup evaporated cane juice
9½ cups all-purpose flour, plus extra for rolling the dough
1 tablespoon sea salt
2 tablespoons unsweetened soy milk

3 tablespoons ground cinnamon
1 teaspoon ground cardamom
Canola oil, for frying

1 **Make the tamarind-plum glaze:** Place the plums, soy milk, tamarind concentrate, and brown rice syrup in a blender. Blend on high for 30 to 45 seconds, until the plums are totally broken down. Transfer the contents of the blender to a stand mixer fitted with a whisk attachment and whisk together with the powdered sugar until smooth.

2 **Make the cardamom glaze:** In the bowl of a stand mixer fitted with the whisk attachment, beat together the powdered sugar, soy milk, agave nectar, cardamom, and rosewater until smooth.

3 **Make the twists:** In a large saucepan over low heat, warm the tea, orange zest, and coconut oil to 95°F, or just until a little warm to the touch. Turn off the heat, sprinkle on the yeast, and sprinkle the evaporated cane juice on top of the yeast. Allow the yeast to activate for 5 minutes, until it foams up. Add the flour and salt and knead together on a floured work surface for about 4 minutes to form a smooth dough. Place the dough in a medium bowl and allow the dough to rest, covered, for 1 hour, until the dough has just about doubled in size. (If the room temperature is cool, allow for slightly more time.)

4 Transfer the dough to a floured work surface and knead together for 40 seconds into a smooth, workable ball. Roll the dough out into a ½-inch-thick, 10-inch-long rectangle, as wide as possible. Brush the surface of the dough with the soy milk and sprinkle evenly with the cinnamon and cardamom. Fold the rectangle in half the shorter way, and cut it into 1-inch-wide by 10-inch-long strips.

5 Lightly dust a baking sheet with flour. Twist the strips a few times, and transfer them onto the baking sheet. (Gently press the ends down, so that the twists do not unravel.) Place the sheet with the twists in a proofer (or in your oven, see page 226) for 20 minutes, until puffed and increased in size.

6 Fill a deep fryer or a deep-sided frying pan with 2 to 3 inches of canola oil and heat the oil to 360°F. Working in batches to prevent crowding, fry the proofed twists for 2½ to 3 minutes on each side. Check the first donut with a knife to ensure that the center has cooked through perfectly. The centermost dough should be risen and bready, without the outsides being overcooked. Transfer the finished donuts to a cooling rack to drain and cool.

7 Dip both sides of the cooled twists in the cardamom glaze. Drip off excess glaze before placing the twists on a wire cooling rack and allow the glaze to set for 5 minutes. Drizzle with the tamarind-plum glaze.

Peanut Butter-Chocolate Cheesecake Donuts and Snails

I always try to think of an extra element that can raise a food up a notch. These donuts and snails are made so by the filling for our Mini Peanut Butter–Chocolate Cheesecakes (page 204), which lets them ascend into decadent dessert hyperspace. We make these as donuts and snails, so I've given you the recipe for both. Either way, they are sure to please PB-CHOCO fiends like superstar Snail fan Abby "Mean" Bean (and her mommy).

MAKES 24 DONUTS OR 20 SNAILS

All-purpose flour, for rolling out the dough

1 batch of Master Raised Dough (page 229)

Canola oil, for frying

2 cups chocolate glaze (see page 248)

1½ cups chocolate ganache (see page 248)

1 batch of peanut butter–chocolate cheesecake filling (see page 204)

1 cup ground vegan dark chocolate chips, for garnish

½ cup chopped roasted peanuts (optional; for garnish)

1 cup Vanilla Glaze (page 230)

1 To make donuts: On a lightly floured work surface, roll out the dough until it is about ½ inch thick. Cut with a 3-inch biscuit cutter and transfer the circles of dough onto a lightly floured baking sheet. Reroll any scraps to form more donuts. Place the donuts in a proofer for 25 minutes (or proof in your oven, see page 226).

2 Fry the donuts: Fill a deep fryer or deep-sided pan with 2 to 3 inches of canola oil and heat the oil to 360°F. Working in batches, fry the proofed donuts for 2½ to 3 minutes on each side. Check the first donut with a knife to ensure that the center has cooked through. Transfer the finished donuts to a cooling rack.

3 Fill the donuts: Using both thumbs, create a crater in the center of each cooled donut on one side. Glaze the top side (with the cavity) of each donut with the chocolate glaze. Stuff the center of each donut with 1 tablespoon of the ganache, then top with 2 tablespoons of the peanut butter–cheesecake filling. While the glaze is still wet, garnish the donuts with the ground chocolate chips and the chopped peanuts, if using. Finish by drizzling the vanilla glaze over the garnishes.

4 To make snails: Line a baking sheet with parchment paper and lightly oil the paper. On a lightly floured work surface, roll the dough into a 16 by 20-inch rectangle, ½ inch thick, with a long edge facing you. Spread the peanut butter–cheesecake filling evenly over the surface of the dough. About 2 inches from the long edge of dough closest to you, evenly spread a line of chocolate ganache along the length of the dough. Starting at the same long edge, roll the rectangle into a cylinder 3½ inches in diameter. Cut the roll crosswise into ¾-inch-thick slices. Place the slices at least 1½ inches apart on the prepared baking sheet and allow to proof in a warm, humid environment for 15 to 30 minutes, until they have doubled in height.

5 Preheat the oven to 350°F. Bake the proofed snails for 15 to 18 minutes, until golden brown and no longer doughy to the touch. Drizzle each of the snails with about 2 tablespoons of each type of glaze, and garnish with the dark chocolate and peanuts (if using).

DONUT SHOP-STYLE FRITTERS

One of my favorite desserts in the world is the apple fritter from Ronald's Donuts in Las Vegas. It looks so gross, like a chopped-up baseball mitt. But don't be scared: This is the most heavenly fritter ever.

There are a couple of types of fritters out there, including fresh slices of fruit dipped in a thin batter; dropped batter–style fritters; and the holy grail of fritters, the old-timey donut shop fritters. When forming these fritters, keep the outer edges rough and irregular, and do NOT form them too thick—just an inch thick at most. They will get larger when they proof, and you don't want them so thick that they need to fry excessively to cook. Once you know what you are doing with fritters, allow yourself to play with them. Use whatever is seasonal and amazing. Let the fritters be a canvas to show off the best fresh fruit you can find. It makes a difference.

MAKES 16

All-purpose flour, for rolling out the dough
1 batch of Master Raised Dough (see page 229)
2 cups fresh chopped fruit, or filling of your choice (see suggestions on page 242)
3 tablespoons ground cinnamon (optional)
¼ cup evaporated cane juice (optional)
Vegetable oil, for frying
2 cups of your favorite donut glaze (see suggestions on page 230)
Grated citrus zest or other garnish of your choice (optional)

1 On a lightly floured work surface, roll the prepared dough out into a ½-inch-thick rectangle, 14 to 16 inches wide by about 20 inches long. Spread the fruit or fruit filling on the half of the dough closest to you. (If you are working with just plain chopped fruit or berries instead of one of the fillings listed below, you may want to add the cinnamon and evaporated cane juice. If your filling is very wet and messy, sprinkle on additional flour to dry up the filling.) Fold the plain half of the dough over the half with the filling on it, forming a narrow, long rectangle.

Using a knife or bench scraper, roughly chop up the dough into irregular inch-size squares.

2 Lightly dust a baking sheet with flour. Taking a handful (roughly ⅔ to 1 full cup) of the chopped dough, gently squeeze the dough together, and lightly press the handful down onto the prepared sheet pan. Make sure to leave the outer edges rough. Repeat with the remaining dough to make 16 fritters. Do not be tempted to press the fritters down into smooth, patty-shaped disks. Allow the fritters to proof for 15 to 20 minutes, until puffed and increased in size.

3 Fill a deep fryer or a deep-sided frying pan with 2 to 3 inches of vegetable oil and heat the oil to 360°F. Working in batches to prevent crowding, fry the fritters for 1 to 1½ minutes on each side, until golden. Drain on a wire rack. Test the first fritter with a knife to ensure that the internal dough is thoroughly cooked. Once the fritters are all fried, glaze them in warm thin glaze, and garnish as desired.

Suggested Fillings and Flavors for Fritters

The double-edged sword of fritter making is that the filling is partially exposed while the donuts fry. This means the pears or peaches or cherries you fill the fritters with will get nicely cooked and tender from being in contact with the oil. The downside is that you will lose small bits of fruit to the oil, as some pieces of fruit may float away while frying. To avoid too much of that, make sure the fillings you create aren't too loose, or just try one of the suggested filling and glaze combos that follow. Use the instructions for Donut Shop–Style Fritters (page 241) for all of these variations.

Bing Cherry Fritters (GF)

2½ cups fresh Bing cherries, pitted and coarsely chopped
Grated zest of 2 lemons, plus more for dusting if desired
1 tablespoon chopped fresh rosemary leaves, plus more for dusting if desired
3 tablespoons evaporated cane juice
3 tablespoons cherry jam
Vanilla Glaze (page 230), warmed
Ground cinnamon, for dusting (optional)

1 In a small mixing bowl, combine the cherries with the lemon zest, rosemary, and evaporated cane juice. Fill the fritters with this mixture before proofing.

2 In a separate bowl, mix the cherry jam thoroughly with the vanilla glaze and keep warm. Brush the finished fritters with the glaze. Top the fritters with a light dusting of cinnamon, or of lemon zest and chopped rosemary, if desired.

Plum Chestnut Fritters (GF)

4 fresh plums, pitted and chopped
1 cup chopped roasted chestnuts
¼ cup Sucanat
3 tablespoons slivovitz (plum brandy) or prune juice
1 teaspoon pure vanilla extract
¼ cup chestnut flour
Vanilla Glaze (page 230), warmed

For the filling, combine the plums, chestnuts, Sucanat, slivovitz, vanilla, and chestnut flour in a medium bowl. Fill the fritters with this mixture before proofing. Brush the finished fritters with the vanilla glaze.

Cinnamon Apple Fritters

2 tablespoons vegan margarine (such as Earth Balance)

3 apples of your choice, sliced

Grated zest and juice of 1 lemon

3 tablespoons evaporated cane juice

1 teaspoon molasses

2 teaspoons ground cinnamon, plus more for dusting

½ teaspoon ground nutmeg

2 tablespoons all-purpose flour

Vanilla Glaze (page 230), warmed

1 In a pan over medium heat, melt the margarine. When it is hot, sauté the apple slices, stirring, for 2 minutes. Remove the pan from the heat and add the lemon zest and juice, evaporated cane juice, molasses, cinnamon, and nutmeg, and toss together for an additional 2 minutes. Sprinkle the filling with the flour. Cool the apple filling to room temperature. Fill the dough with the filling before forming, proofing, and frying.

2 When the fritters have fried and cooled, coat with the vanilla glaze, and dust liberally with cinnamon.

Blueberry–Pine Nut Fritters GF

3 tablespoons extra-virgin olive oil

⅔ cup pine nuts

2 cups fresh blueberries

10 fresh mint leaves, coarsely chopped

3 tablespoons evaporated cane juice

1 tablespoon balsamic vinegar

¼ cup blueberry jam

Vanilla Glaze (page 230), warmed

1 Warm the olive oil in a saucepan over medium heat. Add the pine nuts and sauté for 2 to 3 minutes, stirring, until the pine nuts become evenly golden and fragrant. Add the blueberries, mint, evaporated cane juice, and balsamic vinegar. Simmer for a couple of minutes, until the outsides of the berries become cracked and softened. Remove from the heat and allow the filling to cool to room temperature. Fill the dough with the filling before forming, proofing, and frying.

2 Mix the blueberry jam with the vanilla glaze in a small bowl and keep warm. Brush the fritters with the thin glaze.

LaVENder Pear FritteRS
WITH MEYER LEMON GLaZE

This is one of my favorite fritters we offer on the truck. I really love the way lavender, pears, and lemon zest complement one another's delicate flavors.
MAKES 12

2 ripe pears, halved, seeded, and stemmed

2 tablespoons extra-virgin olive oil

1 tablespoon dried lavender flowers (or 1 tablespoon minced fresh lavender)

2 tablespoons freshly squeezed lemon juice

3 tablespoons Sucanat

1 batch of Master Raised Dough (page 229), prepared as Donut Shop–Style Fritters (page 241)

Vegetable oil, for frying

Meyer Lemon Glaze (recipe follows)

¼ cup minced candied lemon rind (optional; for garnish)

1 tablespoon grated lemon zest (optional; for garnish)

1 Slice the pears into ¼-inch-thick slices. In a saucepan, warm the olive oil over medium heat. Add the pears, lavender, lemon juice, and Sucanat to the pan. Cook for about 2 minutes, stirring, until the pears soften a little and the Sucanat dissolves. Remove the mixture from the pan and set it aside (chill it if you are not completing the recipe right away).

2 Fill the fritters with the pear filling, proof them, and fry them, then let them cool. Submerge the cooled fritters in the Meyer lemon glaze. Sprinkle the donuts with the minced candied lemon rind or fresh lemon zest, if desired, while the glaze is still wet. Allow the glaze to set before serving.

Meyer Lemon Glaze

MAKES ENOUGH FOR 12 FRITTERS OR 24 DONUTS

5 cups vegan powdered sugar

⅓ cup unsweetened soy milk

¼ cup store-bought Meyer lemon puree

Grated zest of 1 lemon

⅛ teaspoon ground turmeric

1 teaspoon pure vanilla extract

In the bowl of a stand mixer fitted with the whisk attachment, beat together the powdered sugar, soy milk, lemon puree, lemon zest, turmeric, and vanilla until smooth. Use immediately, or store in an airtight container in the refrigerator for up to 3 weeks. Before using, gently warm in a double boiler to just above room temperature.

VANILLA-BOURBON CRÈME BRÛLÉE DONUTS

We won the 2011 Vendy Award for these extra-yummy bourbon-spiked custard-filled monsters. What I love about them is the contrast in textures between the crisp, crunchy caramelized top and the soft custard filling. Yes, these are a bit of a pain to make, but they are one impressive dessert. Our crème brûlée donuts have become the gateway drug to veganism for many skeptical carnivores.

The bourbon provides a great woody flavor, but if you don't want to use it, you can replace it with an equal amount of coconut milk.

MAKES 24

3 cups coconut milk

½ cup bourbon (we use Maker's Mark)

¼ teaspoon sea salt

1 teaspoon pure vanilla extract

¼ cup plus 1½ cups evaporated cane juice

5 saffron threads

½ teaspoon agar-agar powder

All-purpose flour, for rolling out the dough

1 batch of Master Raised Dough (page 229)

Canola oil, for frying

1 batch of Vanilla Glaze (page 230)

1 **Make the custard:** Bring the coconut milk, bourbon, salt, vanilla, and the ¼ cup of evaporated cane juice to a boil in a 2- to 4-quart saucepan. Stir in the saffron and agar-agar powder and continue to cook for 5 minutes, whisking frequently. Remove the pan from the heat and allow the mixture to cool for 15 minutes. Whisk the mixture once more before pouring it into a plastic storage container. Chill the custard for at least 4 hours so it can thicken.

2 **Shape and fry the donuts:** Sprinkle a baking sheet with flour. On a lightly floured work surface, roll the dough out into a ½-inch thickness. Cut with a 3-inch biscuit cutter and transfer the circles of dough onto the baking sheet. (Reroll the dough and cut out more donuts as you go.) Place the donuts in a proofer for 25 minutes (or proof in your oven, see page 226).

3 Fill a deep fryer or a deep-sided pan with 2 to 3 inches of canola oil and heat the oil to 360°F. Working in batches, fry the proofed donuts for 2½ to 3 minutes on each side. Check the first donut with a knife to ensure that the center has cooked through perfectly. Transfer the finished donuts to a wire rack to drain and cool.

4 **Fill the donuts:** Once all the donuts are fried, use both thumbs to pinch out and widen a crater in the center of each donut on one side, being careful not to go through the other side of the donut. Brush the top side (with the cavity) with the vanilla glaze. Spoon a heaping tablespoon of custard filling into each donut center. Sprinkle each donut with 1 tablespoon of the remaining evaporated cane juice and carefully torch the top of each donut individually with a butane torch. The donuts are finished when the tops are evenly torched with a golden brown crust.

CRÈME BRÛLÉE VANDALISM

Back when I was a kid, I used to sneak out of my parents' house in the middle of the night to paint murals and otherwise vandalize New York City (yes, I know, I was a very bad little boy, and I'm sorry if that was your building and you didn't like my mural). I learned quickly that to avoid drips of paint, you need special spray can technique: If you want a more opaquely colored area, you need to keep the can moving and keep going back to apply more light layers of paint. The paint needs a moment to dry between dustings of sprayed paint particles, otherwise it pools up wet and starts dripping all over your nice mural.

The same technique goes for rocking a butane torch for the tops of crème brûlée: The heat from the torch melts the sugar and caramelizes it. If you don't keep the torch moving, the sugar melt unevenly, some parts becoming runny and deeply burnt while you try to get the sugar crystals around it to break down and melt. So be patient, keep a little distance from the donut, and keep moving the torch in circular patterns around the surface of the pastry to obtain a perfect golden finish.

Chocolate Ganache-Stuffed S'MORES Donuts

We made these donuts for our first year as a finalist at the Vendy Awards. Years later, they continue to be one of our customers' favorites among our special filled donuts. We use vegan marshmallows and grahams by Sweet & Sara, a rocking vegan marshmallow company based in New York City, and our own extra-rich vegan ganache.

MAKES 24

For the chocolate ganache
1 cup coconut milk
3 tablespoons brown rice syrup
2 cups vegan chocolate chips

For the donuts
All-purpose flour, for rolling out the dough
1 batch of Master Raised Dough (page 229)
Canola oil, for frying
1½ cups mini vegan marshmallows (or chopped vegan marshmallows)
1 cup smashed vegan graham crackers
½ cup Vanilla Glaze (page 230; optional)
½ cup ground vegan dark chocolate chips (optional)

For the chocolate glaze
¾ cup sifted Dutch-process cocoa powder
6 cups vegan powdered sugar
¾ cup unsweetened soy milk

1 **Make the ganache:** In a large saucepan set over medium heat, bring the coconut milk and brown rice syrup almost to a boil. Place the chocolate chips in a heat-proof bowl. When the milk starts bubbling and rising, pour it on top of the chocolate chips, and vigorously whisk together until the chips have completely broken down and the mixture is totally smooth. Chill the ganache for at least 3 hours. Use immediately, or store in an airtight container in the refrigerator for up to 10 days.

2 **Roll out the donuts:** Lightly dust a baking sheet with flour. On a lightly floured work surface, roll the dough into a ½-inch thickness. Cut with a 3-inch biscuit cutter and transfer the circles of dough onto the floured baking sheet. Reroll any scraps to form more donuts. Place the donuts in a proofer for 25 minutes (or proof in your oven, see page 226).

3 **Make the chocolate glaze:.** In the small bowl of a stand mixer fitted with the whisk attachment, beat together the cocoa powder, powdered sugar, and soy milk.

4 **Fry the donuts:** Fill a deep fryer or deep-sided frying pan with 2 to 3 inches of canola oil and heat the oil to 360°F. Working in batches to avoid crowding, fry the proofed donuts for 2½ to 3 minutes on each side. Check the first donut with a knife to ensure that the center has cooked through perfectly. Transfer the finished donuts to a cooling rack to dry and cool.

5 **Fill the donuts:** Once all the donuts are fried, using both thumbs, pinch out and widen a crater in the center of each donut on one side. Glaze the top side (the side with the cavity) of each donut with chocolate glaze. Stuff the center of each donut with 2 tablespoons of the ganache. While the glaze is still wet, place 5 or 6 marshmallows atop each donut and sprinkle with crushed grahams. Drizzle 1 tablespoon of the vanilla glaze and sprinkle 1 tablespoon of the ground chocolate chips, if using, onto each donut. For ultimate-maximum-incredible-campfire bonus points, do what we do, and lightly toast the marshmallows on top with a butane torch.

SARA'S BOMB 'MALLOWS

Sweet & Sara was the first commercially available vegan marshmallow on the market. Run by Sara Sohn and her amazing Korean family, this is a company totally committed to bringing the vegan lifestyle to the masses. Sara and her family are such a huge inspiration to me: She is probably the hardest-working vegan anywhere. I have watched S&S go from a tiny boutique operation to being distributed to almost every Whole Foods in the country, to mainstream supermarkets, and now to international locations. I am so, *so* proud to know Sara and her family, and to help support her fantastic business. We go to pick up the 'mallows in person with our kids. What could possibly be more exciting for a vegan kid than visiting an all-vegan-marshmallow factory!?! IT'S HEAVEN.

WASABI
MAYONNAISE

CHIPOTLE
MAYONNAISE

HABANERO
AIOLI

THE
Saucy Stuff

253 Ginger Stout Syrup

253 Red Wine Syrup

254 Perfect Homemade Applesauce

254 Pumpkin Brown Butter

255 Pine Nut Butter

256 Easy Yummy Flavored Mayonnaises

    256 Chipotle Mayonnaise

    256 Wasabi Mayonnaise

    256 Sriracha Mayonnaise

257 Habanero Aioli

257 Black Sesame Gomasio

259 Roasted Tomatillo Salsa Verde

259 Niçoise Olive Tapenade

260 Grilled Mango Salsa

261 Truffled Cashew Cheese

262 Habanero Apricot Glaze

HUGE LONG LINES HAVE BECOME OUR SPECIALTY, but in the beginning, we learned to deal with endless lines of people the hard way, at some pretty kooky events.

Over the years we've taken part in a series of food truck festivals, called Parked!, put together by MeanRed productions, and they're always an adventure. After the lease was lost for the original Parked! property, once located in an abandoned industrial yard with a scenic view of the contaminated Gowanus Canal, the promoters moved the event to Governors Island in 2010. I convinced my friend Sean to tag along and be my window person—he didn't have restaurant or cooking experience, but he was really good with people, and I was really in a jam.

As it turned out, that event was probably the most infamous food truck festival in New York City history. The island was crowded with more than ten thousand people. Ferries only appeared twice an hour, and the waiting time to get on a ferry was almost two hours long. Upon arriving, you faced more hour-long lines to get into the area with the food trucks. The organizers had done an epic job of promoting the event, but most vendors were selling only beverages or light snacks,

leaving us and a few other trucks as the sole option offering actual meals. Every vendor was SLAMMED with heavy wait times to order and deliver the food, and most sold out and were left to face the angry, hungry customers. At one point our line must have had two hundred people on it. And at that exact moment, a health inspector started going around to all of the trucks. We had to completely stop serving the line to show him our paperwork.

Every day since then, Parked! is the benchmark to which we compare our busiest days. At the end of that day, there wasn't a single piece of food left on the truck, and the inside of the truck looked like a bomb had gone off in it. But in spite of it all, people had lots of good things to say about our food, and the event started a buzz about our little truck. Sean rocked so hard on the truck that day, and he became one of my first full-time employees. If he could survive Parked!, everything else would be a breeze.

Ginger Stout Syrup

The deep malty flavor of stout creates a decadent syrup that performs a sensuous, intoxicated dance with bourbon candied hazelnuts (see page 28). You can use any favorite vegan stout or porter for this syrup. Not sure if a beer is vegan? Look it up on Barnivore.com to be sure (quite a lot of beers are made with FISH BLADDERS—yuck!).

MAKES 1 PINT

1 tablespoon ground ginger

1 tablespoon finely grated peeled fresh ginger (grated with a Microplane)

1 teaspoon ground cinnamon

½ teaspoon freshly ground black pepper

One 12-ounce bottle of stout or porter

2 cups pure maple syrup

Place the ground ginger, grated ginger, cinnamon, and pepper in a large saucepan. Whisking continuously to avoid clumping, slowly pour in the stout and maple syrup. Bring the mixture to a boil over medium heat, then turn the heat down to low and simmer, uncovered, for 20 minutes, until the syrup reduces to the desired thickness. Store in a bottle or airtight container in the refrigerator for up to 3 weeks.

Red Wine Syrup

Because of its deep burgundy color and complex sophisticated flavor, this syrup is lovely on a Valentine's breakfast, to plate a romantic dessert, or poured all over your dad from a barrel that's been carefully booby-trapped to the top of his golf cart.

MAKES 1 PINT (GF)

1 cup red wine

1 cup brown rice syrup

2 tablespoons balsamic vinegar

2 tablespoons unsulfured molasses

¼ teaspoon freshly ground black pepper

Bring the red wine to a boil in a small pot set over medium heat. Once boiling, lower the heat to medium low and allow the wine to reduce for 5 minutes. Stir in the rice syrup, vinegar, molasses, and pepper, remove from heat, and let cool. Use the syrup immediately, or store in an airtight container in the refrigerator for up to 2 weeks.

PERFECT HOMEMADE APPLESAUCE

To make perfect applesauce, you need only two things: a food mill and great apples. Opt for a crisp local apple that has a strong balance of sweet and tart. I prefer Braeburn, Honeycrisp, or Pink Lady apples for applesauce. My mother uses Empire, which produce a beautiful pink applesauce from the color of the skins. Empire and Honeycrisp aren't too easy to come by, though, so pick your favorite or a combination of varieties.

MAKES ABOUT 2 CUPS (GF)

5 apples of your choice
Dash of pure maple syrup or pinch of ground cinnamon (optional)

1 Quarter the apples, leaving the stem and seeds in. Place the cut apples and 2 tablespoons water into a large pot over medium heat and cover. Heat the mixture over a medium flame for about 8 minutes until it is actively steaming, then lower the heat to a simmer and allow the apples to steam for 10 minutes.

2 Place a food mill over a bowl and dump the apples and any remaining liquid into it. Grind the apples through the food mill and taste; if you desire, you can add a tiny dash of maple syrup or a pinch of cinnamon. You can store the applesauce in an airtight container in the refrigerator for up to 4 days. I like to warm it up before serving it, and add a dash of cinnamon on top.

PUMPKIN Brown Butter

This is a fall-themed pancake butter that's awesome on Beer-Battered French Toast (page 46), on waffles, or even on top of a hot bowl of oatmeal. It's lightly sweet and spiced, almost like a melty pumpkin pie.

MAKES ½ CUP (GF)

6 tablespoons melted coconut oil
2 tablespoons canned pumpkin puree
2 tablespoons pure maple syrup
½ teaspoon ground cinnamon
¼ teaspoon ground nutmeg
¼ teaspoon sea salt

Place the coconut oil, pumpkin puree, maple syrup, cinnamon, nutmeg, and salt in a high-speed blender and blend on high for 60 seconds, until smooth and emulsified. Pour into an airtight container and chill for at least 3 hours. (The butter can be kept refrigerated for up to 2 weeks.)

 254

Pine Nut Butter

We sneak this buttery condiment onto a bunch of special pancakes, French toasts, and waffles that we serve on the truck. The ground toasted pine nuts contribute an almost caramel-like richness that makes the topping fantastic. Also, because pine nuts complement berries so nicely, it's a natural accompaniment for pancakes and waffles that are bursting with fresh blueberries, raspberries, or figs.
MAKES 1 CUP (GF)

¼ cup pine nuts

⅓ cup coconut oil

½ cup vegan margarine (such as Earth Balance)

¼ teaspoon sea salt

¼ teaspoon ground cinnamon

1 teaspoon agave nectar

1 In a dry sauté pan set over medium-low heat, toast the pine nuts until lightly golden all over, about 6 minutes. Transfer them to the empty bowl of a food processor.

2 Add the coconut oil, margarine, salt, cinnamon, and agave nectar to the now-empty sauté pan and melt them together over medium heat.

3 Pulse the toasted pine nuts in the food processor several times to yield coarse fragments. Stir in the coconut oil mixture, then scrape out the food processor's contents into a small bowl. Refrigerate and let cool until the fats have solidified (about 1 hour). Using a rubber spatula, mix everything together (the pine nuts may have settled during the initial chilling). Use the pine nut butter immediately, or store in an airtight container for later use. (The butter will keep in the refrigerator for months, if it isn't eaten well before then.)

Easy Yummy Flavored Mayonnaises

Yummy flavored mayonnaise, you complete so many sandwiches with your rich, mouthwatering goodness. You are great as a dip for homemade French fries or roasted sweet potatoes. Even better, you make spicy aiolis for spreading on ridiculous tacos—oh baby. Vegan mayonnaises of the world, will you marry me? I think we can get married legally somewhere in the Midwest. Is that okay?

Chipotle Mayonnaise (GF)

MAKES 1 PINT

Here is a spicy mayonnaise that can be made quickly from scratch, without relying on store-bought vegan brands. The chipotle powder adds a smoky flavor that goes great on grilled food, as a condiment on tacos, or slathered on bread for Mexican-inspired tortas.

One 12-ounce block silken tofu
4 teaspoons brown rice vinegar
1 tablespoon tomato paste
2 teaspoons chipotle powder
1 teaspoon agave nectar
1 tablespoon mirin
½ teaspoon sea salt
¼ cup extra-virgin olive oil

Break the silken tofu into a few small pieces and place it into a high-speed blender along with the rice vinegar, tomato paste, chipotle powder, agave nectar, mirin, and salt. Blend at high speed for 60 seconds. Continue blending at high speed while drizzling in the olive oil until fully emulsified, over the course of 30 seconds. Use immediately, or store in an airtight container in the refrigerator for up to 5 days.

Wasabi Mayonnaise (GF)

MAKES 1 PINT

This has just enough wasabi for a horseradishy punch, without making your glasses fall off. The mirin and rice syrup help keep everything cool and balanced.

1¾ cups vegan mayonnaise
3 tablespoons natural wasabi powder
¼ cup mirin
2 teaspoons tamari
1 tablespoon brown rice syrup

In a medium bowl, rapidly whisk together the mayonnaise, wasabi powder, mirin, tamari, and brown rice syrup until smooth. (This mayonnaise will stay fresh for up to 3 weeks when stored in an airtight container in the refrigerator.)

Sriracha Mayonnaise (GF)

MAKES 1 PINT

Sriracha is a Vietnamese-Cambodian–inspired hot sauce with an addictive chile flavor and lots of bite. This mayonnaise is a great way to turn up the heat on Asian-style sandwiches such as banh mi, on our Thai Barbecue Seitan Ribs (page 124), or on the Chinese-style steamed buns in our Bangin' Bao (page 134).

2 cups vegan mayonnaise
¼ cup Sriracha
2 teaspoons evaporated cane juice

Combine the mayonnaise, Sriracha, and evaporated cane juice in a medium bowl. Store in an airtight container in the refrigerator for up to 3 weeks.

Habanero Aioli

Habaneros have an earthy flavorful heat that makes for a kick-ass sandwich condiment. This aioli also packs some cooked garlic, scallions, and carrots for a diverse and balanced flavor. Plum vinegar provides just the right amount of tanginess.

MAKES 1½ CUPS (GF)

¼ cup extra-virgin olive oil

1 medium habanero pepper, stem and seeds removed

6 garlic cloves

2 scallions, light green and white parts

¼ cup shredded carrot

¼ cup mirin

2 tablespoons brown rice vinegar

2 tablespoons umeboshi plum vinegar

1 teaspoon smoked paprika

½ block soft tofu, drained

1 Heat the olive oil in a small sauté pan over medium heat. Sauté the habanero pepper and whole garlic cloves in the hot oil, stirring frequently, for about 5 minutes, until the garlic becomes lightly golden in color. Stir in the scallions and shredded carrot. Continue sautéing for about 4 minutes, until the carrots soften. Add the mirin, rice vinegar, plum vinegar, and paprika. Allow the liquids to heat up and bubble, and then turn the heat off.

2 Pour the mixture into a high-speed blender. Crumble the tofu into the blender, and blend at high speed for 60 seconds to form a smooth puree. Scrape down the sides of the blender with a rubber spatula, and pulse again until everything is smooth and incorporated. Use immediately, or store in an airtight container in the refrigerator for up to 5 days.

Black Sesame Gomasio

Gomasio is a dry condiment made from toasted sesame seeds that tastes distinctly Japanese. It is a more flavorful, nutritious way to salt a finished dish. This one is great for adding a nutty, salty garnish to salads, stir-fries, soups, or our Gochujang Burger Deluxe (page 145).

MAKES ¼ CUP (ENOUGH FOR 4 BURGERS) (GF)

¼ cup black sesame seeds

½ teaspoon sea salt

¼ teaspoon ground cloves

¼ teaspoon cayenne pepper

Toast the sesame seeds, salt, cloves, and cayenne in a small sauté pan over medium-low heat, stirring for about 5 minutes, until the seeds are aromatic. Place the mixture into a blender and blend at high speed for about 40 seconds to form a powder. Use immediately, or store in an airtight container at room temperature for up to a month.

ROASTED TOMATILLO
SALSA VERDE

Roasted Tomatillo Salsa Verde

When roasted, the combination of tomatillos, jalapeños, and garlic forms a robust base for this salsa. It's simple to make, and it tastes great on nachos, tacos, grilled veggies, or sandwiches like our Blue Corn and Hemp Seed–Crusted Tempeh (page 140).

MAKES 1 CUP (GF)

3 tablespoons freshly squeezed lime juice

2 tablespoons extra-virgin olive oil

½ teaspoon sea salt

4 medium tomatillos, husked and cut into quarters

½ medium jalapeño pepper, stem and seeds removed

2 garlic cloves

⅓ cup chopped fresh cilantro leaves

1 teaspoon ground coriander

1 teaspoon ground cumin

1 Preheat the oven to 350°F.

2 In a small mixing bowl, combine the lime juice, olive oil, salt, tomatillos, jalapeño, and garlic. Place the ingredients in a small roasting pan and bake for 18 minutes. Allow to cool for 8 to 10 minutes.

3 Place the hot roasted vegetables into a food processor along with the cilantro, coriander, and cumin. Process for about a minute, until the mixture is free of any large chunks. Use immediately, or store in an airtight container in the refrigerator for up to 5 days.

Niçoise Olive Tapenade

The tapenade is made with tiny olives from the South of France and features Provençal flavors like lavender, fresh rosemary, and lemon. It's great on our Sage Tempeh Sausage Sliders (page 137), tossed with hot pasta, or as a stand-alone dip to serve with crackers, crudité, or bread.

MAKES 1 CUP (GF)

1½ cups pitted Niçoise olives (or other olive of your preference)

⅓ cup extra-virgin olive oil

Grated zest and juice of 2 lemons

½ teaspoon freshly ground black pepper

1 tablespoon minced fresh rosemary leaves

2 teaspoons dried lavender flowers

Place the olives, olive oil, lemon zest and juice, and pepper into a food processor and process for 2 minutes to form a mostly smooth olive paste. Add the rosemary and lavender, and continue to process for 20 seconds. Use immediately, or store in an airtight container in the refrigerator for up to 3 weeks.

Grilled Mango Salsa

This is a milder salsa that gets a sweet and smoky flavor from grilled mangos. It's great to serve at a barbecue (when you are firing up your grill anyway) as a dip for tortilla chips. It's also the bomb on top of our Ginger Island Tofu (page 166), completing the dish with its Caribbean flair.

MAKES 1 PINT (GF)

¼ to ½ medium habanero pepper, stem and seeds removed, minced

1 garlic clove, minced

2 tablespoons freshly squeezed lime juice

2 tablespoons tamari

3 tablespoons Sucanat (or other brown sugar)

3 tablespoons extra-virgin olive oil

2 medium mangos, not fully ripe

½ small red onion, cut into thick rings

½ medium red bell pepper, stem and seeds removed

¼ cup chopped fresh cilantro leaves

2 scallions, light green and white parts, finely chopped

Sea salt

1 Preheat an outdoor grill, stovetop grill, or grill pan.

2 In a mixing bowl, combine the habanero, garlic, lime juice, tamari, Sucanat, and olive oil. Remove the skin from the mangos, and cut the two halves of fruit from the pit of each.

3 Toss the skinned mango pieces, onion rings, and bell pepper in the marinade. With a slotted spoon, remove the mango pieces, onion rings, and bell pepper from the marinade, letting excess liquid drip back into the bowl. Reserve the marinade. Grill the mango and vegetables on all sides for 2 to 4 minutes to obtain dark grill marks all over. Return the grilled pieces to the bowl with the reserved marinade to cool for at least 30 minutes.

4 Remove the mango and vegetables from the marinade and chop them into pieces no bigger than ¼ inch, then transfer to a clean bowl. Discard any remaining marinade. Toss the cilantro and scallions into the bowl of chopped mango and vegetables. If you desire a less chunky salsa, pulse the salsa a couple of times in a blender or food processor. Season with salt to taste. Use immediately, or store in an airtight container in the refrigerator for up to 2 days.

tRuffLED CaSHEW CHeeSE

If you love truffles, you are going to want to use this spreadable cashew cheese all over everything. It's an addictive condiment for crudité, or just smeared on grilled bread to have with a salad. Because its sophisticated flavor pairs so nicely with sage and olives, it goes naturally on our Sage Tempeh Sausage Sliders (page 137). Best of all, when you use truffle oil, you get a really strong truffly flavor with just a few drops—better than spending all your savings on a king-size truffle!

MAKES 2 CUPS

2 cups unroasted cashew pieces, soaked in water for 20 to 30 minutes

¼ cup extra-virgin olive oil

2 tablespoons white miso paste

2 tablespoons umeboshi plum vinegar

3 tablespoons truffle oil

2 tablespoons chopped fresh basil leaves

1 teaspoon dried thyme

1 teaspoon asafetida

Drain the cashews, discarding the soaking water. Place the cashews into a blender along with the olive oil, miso paste, plum vinegar, truffle oil, basil, thyme, and asafetida and blend at high speed for 90 seconds to form a very smooth puree. (You may need to stop and scrape down the sides once or twice during the blending, to re-incorporate any stray pieces of cashew.) Use immediately, or store in an airtight container in the refrigerator for up to 4 days.

Habanero apricot Glaze

3 tablespoons extra-virgin olive oil

½ medium habanero pepper, stem and seeds removed

2 tablespoons minced peeled fresh ginger

¼ cup agave nectar

¼ cup brown rice vinegar

⅓ cup apricot preserves

Pour the olive oil into a small sauté pan set over medium heat. Place the pepper and ginger in the pan and cook, stirring, for about 2 minutes, until the ginger becomes golden. Add the agave nectar, vinegar, preserves, and ⅔ cup water and cook for 5 more minutes to soften the pepper. Transfer the mixture to a blender and blend on high speed for 30 seconds, until it forms a smooth glaze. Pour the glaze into an airtight container and chill until you're ready to serve. (Refrigerated, the glaze will stay fresh for up to 8 days.)

This is like duck sauce on PCP. I wish I could say that more often about more things . . . don't you want to live in a world where more things were like duck sauce on PCP? Well, now is your chance to make that world a reality! This sweet, spicy, gingery sauce is great on our Pan-Fried Kimchi Dumplings (page 73), spring rolls, or other dipable appetizers and snacks.

MAKES 1 CUP (GF)

ACKNOWLEDGMENTS

Making this book was a huge, huge, huge homework assignment for me for a couple of years, while I was also running the truck, teaching cooking and yoga classes, and trying to be a good dad and husband. This book wouldn't have been possible without the help, understanding, and encouragement from these folks and others:

Maha-high-five to Sri Dharma Mittra for inspiring me to share my knowledge of vegan cooking with the world.

I make chocolate sculptures of gratitude to the softest, snuggliest wife in the world, Ms. Chickpea "Ogilvie Home Perm" Smith, and bestow thankful mountains of vegan marshmallows to my kids, Yozin Dozzin and Deegie Stoogie, for putting up with me spending so many hours working on this book instead of snuggling and wearing a cape that says "Dad" on the back.

Well-coordinated Superbowl Halftime-caliber celebration dances to my amazing staff, now becoming too numerous to name all in one spot, for holding down the fort in weeks when I was consumed by book-related stuff. Thanks for prepping some of the components used in the photography in the book too, y'all! Kaboodles of strudels to my dear friend Greggie, who lives in a smelly old windmill and designed the beautiful artwork that adorns our trucks. May you be serenaded by Hootie & the Blowfish forever, you goofy old turkey.

A giant-size set of lips bigger than buildings for the smooches for Kim Ima from the Treats Truck, for all her mentoring and support. You are my food truck mommy.

Huge hugs to my awesome editor at Potter, Jessica Freeman-Slade, aka "Sladerunner." In fact, thanks to the entire Potter team: Aaron Wehner, Doris Cooper, Danielle Deschenes, Gabriel Levine, and Sigi Nacson.

Mega-belly bumps with supreme optical ventriloquist Kate Lewis for making my food look even yummier than it does in real life, with her photographic wizardry. I'm sorry my bad dog ate some of the appetizers we tried to shoot in my home!

The galaxy's biggest high-five to all of the folks who did recipe testing for the book. Thanks for catching some of my stupid mistakes!

Big thanks to Julian David Kurt Wiener Schmalun for teaching me how to rap so well.

Oodles of poodles to my mommy and literary agent, Judith Weber, for helping me find a wonderful publisher to work with, and for the guidance and wisdom that she poured into the formulation of this here book.

Ten thousand diamond-encrusted salutations to Sean and everyone over at the Street Vendor Project for fighting for our right to party.

I quack like a duck at the president, and lovingly give him a wedgie. And I bow at the feet of everyone fighting hard for animal and human liberation.

INDEX

NOTE: PAGE REFERENCES IN *ITALICS* INDICATE RECIPE PHOTOGRAPHS.

----------------- A -----------------

Agar agar, about, 17
Agave nectar, about, 16
Agua Frescas, 63
Aioli, Habanero, 250, 257
Almond(s)
  milk, about, 15
  Raw Raspberry–Chocolate Fudge Tart, 211
  Roasted, Cauliflower Soup, Creamy, 107
  Supreme Raw Fudge Brownie Milk Shake, 61
Amaranth flour, about, 16
Appetizers, list of, 71
Apple(s)
  Cashew Oat Waffles, 48, 49
  Cinnamon Fritters, 243
  Perfect Homemade Applesauce, 254
Apricot Habanero Glaze, 262, 262
Arrowroot starch, about, 17
Asafetida, about, 18

----------------- B -----------------

Balsamic Figs and Parsnips Pizza, 162, 165
Bao Buns
  Bangin' Bao, 134
  Oyster Mushroom, 135, 136
  Peking Seitan, 135, 136
  Sesame Bean Paste, 135, 135
Bars
  Gooey Salted-Caramel Pecan Turtle, 196, 197
  Jalapeño Raw Brownies, 215, 215
  Raw Brownies, 214
Basil, Thai
  about, 159
  –Coconut Donuts, 230
Bean(s)
  Jalapeño Corn Chowdah, 99
  New England–Style Chickpea "Crab" Cakes, 74–75, 75

Red, Ancho and Seitan Asada Chili, 117–18, 119
Red, –Scallion Pancakes, 158–59
Red Wine Minestrone, 110, 111
Sesame Bean Paste Bao Buns, 135, 135
String, Ramen, Live Szechuan, 160, 161
Tequila Lime Tostones, 90–91
Thai Coconut Curry Soup, 96, 103
White, Rosemary Croquettes, 81–82, 83
Beer
  -Battered Habanero Buffalo Wings, 70, 79–80
  Ginger Stout Syrup, 253
Beverages, list of recipes, 53
Bing Cherry Fritters, 242
Blackberry Lemonade, Maple-Mashed, 64, 65
Black Sesame Gomasio, 257
Blintzes, Kasha and Fried Onion, 38–40, 39
Blueberry
  -Lemon Cheesecake, Raw, 216, 217
  –Pine Nut Fritters, 243
Bok Choy
  Ginger Laphing, 106
Bourbon
  -Blanched Mustard Greens, 187
  –Brown Sugar Glazed Seitan, 132–33
  Hazelnut Pancakes, 20, 28–29
  -Vanilla Crème Brûlée Donuts, 246, 246–47
Brazil Nut
  Cranberry Granola, 36, 37
  Milk, 52, 58
Breads
  Almond Milk French Toast, 41–42, 43
  Beer-Battered French Toast, 46–47
  Grilled Tomato–Olive Bruschetta, 84
  Poached Pear–Stuffed French Toast, 34–35, 35
Breakfast dishes, list of, 21
Broccoli Beer Soup, Cheesy, 114, 115

Brownies
  Raw, 214
  Raw, Jalapeño, 215, 215
Bruschetta, Grilled Tomato–Olive, 84
Brussels Sprouts, Raw Maple Miso, 178, 179
Buckwheat flour, about, 17

----------------- C -----------------

Cabbage
  Maple Barbecue Tempeh, 142–43
  Napa, and Radish Kimchi, Basic, 172, 175
  Spicy Kimchi with Mustard Greens and Carrot, 176
Cacao
  about, 17, 57
  butter, about, 18
  Chocolate Cashew Milk, 52, 57
  Jalapeño Raw Brownies, 215, 215
  Mint Matlock Took All His Clothes Off, 202
  Raw Brownies, 214
  Raw Chocolate Pudding, 199
  Raw Raspberry–Chocolate Fudge Tart, 211
  Supreme Raw Fudge Brownie Milk Shake, 61
Cakes
  Mini Peanut Butter–Chocolate Cheesecakes, 204, 205
  Raspberry Coconut Frou Frous, 198–99
  Raw Lemon-Blueberry Cheesecake, 216, 217
Cane juice, evaporated, about, 16
Carrot(s)
  Live Pumpkinish Pie, 206, 207
  and Mustard Greens, Spicy Kimchi with, 176
Cashew(s)
  Cheese, Truffled, 261

Cheese Wedges, Polenta Sage, *76,*
77–78
Chocolate Milk, *52,* 57
Jalapeño Raw Brownies, 215, *215*
Jalapeño Roasted Corn–Stuffed Red
Quinoa Croquettes, 168–70, *171*
Lemongrass Five-Spice Seitan, 127–29,
128
Live Pumpkinish Pie, *206, 207*
Oat Waffles, 48, *49*
Raw Brownies, 214
Raw Chocolate Pudding, 199
Raw Lemon-Blueberry Cheesecake,
216, 217
Raw Pizza, *162,* 163–64
Raw Raspberry–Chocolate Fudge Tart,
211
Supreme Raw Fudge Brownie Milk
Shake, 61
Cauliflower Roasted Almond Soup,
Creamy, 107
Celery root
Shredded Root Vegetable Hash
Browns, *50,* 51
Chamomile Pine Nut Milk, *52,* 60
Cheesecake, Raw Lemon-Blueberry, *216,*
217
Cheesy Broccoli Beer Soup, *114,* 115
Cherry
Bing, Fritters, 242
and Yacón Pancakes, 32–33
Chestnut
flour, about, 17
Plum Fritters, 242
Roasted, Cake Donuts, 236, *237*
Chiles
Beer-Battered Habanero Buffalo
Wings, *70,* 79–80
Chipotle Mayonnaise, *250,* 256
ground, Korean, about, 19
Habanero Aioli, *250,* 257
Habanero Apricot Glaze, 262, *262*
Jalapeño Corn Chowdah, 99
Jalapeño Raw Brownies, 215, *215*
Jalapeño Roasted Corn–Stuffed Red
Quinoa Croquettes, 168–70, *171*
Live Habanero Tomato Soup, *100,* 101
Seitan Asada and Ancho Red Bean
Chili, 117–18, *119*

Smoky Portobello– and Potato–
Stuffed Poblanos, 86–87
Watermelon Habanero Refresco, 63
Chili
Seitan Asada and Ancho Red Bean,
117–18, *119*
Stuffed Potato Skins, 118–19, *119*
Chimichurri Tempeh Empanadas,
94–95
Chinese ingredients, 18–19
Chocolate. *See also* Cacao
Cake Donuts, 234
Coffee Ice Cream Sundae Donuts, 231
Ganache–Roasted Mandarin Tart,
188, 193
Ganache–Stuffed S'mores Donuts,
248–49, *249*
Gooey Salted-Caramel Pecan Turtle
Bars, 196, *197*
Hot, Peppermint, 69
Hot, Toasted Hazelnut, *68,* 69
Mexican Hot, –Glazed Twists, 235
Mint Matlock Took All His Clothes
Off, 202
–Peanut Butter Cheesecake Donuts,
240
–Peanut Butter Cheesecakes, Mini,
204, *205*
–Peanut Butter Ganache Pop Tarts 'n'
Hearts, *190,* 192
Sambuca Cookies, *212,* 213
White, Macadamia Granola, *44,* 45
White, –Macadamia Twinkies,
194–95
Cinnamon
Apple Fritters, 243
Coconut Cream, *206, 207*
Snails, *232,* 233
Coconut
Blue Corn–Hemp Seed–Crusted
Tempeh, 140–41, *141*
Cream, Cinnamon, *206,* 207
Creamy Strawberry Pink Drink, 62, *62*
Curry Soup, Thai, *96,* 103
flakes, about, 16
Jalapeño Raw Brownies, 215, *215*
milk, about, 15
oil, about, 15
Raspberry Frou Frous, 198–99

Raw Brownies, 214
shredded, about, 16
Star Anise Milk, *52,* 56
–Thai Basil Donuts, 230
young Thai, opening, 56
Coffee Ice Cream Sundae Donuts, 231
Cookies
Chocolate Sambuca, *212,* 213
Mint Matlock Took All His Clothes
Off, 202
Pine Nut Friendlies, 203
Rum-Glazed Pecan, 208, *209*
Corn
Chowdah, Jalapeño, 99
Jalapeño Roasted, –Stuffed Red
Quinoa Croquettes, 168–70, *171*
Cornmeal
Blue Corn–Hemp Seed–Crusted
Tempeh, 140–41, *141*
Blue Corn Pancakes, 23
Cranberry(ies)
Beer-Battered French Toast, 46–47
Brazil Nut Granola, *36,* 37
Fresh, Donuts, 231
Cream cheese, vegan, about, 15
Crème Brûlée, Lavender–Vanilla Bean,
200, 201
Croquettes
Red Quinoa, Jalapeño Roasted Corn–
Stuffed, 168–70, *171*
Rosemary White Bean, 81–82, *83*
Cucumber Ginger Agua Fresca, 63

---------------- D ----------------

Dandelion Greens, Fried, 24, *25*
Desserts, list of, 189
Donuts
list of recipes, 223
preparing, guide to, 225–26
storing, note about, 226
Dumplings, Pan-Fried Kimchi, 73

---------------- E ----------------

Egg replacer powder, about, 16
Empanadas, Chimichurri Tempeh,
94–95
Evaporated cane juice, about, 16

F

Fig(s)
  Fresh, Arnold Palmers, 66, *67*
  Fresh, Pancakes, 30, *31*
  and Parsnips, Balsamic, Pizza, *162*, 165
Five-spice powder, about, 19
Flax meal
  about, 18
  Raw Pizza, *162*, 163–64
Flours, about, 16–17
French Toast
  Almond Milk, 41–42, *43*
  Beer-Battered, 46–47
  Poached Pear–Stuffed, 34–35, *35*
Fritters
  Bing Cherry, 242
  Blueberry–Pine Nut, 243
  Cinnamon Apple, 243
  Donut Shop–Style, 241
  Lavender Pear, *244*, 245
  Plum Chestnut, 242
Fruit. *See also specific fruits*
  Donut Shop–Style Fritters, 241

G

Galangal Pea Pancakes, 153–55, *154*
Garbanzo / fava bean flour, about, 17
Garlic
  Habanero Aioli, *250*, 257
  -Lemon Swiss Chard, 187
Ginger
  Cucumber Agua Fresca, 63
  Island Tofu, 166–67
  Laphing, 106
  Stout Syrup, 253
Glaze, Habanero Apricot, 262, *262*
Gluten-free (appetizers and drinks)
  Agua Frescas, 63
  Brazil Nut Milk, *52*, 58
  Chamomile Pine Nut Milk, *52*, 60
  Chocolate Cashew Milk, *52*, 57
  Coconut Star Anise Milk, *52*, 56
  Creamy Strawberry Pink Drink, 62, *62*
  Fresh Fig Arnold Palmers, 66, *67*
  Hot Ragi, 69
  Peppermint Hot Chocolate, 69

Pistachio Milk, *52*, 60
Several Rad Lemonades, *64*, 64–65
Smoky Portobello– and Potato–
  Stuffed Poblanos, 86–87
Supreme Raw Fudge Brownie Milk
  Shake, 61
Tequila Lime Tostones, 90–91
Toasted Hazelnut Hot Chocolate, *68*, 69
Vanilla Sesame Milk, *52*, 55
Gluten-free (breakfasts)
  Almond Milk French Toast, 41–42, *43*
  Cashew Oat Waffles, 48, *49*
  Fried Dandelion Greens, 24, *25*
  Shredded Root Vegetable Hash
    Browns, *50*, 51
  Yacón and Cherry Pancakes, 32–33
Gluten-free (condiments)
  Black Sesame Gomasio, 257
  Chipotle Mayonnaise, *250*, 256
  Grilled Mango Salsa, 260
  Habanero Aioli, *250*, 257
  Habanero Apricot Glaze, 262, *262*
  Niçoise Olive Tapenade, 259
  Perfect Homemade Applesauce, 254
  Pine Nut Butter, 255
  Pumpkin Brown Butter, 254
  Red Wine Syrup, 253
  Roasted Tomatillo Salsa Verde, *258*, 259
  Sriracha Mayonnaise, 256
  Wasabi Mayonnaise, *250*, 256
Gluten-free (desserts)
  Jalapeño Raw Brownies, 215, *215*
  Lavender–Vanilla Bean Crème Brûlée, *200*, 201
  Live Pumpkinish Pie, *206*, 207
  Raw Brownies, 214
  Raw Chocolate Pudding, 199
  Raw Lemon-Blueberry Cheesecake, *216*, 217
  Raw Raspberry–Chocolate Fudge Tart, 211
Gluten-free (donuts)
  Bing Cherry Fritters, 242
  Blueberry–Pine Nut Fritters, 243
  Coconut–Thai Basil Donuts, 230
  Fresh Cranberry Donuts, 231
  Plum Chestnut Fritters, 242

Vanilla Donuts, 230
Gluten-free flour mixes, about, 17
Gluten-free (main dishes)
  Ginger Island Tofu, 166–67
  Live Szechuan String Bean Ramen, 160, *161*
  Raw Pizza, *162*, 163–64
Gluten-free (side dishes)
  Basic Napa Cabbage and Radish
    Kimchi, *172*, 175
  Bourbon-Blanched Mustard Greens, 187
  Horseradish Mashed Potatoes, 182, *183*
  Lemon-Garlic Swiss Chard, 187
  Lemon-Soy Watercress, 177
  Maple-Roasted Kabocha, 180, *180*
  Raw Maple Miso Brussels Sprouts, 178, *179*
  Simple Marinated Kale, 177
  Spicy Kimchi with Mustard Greens
    and Carrot, 176
Gluten-free (soups)
  Creamy Roasted Almond Cauliflower
    Soup, 107
  French Lentil Soup, 102
  Ginger Laphing, 106
  Jalapeño Corn Chowdah, 99
  Live Habanero Tomato Soup, *100*, 101
  Maple Butternut Squash Soup, 104, *105*
  Thai Coconut Curry Soup, *96*, 103
  Tomato Sage Bisque with Mizuna, 109
  Wild Mushroom, Spinach, and Potato
    Soup, 108
Gochujang
  about, 19
  Burger Deluxe, *144*, 145–46
Gomasio, Black Sesame, 257
Graham crackers
  Chocolate Ganache–Stuffed S'mores
    Donuts, 248–49, *249*
Grains. *See also* Cornmeal; Oat(s)
  Jalapeño Roasted Corn–Stuffed Red
    Quinoa Croquettes, 168–70, *171*
  Kasha and Fried Onion Blintzes, 38–40, *39*
  Polenta Sage Cashew Cheese Wedges, *76*, 77–78

Granola
  Cranberry Brazil Nut, *36*, 37
  White Chocolate Macadamia, *44*, 45
Greens
  Dandelion, Fried, 24, *25*
  Flaky Spinach Pie, *92*, 92–93
  Lemon-Garlic Swiss Chard, 187
  Lemon-Soy Watercress, 177
  Mustard, and Carrot, Spicy Kimchi
    with, 176
  Mustard, Bourbon-Blanched, 187
  Red Wine Minestrone, *110*, 111
  Simple Marinated Kale, 177
  Spinach and Pine Nuts Pizza, *162*, 165
  Tomato Sage Bisque with Mizuna, 109
  Wild Mushroom, Spinach, and Potato
    Soup, 108

---------------- **H** ----------------

Hash Browns, Shredded Root Vegetable,
  50, 51
Hazelnut
  Bourbon Pancakes, *20*, 28–29
  Toasted, Hot Chocolate, *68*, 69
Hemp Seed(s)
  about, 18
  –Blue Corn–Crusted Tempeh, 140–41,
    141
  Rosemary, –Crusted Tofu, *148*, 151–52
Hibiscus Limeade, *64*, 65
Hijiki, about, 19
Honeydew Mint Agua Fresca, 63
Horseradish Mashed Potatoes, 182, *183*

---------------- **I** ----------------

Indian ingredients, 18

---------------- **J** ----------------

Japanese ingredients, 18–19
Jicama
  Rosemary Faux-Tato Pizza, *162*, 165

---------------- **K** ----------------

Kaffir lime leaves, about, 18
Kale, Simple Marinated, 177

Kasha and Fried Onion Blintzes, 38–40,
  39
Kimchi
  about, 19
  Dumplings, Pan-Fried, 73
  Korean Barbecue Seitan, 130
  Napa Cabbage and Radish, Basic, *172*,
    175
  Soup, Korean, 112, *113*
  Spicy, with Mustard Greens and
    Carrot, 176
Kombu, about, 19
Korean ingredients, 19

---------------- **L** ----------------

Lavender
  Pear Fritters, *244*, 245
  -Raspberry Pop Tarts 'n' Hearts, *190*,
    192
  –Vanilla Bean Crème Brûlée, *200*, 201
Lemonades, Several Rad, *64*, 64–65
Lemongrass
  about, 18
  Five-Spice Seitan, 127–29, *128*
  Mango Donuts, 231
Lemon(s)
  -Blueberry Cheesecake, Raw, *216*, 217
  Fresh Fig Arnold Palmers, 66, *67*
  -Garlic Swiss Chard, 187
  Maple-Mashed Blackberry Lemonade,
    64, 65
  Plain Old Agave-Sweetened Fresh
    Lemonade, 65
  -Soy Watercress, 177
Lentil, French, Soup, 102
Limeade, Hibiscus, *64*, 65
Lucuma, about, 17

---------------- **M** ----------------

Maca, about, 17
Macadamia
  White Chocolate Granola, *44*, 45
  –White Chocolate Twinkies, 194–95
Mango
  Grilled, Salsa, 260
  Lemongrass Donuts, 231
Maple

Barbecue Tempeh, 142–43
  Butternut Squash Soup, 104, *105*
  -Mashed Blackberry Lemonade, *64*, 65
  Miso Brussels Sprouts, Raw, 178, *179*
  Mustard Breakfast Seitan Strips, 26,
    27
  -Roasted Kabocha, 180, *180*
Margarine, vegan, about, 15
Marshmallows
  Chocolate Ganache–Stuffed S'mores
    Donuts, 248–49, *249*
  vegan, buying, 249
Mayonnaise
  Chipotle, *250*, 256
  Sriracha, 256
  vegan, about, 15
  Wasabi, *250*, 256
Melon
  Honeydew Mint Agua Fresca, 63
  Watermelon Habanero Refresco, 63
Milks
  Brazil Nut, *52*, 58
  Chamomile Pine Nut, *52*, 60
  Chocolate Cashew, *52*, 57
  Coconut Star Anise, *52*, 56
  Pistachio, *52*, 60
  strained pulp from, uses for, 55
  Vanilla Sesame, *52*, 55
  vegan, types of, 15
Minestrone, Red Wine, *110*, 111
Mint Matlock Took All His Clothes Off,
  202
Mirin, about, 19
Miso
  about, 19
  Maple Brussels Sprouts, Raw, 178, *179*
  Sesame Bean Paste Bao Buns, 135, *135*
  Teriyaki Seitan, 123
Mushroom(s)
  health benefits, 108
  Live Szechuan String Bean Ramen,
    160, *161*
  Oyster, Bao Buns, *135*, 136
  Pecan-Crusted Seitan, 156–57
  Peppers, and Basil Pizza, *162*, 165
  Smoky Portobello– and Potato–
    Stuffed Poblanos, 86–87
  Wild, Spinach, and Potato Soup, 108

Mustard Greens
    Bourbon-Blanched, 187
    and Carrot, Spicy Kimchi with, 176

----------------- N -----------------

Noodles
    Ginger Laphing, 106
    Korean Kimchi Soup, 112, *113*
    Live Szechuan String Bean Ramen,
        160, *161*
Nut(s). *See also* Cashew(s); Pine Nut(s)
    Bourbon Hazelnut Pancakes, *20*,
        28–29
    Brazil, Cranberry Granola, *36*, 37
    Brazil, Milk, *52*, 58
    Gooey Salted-Caramel Pecan Turtle
        Bars, 196, *197*
    Live Pumpkinish Pie, *206*, 207
    Macadamia–White Chocolate
        Twinkies, 194–95
    Pecan-Crusted Seitan, 156–57
    Pistachio Milk, *52*, 60
    Plum Chestnut Fritters, 242
    Raw Lemon-Blueberry Cheesecake,
        216, 217
    Raw Raspberry–Chocolate Fudge Tart,
        211
    Roasted Chestnut Cake Donuts, 236,
        237
    Rum-Glazed Pecan Cookies, 208, *209*
    Toasted Hazelnut Hot Chocolate, *68*, 69
    White Chocolate Macadamia Granola,
        44, 45

----------------- O -----------------

Oat(s)
    Cashew, Waffles, 48, *49*
    Cranberry Brazil Nut Granola, *36*, 37
    White Chocolate Macadamia Granola,
        44, 45
Oils, types of, 15
Olive(s)
    –Grilled Tomato Bruschetta, 84
    Niçoise, Tapenade, 259
    Raw Pizza, *162*, 163–64
    Shredded Root Vegetable Hash
        Browns, *50*, 51

Onion
    Fried, and Kasha Blintzes, 38–40, *39*
    Fried, and Potato Pierogies, Truffled,
        88–89
Oranges
    Roasted Mandarin–Chocolate
        Ganache Tart, *188*, 193

----------------- P -----------------

Pancakes
    Blue Corn, 23
    Bourbon Hazelnut, *20*, 28–29
    Fresh Fig, 30, *31*
    Galangal Pea, 153–55, *154*
    Red Bean–Scallion, 158–59
    Yacón and Cherry, 32–33
Parsnips
    and Figs, Balsamic, Pizza, *162*, 165
    Pecan-Crusted Seitan, 156–57
    Shredded Root Vegetable Hash
        Browns, *50*, 51
Pasta and noodles
    Ginger Laphing, 106
    Korean Kimchi Soup, 112, *113*
    Live Szechuan String Bean Ramen,
        160, *161*
    Red Wine Minestrone, *110*, 111
Peanut Butter
    –Chocolate Cheesecake Donuts, 240
    –Chocolate Cheesecakes, Mini, 204,
        205
    –Chocolate Ganache Pop Tarts 'n'
        Hearts, *190*, 192
Pea Pancakes, Galangal, 153–55, *154*
Pear
    Lavender Fritters, *244*, 245
    Poached, –Stuffed French Toast,
        34–35, *35*
Pecan(s)
    Cookies, Rum-Glazed, 208, *209*
    -Crusted Seitan, 156–57
    Live Pumpkinish Pie, *206*, 207
    Raw Lemon-Blueberry Cheesecake,
        216, 217
    Salted-Caramel Turtle Bars, Gooey,
        196, *197*
Peppermint Hot Chocolate, 69
Peppers. *See also* Chiles

Mushrooms, and Basil Pizza, *162*, 165
Pierogies, Truffled Potato and Fried
    Onion, 88–89
Pies
    Pumpkinish, Live, *206*, 207
    Rum Pumpkin Chiffon, 210
Pine Nut(s)
    –Blueberry Fritters, 243
    Butter, 255
    Chamomile Milk, *52*, 60
    French Lentil Soup, 102
    Friendlies, 203
    and Spinach Pizza, *162*, 165
Pistachio Milk, *52*, 60
Pizza, Raw, *162*, 163–64
Pizza toppings
    Balsamic Figs and Parsnips, *162*, 165
    Peppers, Mushrooms, and Basil, *162*,
        165
    Rosemary Faux-Tato, *162*, 165
    Spinach and Pine Nuts, *162*, 165
Plantains
    Tequila Lime Tostones, 90–91
Plum Chestnut Fritters, 242
Polenta Sage Cashew Cheese Wedges,
    76, 77–78
Pop Tarts 'n' Hearts, *190*, 191–92
Potato(es)
    – and Smoky Portobello–Stuffed
        Poblanos, 86–87
    Cheesy Broccoli Beer Soup, *114*, 115
    Fried Dandelion Greens, 24, *25*
    and Fried Onion Pierogies, Truffled,
        88–89
    Horseradish Mashed, 182, *183*
    Jalapeño Roasted Corn–Stuffed Red
        Quinoa Croquettes, 168–70, *171*
    Live Pumpkinish Pie, *206*, 207
    Shredded Root Vegetable Hash
        Browns, *50*, 51
    Skins, Stuffed, 118–19, *119*
    Wild Mushroom, and Spinach Soup,
        108
Protein, non-meat, types of, 14
Pudding, Raw Chocolate, 199
Pumpkin
    Brown Butter, 254
    Rum Chiffon Pie, 210

---------------- Q ----------------

Quinoa, Red, Croquettes, Jalapeño
    Roasted Corn–Stuffed, 168–70, *171*

---------------- R ----------------

Radish(es)
    and Napa Cabbage Kimchi, Basic,
        172, 175
    Spicy Kimchi with Mustard Greens
        and Carrot, 176
Ragi, Hot, 69
Raspberry(ies)
    Almond Milk French Toast, 41–42, *43*
    –Chocolate Fudge Tart, Raw, 211
    Coconut Frou Frous, 198–99
    -Lavender Pop Tarts 'n' Hearts, *190*,
        192
Red curry paste, about, 18
Red Wine Syrup, 253
Rhubarb-Strawberry Pop Tarts 'n'
    Hearts, *190*, 192
Rice flour, about, 17
Rice vinegar, about, 15
Rosemary
    Faux-Tato Pizza, *162*, 165
    Hemp Seed–Crusted Tofu, *148*,
        151–52
Rum
    -Glazed Pecan Cookies, 208, *209*
    Pumpkin Chiffon Pie, 210

---------------- S ----------------

Sage Tempeh Sausage Sliders, 137–39,
    138
Salsa
    Grilled Mango, 260
    Verde, Roasted Tomatillo, *258*, 259
Salted-Caramel Pecan Turtle Bars,
    Gooey, 196, *197*
Sambar masala, about, 18
Sambuca Chocolate Cookies, *212*, 213
Sandwiches, list of recipes, 121
Sauces
    bottled, vegan, 15–16
    Grilled Mango Salsa, 260

Roasted Tomatillo Salsa Verde, *258*,
    259
Seitan
    about, 14
    Asada and Ancho Red Bean Chili,
        117–18, *119*
    Brown Sugar–Bourbon Glazed, 132–33
    Galangal Pea Pancakes, 153–55, *154*
    Gochujang Burger Deluxe, *144*,
        145–46
    Korean Barbecue, 130
    Lemongrass Five-Spice, 127–29, *128*
    Miso Teriyaki, 123
    Pecan-Crusted, 156–57
    Peking, Bao Buns, *135*, 136
    Ribs, Thai Barbecue, 124–26, *125*
    Strips, Maple Mustard Breakfast, *26*,
        27
Sesame oil, toasted, about, 15
Sesame seeds
    Black Sesame Gomasio, 257
    Miso Teriyaki Seitan, 123
    Sesame Bean Paste Bao Buns, 135, *135*
    Vanilla Sesame Milk, *52*, 55
Sorghum flour, about, 17
Soups, list of recipes, 97
Soy milk
    about, 15
    curdled, cooking with, 151
Soy sauce, about, 18
Spelt flour, about, 16
Spinach
    Pie, Flaky, *92*, 92–93
    and Pine Nuts Pizza, *162*, 165
    Wild Mushroom, and Potato Soup, 108
Spreads
    Chipotle Mayonnaise, *250*, 256
    Habanero Aioli, *250*, 257
    Niçoise Olive Tapenade, 259
    Pine Nut Butter, 255
    Pumpkin Brown Butter, 254
    Sriracha Mayonnaise, 256
    Truffled Cashew Cheese, 261
    Wasabi Mayonnaise, *250*, 256
Squash
    Butternut, Maple Soup, 104, *105*
    Maple-Roasted Kabocha, 180, *180*
    Pumpkin Brown Butter, 254
    Rum Pumpkin Chiffon Pie, 210

Sriracha Mayonnaise, 256
Star Anise Coconut Milk, *52*, 56
Strawberry
    Pink Drink, Creamy, 62, *62*
    -Rhubarb Pop Tarts 'n' Hearts, *190*,
        192
Sucanat, about, 16
Sunflower seeds
    Cheesy Broccoli Beer Soup, *114*, 115
    Miso Teriyaki Seitan, 123
    Raw Pizza, *162*, 163–64
Sweet potatoes
    Jalapeño Roasted Corn–Stuffed Red
        Quinoa Croquettes, 168–70, *171*
    Live Pumpkinish Pie, *206*, 207
Swiss Chard
    Lemon-Garlic, 187
    Red Wine Minestrone, *110*, 111
Syrups
    Ginger Stout, 253
    Red Wine, 253

---------------- T ----------------

Tamarind concentrate, about, 18
Tapenade, Niçoise Olive, 259
Tarts
    Raspberry–Chocolate Fudge, Raw, 211
    Roasted Mandarin–Chocolate
        Ganache, *188*, 193
Tea
    Black, Twists, 238–39
    Fresh Fig Arnold Palmers, 66, *67*
Tempeh
    about, 14
    Blue Corn–Hemp Seed–Crusted,
        140–41, *141*
    Empanadas, Chimichurri, 94–95
    Maple Barbecue, 142–43
    Sage, Sausage Sliders, 137–39, *138*
Tequila Lime Tostones, 90–91
Thai Basil
    about, 159
    –Coconut Donuts, 230
Thai ingredients, 18
Toasted sesame oil, about, 15
Tocotrienols, about, 58

Tofu
    about, 14
    Beer-Battered Habanero Buffalo
        Wings, *70, 79*–80
    Chipotle Mayonnaise, *250,* 256
    cream cheese, about, 15
    Ginger Island, 166–67
    Habanero Aioli, *250,* 257
    Korean Kimchi Soup, 112, *113*
    Mini Peanut Butter–Chocolate
        Cheesecakes, 204, *205*
    Red Bean–Scallion Pancakes, 158–59
    Rosemary Hemp Seed–Crusted, *148,*
        151–52
    silken, about, 14
    Thai Barbecue Seitan Ribs, 124–26,
        125
Tomatillo, Roasted, Salsa Verde, *258,*
    259
Tomato(es)
    Grilled, –Olive Bruschetta, 84
    Habanero Soup, Live, *100,* 101
    Raw Pizza, *162,* 163–64
    Sage Bisque with Mizuna, 109
Tostones, Tequila Lime, 90–91
Truffled Cashew Cheese, 261
Truffled Potato and Fried Onion
    Pierogies, 88–89
Truffle oil, about, 89
Turnips
    Shredded Root Vegetable Hash
        Browns, *50,* 51
Twinkies, Macadamia–White
    Chocolate, 194–95

---------------- U ----------------

Umeboshi plum vinegar, about, 15

---------------- V ----------------

Vanilla
    -Bourbon Crème Brûlée Donuts, *246,*
        246–47
    Donuts, 230
Vegetable(s)
    Red Wine Minestrone, *110,* 111
    Root, Shredded, Hash Browns, *50,* 51
Vinegars, types of, 15

Vital wheat gluten. *See also* Seitan
    about, 16–17
    Thai Barbecue Seitan Ribs, 124–26,
        125

---------------- W ----------------

Waffles, Cashew Oat, 48, *49*
Wasabi
    Mayonnaise, *250,* 256
    powder, about, 18
Watercress, Lemon-Soy, 177
Watermelon Habanero Refresco, 63
White Chocolate
    Macadamia Granola, *44,* 45
    –Macadamia Twinkies, 194–95
Wine, Red, Syrup, 253

---------------- X ----------------

Xanthan gum, about, 17

---------------- Z ----------------

Yacón syrup, about, 16
Yams
    Ginger Island Tofu, 166–67